Politically Incorrect Essays by a Concerned Activist

Book 1

MIA A TRÉSTROPE

Copies of this book can be ordered via www.doctorzed.com, booksellers or by contacting:

DoctorZed Publishing
10 Vista Ave, Skye,
South Australia 5072
www.doctorzed.com

ISBN: 978-0-6451840-5-1 (sc)
ISBN: 978-0-6451840-6-8 (e)

A CiP number is available at the National Library of Australia.

Cover images © Mia A Tréstrope

Printed in Australia, UK and USA

rev. date: 21/06/2021

To my four sisters, who gave my life depth.

The youngest and oldest both died in the same year, far too young,
from the ravages of the cruel autoimmune disease, rheumatoid
arthritis. The wonderful second oldest, even though there was
a world war between our births, was like a second mother.
Her strong Christian faith was like a wall of strength
for me. Finally, to my dear younger sister, whose
organised and clever 'left-brain' dominance,
gave order to my slightly less organised,
but creative, 'right-brain'
dominated life.

Good people are at the heart of this world.
When wars, or horrible acts, rain down upon them,
regardless of colour, creed or language,
they gather together as one.

Do not turn away from godliness,
for that is just another word for possession of a soul.
A soul makes us capable of great love, empathy,
and gives us conscience and remorse.

It is hope and strength that divides us from the godless,
those that slither amongst us, the evil and inhumane,
who choose to remain contemptuous of qualities,
which are the bedrock of this precious land.

We must have faith in that mysterious force, the soul,
so uniquely human, that empowers us and drives us on.
It gives us courage to fight against the soulless,
who continue to bring terror to replace calm.

Preserving freedom, peace and comfort,
to see wickedness and strive to change it,
will always be mankind's greatest test.
A drive that must never, ever rest.

Goodness, so battle scarred and weary,
must always win, against pure evil.
This world shall always survive,
when that eternal fight
continues.

22/11/2015
Mia A Tréstrope

Contents

~ Preface ~
Stirring the pot

'Freedom and not servitude is the cure of anarchy.'
— **Edmund Burke**

On *September* 11, 2001, along with the rest of the world, I watched in horror as a few evil men changed the Western world forever. In Australia, it was past 11:00 p.m. and I was packing away my sculpting clay. A newsflash appeared on the small TV screen in my studio. My hand hovered over the remote as the shocking visual of one of the Twin Towers, billowing smoke, appeared with a gaping hole where the first aircraft had slammed into it. My initial thoughts were of some massive equipment failure or air traffic error. Then a second plane appeared and in a steady, controlled manner, flew directly into the second tower. Goosebumps crawled up my arms as the realisation sank in that this was no error.

I pulled back the clay to keep my hands busy while the gut-wrenching drama unfolded. The book of Revelations (6:1-17), with its symbolic warning of the Four Horsemen of the Apocalypse and the uprising of the antichrist, was revealed in this act of pure evil. According to this book, the four riders represented the evils to come at the end of the world. They rode out on horses that were white, red, black and pale. These horses symbolised Conquest, War, Famine, and Death, in that order.

For people not familiar with the prophetic symbolism of the horsemen, the rider of the white horse, was seen as the 'Spirit of Christ' conquering and converting non-believers.[1&2] The horses that followed showed the major problems to follow, in the passage of life on this planet, as people who were anti-faith, hence antichrist, fell away from the values of faith.

The rider of the first horse was given a crown and had as its 'conquest', to bring righteousness to the world—striving to conquer barbarism. Then there was the gradual decline by factors introduced by the following horsemen, War, Famine and the last horse, named Death, which would bring destruction that included plague. While some see the rider of the first horse as the 'antichrist'[3] representing the rise of religious deception, a later verse in Revelations appears to discount this theory:

> Revelations 19:11: 'Then I saw heaven opened, and behold, a white horse! He who sat upon it is called Faithful and True, and in righteousness he judges and makes war.[4]

White is a representation of righteousness and there are numerous references in the Bible connecting white with good deeds, rather than evil. In 2 Peter 2:1 there had been a warning of deception by false prophets, who distorted the prophesies bringing destructive deviations, even denying the 'Master' who bought them:

> 2 Peter 2:1: But false prophets also arose among the people, just as there will be false teachers among you, who will secretly bring in destructive heresies, even denying the Master who bought them, bringing upon themselves swift destruction.[5]

With a world now littered with deceptive, manipulative white-collar psychopaths (WCPs), who put profit before people, we have allowed almost irretrievable damage to this world. The rider of the red horse, representing War, was permitted to 'take peace from the earth'. It warned of a time of murder, assassination, bloodshed and revolution. The black horse rider carried a pair of scales and symbolised Famine, which included pestilence, disease and earthquakes. The article written by DA Cleland, *Why the Black Horse of Revelation CANNOT be the Horse of Famine*,[6] argues the third horse brought the warning of famine, as it was the rider of the pale horse that would kill by 'sword, famine and plague'.

The scales represented drought conditions that would wipe out wheat and barley supplies, curiously, oil and grape vines would be spared (Revelation 6:5-6). It warned of a time where people would work long hours for just enough food to survive, while the luxuries of the wealthy remained untouched.[7] The current massive wealth discrepancy and corrupt tax havens are harsh realities of this warning of extreme greed and dishonesty. The rider of the last horse was described in Revelation 6:8:

> I looked, and there before me was a pale horse! Its rider was named Death, and Hades was following close behind him. They were given power over a fourth of the earth, to kill by sword, famine and plague, and by the wild beasts of the earth.

The rise of terrorists, serial murderers and rapists and COVID in our time has been proof of this horrific prophesy. At 5:00 a.m., after seeing innocent people jumping to their deaths and listening to reports of a flight brought down by brave westerners before it reached its target, I switched off the television. I had witnessed one of the most inhumane acts against humanity this world will ever see and, as I pushed the finished sculpture aside, I realised the significance of choosing to mould a horse, the symbolic creature used in the warning of a future apocalypse. The pale horse, with its rider named Death with Hades following close behind, had arrived. It was the last horse, which was prophesied as having power over one quarter of the earth.

On 9/11 the seeds for this book were planted and my sculpture, the pale horse can be seen on the book cover. Though, at the time, the object choice had been completely random, in retrospect, it was a curious coincidence that of all things I could have selected to mould from clay, while extremists tore apart the free world, I chose to mould the pale-coloured horse: the symbol of death.

Was it just an ironic coincidence that Adherents.com, in their 2012 estimates showed that Christians made up 33 per cent of people of faith, 11.9 per cent were ethnic religions such as Judaism, Buddhism, Shinto, African, Chinese religions and others, 16 per cent were individuals recorded as secular, nonreligious, agnostic or atheist, while 15 per cent were followers of Hinduism, a total of 75.9 per cent.[8&9] Islam, a religion that has become seriously corrupted by false hadiths, has 1.8 billion followers, which makes up virtually one fourth of the earth's 'religious' adherents (24.1 per cent).

The five books of Sunnah, introduced by autocratic tribal men, which overwrite the Quran, are the false hadiths, corrupt fabrications of which Muhammad warned against in his historically famous final sermon.[10] They are rules that distort the words within the Quran (6:112-113) because they are the rules made by tribal men, not God/Allah. They reintroduced, under the guise of faith, almost every barbarous tribal rule Muhammad had tried to change. Every book is in effect contempt of the Prophet Muhammad's wishes and they are the major cause his 'religion of peace' has been corrupted into one of the most dangerous religions on earth.

Let's hope, for the sake of moderate Muslims, that percentage does not have actual relevance to that of old prophecy, which gave the rider of the pale horse the power over a fourth of the earth, to kill by sword, famine and plague.

I had a mould made of my sculpture of the pale horse reproduced in an off-white mortar mix. It now sits on my desk as a reminder of my commitment to stir the pot and stimulate social conscience. We need to make changes and restore hope in the future. Houses of God should be open to all people, of all faiths. Secrecy and male domination should be completely exorcised. If not, and the Sunni 'hadith Islam' corruption of true Islam remains, the world may be witness to yet another shocking genocide war. While 'Death' rode upon the pale horse, do not let 'Apathy' be the name of that horse, in this chillingly accurate religious prophesy.

I was born in South Australia, the state that did not have convict settlement. Families were generally from Protestant faiths, predominantly Lutheran or Methodist, who were seeking religious freedom from the Catholic tyranny of Britain and Europe. Individuals were often more financially secure and many had better education levels than the so-called convicts, who may have done little more than stealing a handkerchief, while working as a servant in the UK. For years South Australians had noticeably better accents, until the 'Ten Pound Poms' brought a broader range of accents, often from the poorer areas where many of the early convicts had been raised. Ten Pound Poms was a colloquial term used in Australia to describe British citizens who migrated to Australia after the Second World War. The migrants were called Ten Pound Poms due to the payment of £10 in processing fees to migrate to Australia. The word Pom is derived from 'pomegranate', Australian rhyming slang for 'immigrant'.

It was SA that gained widespread notoriety for being the first self-governing territory to give women equal franchise on the same terms as it was granted to men. Women gained the right to vote and to stand for parliament in South Australia when the Adult Suffrage Bill passed in 1894. Although South Australia was the second jurisdiction, after New Zealand, to give women the right to vote, NZ still did not have the right for women to stand for parliamentary selection, something which SA women had successfully gained at that time.

I have been an activist since the Vietnam war (1955-1975) because of the disgraceful way soldiers were treated after doing the dangerous work for which they had been trained. Sadly, they were not celebrated on their return unlike soldiers of the past, who had similarly put their lives on the line, had been. It was a time when young people bravely took to the streets to show their anger against unjust political decisions. A time that I thought had sadly passed, courage buried for the last half century, and it was partly the reason I started writing. I was cheered, however, when I saw brave young school children marching against global warming in 2020. Environmental warming, which our narrow-minded politicians, ignorant in the field of agricultural science, ignored–until Australia burned from coast to coast, from September 2019, until February 2020.

As early as the 1980s I was researching for an essay on ZPG (zero population growth) and even at that time scientists were warning us that world population numbers were reaching their peak. Why has the most intelligent species on Earth, now recognised as the apex predator,[11] who were supposed to be the 'shepherds' for this planet, been allowed to reach plague proportions, becoming its most destructive saboteurs? When disastrous fires raged across Australia nonstop for six months, our island continent became an example to the world that nature will wreak horrifying vengeance if we continue to push the environmental boundaries.

Unfortunately, English settlers had introduced crops they were familiar with, which suited a climate of high rainfall and deep topsoil. The Mediterranean climate of Australia, the driest and hottest continent, with shallow topsoil, was cleared and covered with grain crops. On the other hand, olive trees, grown in the Mediterranean areas, with their valuable and healthy fruit, flourish with very little water and cope with far less fertile soil. Grain crops are naturally susceptible to fire and the famine years, whereas olive trees and grapevines root more deeply. Tragically, with thousands of hectares turned into highly flammable grasslands, this contributed to the horrific toll of lost houses and millions of animals burned alive.

Trees are the lungs and the cooling system of the world but many of our English ancestors did not value trees taking up crop space. Developers, to this day, are a big part of the massive deforestation, with an estimated 200,000 trees being bulldozed per day. Australia's land-clearing rate is now amongst the highest in the world.[12&13] I had in the past chained my car to street trees, planted in memory of men who had died in an earlier war, in our small country town. I had been lobbying, with other residents, to get the council to pave dusty foot paths in our main street. Consequently, they decided it was easier to cut down trees than to pave around them. Governments must pour much more money into agricultural science.

We cannot continue to ignore the fact that every environmentally damaging industry is driven by ever increasing human need; overpopulation is now the most destructive aspect of modern life. The COVID-19 virus, which followed our bushfires, has tragically spread with horrifying speed across the world, having the very worst impact in the more heavily overpopulated areas of the world.

I had also taken part in a 24/7 stakeout, to stop Telstra putting a tower between a child-care area and a suburban library. The area was a pretty park in the district where I lived in our capital city and to install this tower, trees would have been removed. It was at a time when no one knew whether it was safe to have these towers close to houses and children. Unfortunately, a journalist from the local paper came at a time during my stakeout shift. As a result, my full name was printed in the paper and, because it is quite unique, it was easy to find in the phonebook. Consequently, the back of my white car, while it was parked in my driveway, was sprayed with a rather nasty message telling me I was a four-letter word, which rhymes with punt. I have had to change to an unlisted number, as activists do make enemies. I write using a pen name, which is an anagram of what I am, not who I am, for the same reason.

I have written numerous essays that I am organising into a series of books. The first delves into psychopathy, which has a genetic component, and sociopathy, an outcome of poverty and inappropriate parenting. Psychopaths are a predatory subset of humanity that range from white-collar to heinous psychopaths: individuals who slither amongst us in all areas from religion (the institution that was formed to transform this evil group), to leaders of businesses that are run for personal profit, not people.

It was predicted in the Bible that false religion would greatly impact the nations in the last days. We have witnessed numerous religious cults that have strayed so far from the simple Abrahamic faith that they have become farce. The 'D3' branch of religion, Scientology and the Westboro Baptist church are three Christian examples of horrific, godless, antichrist administration; the Sunni cult offshoot (which I have called Sunni 'hadith Islam') is the Islamic version. Many of the most heinous of psychopathic personas, paedophiles and dictators, have hidden their crimes under the mask of religion.

We are now also witnessing conquests by godless, white-collar psychopaths, financial whores that have slithered to the upper echelons of business, banking and 'Big Pharma'. The *Big Pharma Conspiracy Theory* consists of conspiracy concepts which claim that pharmaceutical companies, especially the large ones, operate for sinister purposes (i.e. huge profit) and against the public good.[14]

The terrifying SBS documentary, *The Crown Prince of Saudi Arabia*,[15] reveals how the Sunni corruption of Islam, which treats women as badly as dogs (which they kill), has moulded many of the most brutal, murderous maniacs who torture women, with not an iota of guilt or remorse. As Muhammad warned religious clerics, those who adopt hadith fabrications are the godless 'jinn devils' (Quran 6:112-113). They have allowed psychopathic personas, the enemies of Allah, to reverse the Muslim culture to become the brutal, pre-Islamic, tribal rule of appalling gender inequality. The subjugation and shutting down of the voice of the more ethical gender has allowed serpents to destroy the overall quality of life in this culture. When dissidents are tortured and killed, it reveals the growth of the most dangerous subset of all living species, the 'intra-species'.[16] 'Intra-species' predators kill members of their own species, which is quite rare in lesser animal groups.

White-collar psychopaths are spiralling in numbers. As religion is discarded, the warning given in the first book of the Bible, Genesis, of these snakes that would destroy Eden is ignored. As early as 1400 BC, the most dangerous people to walk this earth were described. The Garden of Eden parable described what the modern world now recognises as the psychopathic persona, a deceptive serpent was used as a metaphor for these snakes that slither amongst us–individuals who put profit before people and are slowly destroying our Eden, planet Earth.

Although I lived in a state that allowed religious and political freedom, I questioned fundamentalist dogma from an early age. Religions that read the Bible literally, rather than reading it as historic metaphor and clever symbolism, pushed me towards a more agnostic perspective. However, unlike atheists, I recognised the value of an institution that taught children EQ (emotional intelligence), ingraining morality, empathy, respect and conscience (MERC). These are the qualities that are the foundation of an adult moral compass and must be taught and learned in the first decade of an individual's life. They are not innate.

I was raised in the Methodist faith and the strict, man-made rules of Catholicism shocked me. However, I was always fascinated by science, hence, the literal interpretation of the Bible followed by dogmatic fundamentalists never sat easily with me. I remember asking my mother what the first word I ever said was and she replied, "Mum might have been your first word, but the second one certainly was why!" The latter continues to be the first word that so often springs to my mind. It hovers perpetually, galvanising me into action in my constant search for answers.

As I hadn't been to a church service (apart from weddings and family christenings) since I was sixteen, I was unsure if religions had also begun to question the outdated literal interpretation of the Bible. At the time, I was writing the preface for my first book on corrupted male-dominated religions, primarily Catholicism and Islam. Both religions have supported over-breeding, which has now reached epic proportions, creating immense environmental damage and a prime contributor towards global warming. I had recognised that reading the Bible as literal–factual rather than historical–metaphorical often made it a stumbling block, rather than a book of hope—particularly for those who are across science and totally dedicated to the *Theory of Evolution*, but tend to disregard the *Theory of Intelligent Design* upon which religion is based.

I was hoping to find some support for my radical views against the literal interpretation. Consequently, I was thrilled to find the book written by Marcus J Borg, *Reading the Bible again the first time: taking the Bible seriously but not literally*, agreed with my viewpoint.[17] It confirmed the values I clung to, even if I totally disregarded outdated religious dogma. Not surprisingly, Borg was from a Protestant religion, raised by a Lutheran family in North Dakota, USA. Borg was the Distinguished Professor of Religion and Culture at Oregon State University, until his retirement. This is a lucid and easy-to-read book that should be a must-read for people questioning the value of religion in the modern world.

Antii Balk's book, *Balderdash: a treatise on ethics expands on atheism*, also strips away the 'balderdash' that has been built up around religion.[18] He concludes that there are no atheists 'just secularised Christians' and that practically every Christian-turned-atheist continues to live by an artificial code of ethics that would not exist had Christianity not created it. My book also attempts to strip away religious fabrications from fact. For civilisation to evolve, we needed to adopt the values of GOD.

Throughout my first two books, I use GOD (capitalised) as an acronym for the values of faith—Goodness, Order (including gender and cultural equality) and Decency. These values were introduced by the three early 'messengers', Moses, Jesus and Mohammad, to convert the inhumane towards more humane behaviour. As a result of society failing to ingrain these values in human offspring after discarding early religious training, we have seen spiralling juvenile delinquency and increasing numbers of silver-tongued serpents slithering amongst us.

Atheists and individuals who ignore the historical birth of faith, which attempted to introduce a moral compass and essential emotional development including morality, empathy, respect and conscience, should read three valuable books from the world of modern-day neuroscience. These books explain the danger of the snakes we now call white-collar psychopaths, the 'snakes in suits',[19] individuals who place no value on the essential emotional development (EQ) that religion originally taught.

Academia nurtures IQ, religions nurtured EQ

The first book by Dr Robert Hare, *Without Conscience: the disturbing world of the psychopaths amongst us*,[20] described in substantial scientific detail the psychopathic subset of humanity, from white-collar to heinous, which Moses described in the Garden of Eden parable, in Genesis. A second internationally acclaimed book, by author and science journalist, Daniel Goleman, *Emotional intelligence: why it can matter more than IQ*, should be a must-read for confirmed atheists and people in education.[21]

Developing emotional intelligence (EQ) was the key role of religious institutions, and religious instruction courses at schools. Because this has been largely withdrawn and churches closed, it now falls to academia to develop EQ as well as IQ.

Large numbers of children are not learning the qualities of morality, empathy, respect and conscience (MERC) that form the moral compass. This fact is leading to spiralling levels of juvenile delinquency. We are not born with these qualities. When we abandoned the religious form of EQ training, were we thinking children would start absorbing these qualities by osmosis, without any need for direction? Goleman developed the concept of SEL (Social and Emotional Learning) classes. Such classes have now become essential for children no longer being taught these values by religion or parents. SEL classes should become a compulsory part of education. They have been introduced from kindergarten to tertiary in some states in the USA to educate children in the new atheist world growing up without these values.

The third must-read book is *Brainsex: The real difference between men and women,* by geneticist Anne Moir and David Jessel, which was a book feminists tried to shut down.[22] The powerful feminist 'motherhood-mafia' is very efficient in getting information they do not like repressed. Biologically, skewed hormones in pregnant mothers during the first trimester were found to cause homosexuality. Excessive testosterone, during the same time, caused lesbian behaviour in the female foetus, while excessive oestrogen, which was being pumped into everything by industry, caused homosexuality in the male foetus. Skewed hormones hardwired the brain's sexuality, and it has been shown to be irreversible.

Instead of women wasting their energies in the pursuit of a sort of surrogate masculinity, it is far better to welcome and utilise natural differences between men and women. While the sexes are entirely equal, in human rights and in pay, the actual differences between the two genders have added immensely to humans evolving to become the most intelligent of all animal species. A woman's imagination can solve intractable problems, be they professional or domestic, because of her heightened intuitive skills. While women generally cannot read a map as well as a man, they can usually read a character better.

The acceptance and support of single parenting, ignoring the fact that the roles of father and mother are not interchangeable, has now crippled society for several decades and should have initiated further funding, education and research. Children, robbed from birth of the unconditional love and role model of a father, are left with emotional scars that can last a lifetime. Modern society is witnessing ever increasing numbers of emotionally damaged young children, raised without EQ, who are bullying each other and increasingly committing suicide.[23]

The American activist, Ann Coulter, in the powerful second chapter of her book, *Guilty*,[24] revealed the horrific statistics of single, never-married mothers in the US. This group, raising fatherless children, make up approximately 27 per cent of the population, but their offspring make up approximately 75 per cent of the juvenile crime rate. In Australia, we also have children from single-parent homes filling our juvenile court systems.

Domestic violence has been known to spiral as the offspring of inappropriate parenting can transfer their anger towards innocent partners in later years.[25] Blaming and shaming abusive men is treating the symptoms, not the disease. By the time they reach adulthood in unsuitable early environments, they have often been moulded into monsters. This is generally caused by the fact that bullying other children or cruelty to animals, the earliest signs of psychopathy, are not picked up and treated before mid-teens, by neuroscientists specialising in psychopathic behaviour.[26]

In addition, approximately 82 per cent of people incarcerated in adult jails came from inappropriate early environments, or single parent homes. The statistics were so bad for children raised without a positive male role model in their first decade that some agencies in the USA decided to include divorcees and widows with the single never married parent group, to hide the shocking long-term statistics of this latter group. This added insult to injury to women who had taken steps to provide the best outcomes for their children, until fate intervened. Widows and divorcees were entirely suitable titles, they need not have been drawn into the single never married parent classification, simply to hide the fact children from this group had the very worst outcomes.[27-31]

Unfortunately, children raised by mothers who had a less than amicable divorce often fared worse than unmarried single females. The horror of spiralling domestic violence from men, many of whom had themselves been victims of inappropriate parenting, and the modern trend of discarding two-parent parenting, had been a further area of research for me. While accidents can always happen, to deliberately choose to rob a child of a father is emotional abuse and society is paying the price.

Psychopathy is linked to genes, but sociopathy is definitely linked to dysfunctional early environments. However, both disorders are intensified by unstable early environments, as routines and strong boundaries are required in the first decade of life.[32] The stress-laden life of being the child of a single unmarried female coping alone has created the new stolen generation, children robbed of a lifetime of unconditional love from a father. This can leave emotional scars but may have the even more negative impact of depleting the amazing, but very essential bonding and happiness hormone, oxytocin. Stress, alcohol and drugs inhibit the production of this miracle of life and may also reduce the required oxytocin receptors forming within the bodies of young children, if raised by stressed, unhappy females.[33&34]

~ 1 ~
The enigma of golden light

'It is easier for a camel to pass through the eye of a needle than for a rich man to enter the kingdom of God.'
— **Mark 10:25**

When I first heard of the enigma of 'golden light' some people experience when they are brought back from actual heart stoppage and death, it struck a chord. I recalled only inky blackness while in a coma in intensive care as a result of an attempted suicide, following two years of depression, after my first serious relationship had broken down. I had hated growing up without the unconditional love of a father; it made separating from my first partner even harder. Children of single parents are generally desperate for the love of the gender they were robbed of in their early years. Sadly, many are also victims of domestic violence, as they have fewer positive parental role models in the first and most important decade of their lives. Separation and divorce are much higher for female children from single-parent homes. Statistically, they are also sexually active at an earlier age, and more frequently single parents themselves. They are the group that should be seeing psychologists, not gynaecologists.

My failed suicide left me with a sense of rejection and I was very angry. I felt I had been beaten by a hard taskmaster, who would not let me leave this world which, up until that time, seemed to be a school of hard knocks. When I regained consciousness, I had initially been very angry that I had failed, after weeks of planning. I had quite a strong sensation that my personal choice was taken from me, not by the wonderful medical staff who had treated me, but by a more rigid spiritual overseer, making it fairly obvious my time was not yet done, and that there were things I probably had to do. My carefully planned exit had been foiled when my flatmate, who had intended to go camping for the long weekend, returned to our flat at about midnight because her boyfriend's car had broken down. As I was already unconscious, they called an ambulance.

My father had committed suicide, but had alienated himself from our family years before his death, due to his ownership of and heavy gambling on thoroughbred horses. Shortly before his death, on a Saturday afternoon after the races, he visited the house I shared with friends. This was something he had never done before. Unfortunately, I had been out with friends, but he had printed on the back of a betting ticket, 'Dropped in to see you, sorry I missed you. Love Dad.' He had been raised in a harshly disciplined, rather unloving environment. In my entire life, he had never hugged me or used any affectionate term.

At the same time he had also visited my older sister. He spoke to her about his life, how sad he was for things that had happened and how he had made it so hard for my mother financially, because of his gambling. He then put his head in his hands on her kitchen table and cried. We did not know it at the time, but he was saying goodbye. A day or so later, his brother-in-law, who lived on a neighbouring farm, found his body.

He had hooked a piece of wire, from a roll in the back of his farm ute, around the trigger of his shotgun and pulled it towards his head. I kept his note in an expandable folder with other papers of value, but my house had been robbed some years later. A few things were taken: small electrical items, some jewellery, but the worst loss of all was my expandable folder. Of course, it was never recovered, but I can still close my eyes and see his careful copperplate writing on the back of that small, white card.

A point which adults, especially parents, should not forget when considering suicide, is that it opens a gate for their children, particularly sons, to a path already travelled by a loved one. Psychiatrists have found that close contact to this tragedy familiarises and reduces the fear of it for those left behind. When my medicos realised their patient had a history of suicide in the family, they realised 'bigger guns' had to be called in. More intensive psychiatric treatment, in a psychiatric clinic, was recommended, as the suicide comes from a much stronger, long-term source of pain. My resistance was countered by the fact that suicide was considered a crime and was supposed to be reported at that time, and public servants were vetted for police reports.

It continues to intrigue me why some people experience only dull greyness, while others are drawn to mystical golden light when they leave this life. I was even more perplexed when I found my older sister had witnessed this twice, on the night her first husband had died and when her own heart had stopped after a very difficult birth. In her second marriage, there were complications in the birth of her third child, and she was technically dead for a few minutes. As her heart stopped beating, she heard the concerned nurse taking her pulse saying, 'It's not working'. She then had the sensation of falling, whilst in fact moving upwards towards a golden light. Another band was placed on her upper arm; she felt a huge jolt and then heard the nurse comment, 'This one is working', as her pulse started again. The golden light disappeared. Perhaps as my sister now had three young infants to care for it was not her time—the need to stay on earth was greater. She returned from this experience with greater dedication to the Christian faith and all her children were raised as Christians.

I had two inexplicable incidents in my life that pushed me further along that road towards returning to faith. The first was when my youngest sister was fifty years of age and in hospital. In the last days of her life, she described how she had a dream, a vision where she was walking through a fantastic lush, green forest, filled with tropical ferns and flowers and beautiful birds. I presumed it was a result of the drugs that patients were given for pain, or perhaps a happier vision of paradise lost—planet Earth, the Garden of Eden we have been given, but which careless caretakers have turned from forests and fields of green, to vast areas of concrete, bitumen and dust.

The second incident was on the second day after my mother died. I had a strange dream, in the half-sleep just before waking, on a Saturday morning. The whole scene was golden, the same warm colour one sees when sitting on an outdoor chair, basking in the late-autumn afternoon sun, when you take off sunglasses and close your eyes. The bright gold that comes through eyelids was the colour I saw surrounding two distant golden images standing on a slight incline, which was a slightly darker, earthier gold. These figures were silhouetted behind the brighter gold of the sky, but I recognised the shapes of my father, who had died years earlier, and my mother. They stood motionless for what seemed like a couple of minutes holding hands, they then turned and walked up the incline, still holding hands.

The following day, Sunday morning, my older sister rang to ask if we should bury my mother beside my father, as they had become quite distant in life because of my father's gambling problems, depression and his eventual suicide. I told my sister about this strange dream. I was stunned when she then told me of a similar dream she had the night her husband had died, on their fourth wedding anniversary.

Her husband had died years earlier, a beautiful man inside and out, from a form of leukaemia caused by using what we now know were toxic fumes sprayed in glasshouses. In early days, glasshouses were not properly ventilated, and no one knew masks were needed. They lived in the rural food belt and were market gardeners, with two small children. On the night of his death she thought she had woken because a light had been switched on. The whole room seemed bright with golden light, and her husband stood at the end of the bed with his hands on the bed end. He was smiling and said, 'I am well now, don't worry.' She then drifted back to sleep. When she awoke the next morning, he was not in bed beside her. She went out to the back veranda, which was usually where the toilet was located in old country houses, and found him lying on the veranda floor. He had passed away at about the time my sister had experienced the golden dream. Hence, we decided to bury my mother beside my father.

Religious dogma versus science

Some years later, it had been this sister's first-born son, by then an adult studying science at Adelaide University, who started the conversation that led to my six-hour phone conversation with a friend—and my 'road to Damascus' conversion. I was having a conversation with my nephew about how I thought religion was a waste of time because it continued to reject scientific proof. Although he was in his final year of a science degree, I realised he still had very strong faith in a spiritual Creator.

I was never atheist, but certainly going through an agnostic phase. I had never completely stopped believing there was something more meaningful to life than basic evolution and the short period we spend on this earth. I had studied biology at night-school, so I struggled with religious dogma versus science and found his belief rather astonishing. I had found holes in religious belief that did not relate to science (i.e. virgin births and the longevity of some biblical characters) and was very anti-religion as a result. All arguments from the well-meaning and kind-hearted 'God-botherers' among my family and friends had left me unconvinced.

My nephew questioned the 'Big Bang' *Theory of Evolution*. By simply looking at a pebble, an inanimate object, he was aware that, even if that pebble was broken into pieces, nothing could have evolved from those divided pieces. Science has never really explained how the first living cell, from which all life has been created, was formed; therefore, the most vital element of the *Theory of Evolution*, which is based entirely on cell division, continues to remain unanswered by hard science.

After my nephew went to bed, I made a call to a friend who was, I thought, a lapsed Catholic. Fortunately, she was also an insomniac. We spoke on the topic from 11:00 p.m. to 5:00 a.m., curiously, it was within the same time-frame I watched the horror of 9/11 unfold, years later. She had attended a very expensive and exclusive Catholic girls' college. I had first met her when I was flat hunting, after my return from holidays in Europe. In an early conversation about schools and education she had claimed that, 'The only thing that came out of Catholic colleges was nuns or nymphomaniacs.' I made the comment, 'You're not a nun' and she said, 'No, I am not,' and we both laughed at the inference.

It was a phone call that changed my perspective. Fluent in both Latin and French, my friend was an exceptional wordsmith. To discuss Revelations and other biblical extracts, with a person who put a far more practical interpretation on the convoluted text of the Bible, was like a jigsaw puzzle falling into place for me. I began to read it with different eyes. I had always found Bible reading, from Sunday school days, so confusing with its mixed messages. Being mildly dyslexic, more seriously 'maths' dyslexic (i.e. dyscalculia)—I am more dependent on visual imagery than on verbal literacy. Understanding metaphors and symbolism had appealed to me far more than the literal translation preferred by dogmatic fundamentalism. Reading the Bible in the fundamentalist, literal manner had been like reading a foreign language, I had tended to glaze over when it was quoted. To find two people, my friend as well as my nephew, who were both so modern, well-educated and clever, to be firm believers in that mysterious spiritual presence, had initially shocked me.

A couple of days later, I was walking to my home in Hawthorn after work. It was spring and the street that led to my house was lined with jacaranda trees. It headed west and the glorious purple flowers were bright in the afternoon sun, but for the first time in years I noticed the brilliant blue sky at the end of the street—the gloom I had lived with for years had finally lifted. I remember I felt less empty. Growing up in a dysfunctional home, I had always felt internally hollow, like an unfilled skeleton. I never look back on my teens as happy years. For the first time I felt I was no longer completely alone.

After years of depression and striving to hold onto the faith taught by church ministers, it was a female, lapsed Catholic that turned me around. I have never since felt that complete emptiness again, although depression has hovered from time to time. The difference is that now I know it will pass and I have never again considered suicide. I did not suddenly start attending church, but I felt closer to faith than when I used to attend as a youngster. I was, however, glad that I had that early religious instruction, it felt like returning home. My faith in a spiritual force, on which the *Theory of Intelligent Design* is based, was strengthened, but I still had strong reservations about the corruption in male-dominated religions and the dogmatic religious fundamentalists who have adopted the literal interpretation of the Bible, rather than recognising its historic significance and its clever symbolic imagery.

After surviving my attempted suicide, I went back to university studies. I became less agnostic, but I had to turn away from my love of art, pottery, sculpture, growing olives and renovating houses because I lost strength in my hands due to primary rheumatoid arthritis. English grammar was a subject that I had really disliked at school, but writing had to become my new creative outlet. Fortunately, modern speech apps, the miracle for all dyslexics, not only typed everything I dictated, but reads text back to me when proofreading.

Even more miraculously, I found my subject matter the day Dr Hare's book arrived in my mailbox. In 2011, within the space of a week, two people had said to me, 'Children are growing up without a conscience these days.' Although psychology was my major in an Arts degree, I had started several decades earlier, I naively thought that conscience was something inherent in humans. I had Googled 'no conscience' and Dr Hare's book, *Without Conscience*, came into my life.

Dr Hare is a world-leading specialist in the field of neuroscience and his book should be essential reading for anyone dealing with children: in education departments, the law, psychology and parenting. After Dr Hare's book arrived in my mailbox, I delved deeper into the source of psychopathic behaviour. Psychopathy has many levels, from white-collar to heinous, however, if not recognised and professionally treated, it is beyond total rehabilitation by mid-teens. It has a genetic predisposition, but it is bad or inappropriate parenting that can mould monsters rather than marvels. Magnetic Resonance Imaging (MRI) has shown that psychopaths do not register conscience or empathy (C&E), making them the most dangerous of predators.

Hare's page-turning book opened a Pandora's Box for me, and the toxic tentacles of the terrifying world of psychopathy shook me to the core. As a career woman who had worked for thirty-five years in the Department of Employment, Education and Training (DEET), I found it hard to comprehend that I knew so little about the social predators that mingle invisibly amongst us. Research on psychopaths became a huge part of my life for the next few years. One door closed, another opened.

It occurred to me that we have had warnings of these clever, often charming, but rat-cunning, self-centred, pathologically deceptive personas since circa 1400 BC, from the first messenger, Moses, to whom the first book of the Bible, Genesis, was attributed. The symbolic Garden of Eden parable, in 22 verses (Genesis 3:1-22), accurately described these psychopathic predators—using the serpent as a metaphor for pure evil. The serpent deceptively whispered lies into the ears of the most trusting and vulnerable and 'paradise' was lost. In 1993, the destructive psychopathic personas were described in much greater detail by Dr Hare. Yet we are still ignoring the warning.

The parable was completely symbolic; people no more spoke to actual snakes in those days than they do now. Religious clerics, either extremely misogynist or totally incompetent in interpreting brilliant symbolism, blamed the victim Eve and, like a cancerous growth, the world of religion was damaged for centuries, ruled by some of the most evil of men who preferred to subjugate women rather than see them as equals.

After reading Hare's book, I started to write about the successful white-collar psychopaths (WCPs) that slither amongst us, the metaphorical 'snakes in suits' which the recent Australian Royal Commissions on banking has revealed to the world. *Snakes in suits,*[1] is the title of a book by Paul Babiak and Dr Hare that I also recommend. Recognition of these corrupt men, and occasionally women, who do not have—or are able to repress completely—the two qualities that separate the non-psychopathic persona from the psychopath, conscience and empathy (C&E), have now been revealed by research in the field of neuroscience.

The three Abrahamic religions squabbling amongst themselves about whose prophet is superior, is ludicrous. I never completely discarded my faith, because as an internally angry child from a dysfunctional home with an emotionally distant father, I would not have survived the cold, emptiness of atheism. Faith gave me the feeling that at least a spiritual 'Father' was watching my back 24/7. However, the more I learned about evolution and psychopathy, the more I began to recognise that early religious prophesies matched modern-day outcomes.

Since the 1970s, Australia has had only two psychotic men commit mass murder. One was at Port Arthur in Tasmania, in April 1996, where thirty-five visitors were shot and killed, with twenty-three wounded.[2] The second was an Australian who had travelled to Christchurch in New Zealand. In March 2019, he was responsible for mass shootings in two mosques, killing fifty Muslims with another fifty injured. Unfortunately, the gun restrictions at that time in NZ were more lenient than in Australia, and the killer was easily able to access several military assault rifles.[3]

Within a fortnight of Australia's mass murder at Port Arthur, strict gun control was introduced across all six states and the Northern Territory. Within a fortnight of the extremist assault in New Zealand, they followed Australia's lead and introduced stricter gun laws, banning assault weapons and tightening gun registration. Something which members of America's NRA (National Rifle Association), an association where WCPs put profit before people, should observe, as there were 434 mass shootings in America in 2019 alone.[4]

This averaged 1.19 mass shootings per day in the US. In these shootings, 1,643 people were injured and 517 died, making a total of 2,160 victims. In 2018, 323 mass shootings occurred, resulting in 1,661 people being shot. Of those people, 387 people consequently died.[5] Tragically, this includes an even more disturbing statistic, as they have one to two mass murder events a month in schools.[6] *Everytown*, an independent, non-profit group that studies gun violence, reports it has tracked at least ninety-nine incidents of gunfire on school grounds in 2019 alone, including three suicides and sixty-three injuries.[7] They promote their guns are keeping them safer. Really? It appears mass shootings are increasing. This dictatorial control by the NRA, within a country with a democratically elected government, is a tragedy that good Americans do not deserve—and it shocks the rest of the free world. The gun deaths make America the most dangerous country to visit, in the Western democratic world. It has been reported by the New York Times that a New Yorker is just as likely to be robbed as a Londoner, but the New Yorker is 54 times more likely to be killed in the process. America is about 4.4 per cent of the global population but owns 42 per cent of the world's guns.

What surprised me, after Christchurch, was how Australia and New Zealand were condemned by the Turkish president (where Islam is the major religion), as being guilty of racism and religious persecution. However, I would like to remind society that during the same time (since the 1970s) Islamic terrorists committed over 275 major attacks reported in the world media (refer to Attachment A), against both non-Islamic people and their enemy tribal groups, trying to forge Muslim supremacy. Over 10,000 innocent people have died, and at least another 10,000 injured. In America, 9/11 alone resulted in over 6000 deaths and injuries.

The free world—comprising Judaists, Christians, numerous other religious beliefs and atheists—has been condemned by the Muslim culture for the rise of right-wing extremism and white supremacy, but attacks by Islamic terrorists have also occurred in dozens of countries across the world. What changes do we see made by Sharia law, which rules these cultures? Virtually nothing, because deceptive Islamic religious clerics that formed the cult offshoot of true Islam honour these godless killers by calling them martyrs. I have used the term Sunni 'hadith Islam' for this cult offshoot because it is based on thousands of corrupt tribal hadiths (laws), added under the guise of religion after Muhammad's death and driven primarily by the Sunni tribe.

Muslims have not had the courage that leaders of the Protestant faiths had in the Christian world, where they broke away from the dictatorial control of the Catholic Church, which had introduced sacrilegious rules to increase their power. The character assassination of the third prophet, Muhammad, and the sabotage of his 'religion of peace' by this male-dominant Islam cult offshoot, driven primarily by the Sunni tribal men after his death, sparked my interest. It reminded me of the children's story, *The Emperor's New Clothes*, by Hans Christian Andersen. The world is too afraid to say, 'Enough! You are moulding criminals and thugs, lift your game, or go to prison!'

The shocking and totally godless evil of the terrorist attack of 9/11 in America, prompted me to study corruption within the Islamic religion more closely. I decided to initially write about the psychopathic personas that have risen to the upper echelons of religion, particularly male dominated religions and cults that have formed since the Abrahamic monotheist faith was first introduced.

It concerned me that most people are not interested in religion these days. For this reason, information about so-called WCPs in business, who generally do not kill, seemed more relevant. Then, in March 2019, we witnessed the horror of a mass-murder at Christchurch, New Zealand, where places of worship were attacked by an Australian. That heinous psychopathic behaviour drew me back to the topic of faith versus religion. Religion has attracted many corrupt men, far more interested in earthly power and personal control than in teaching the values of goodness over evil, the foundation of faith. I decided that writing about white collar psychopaths (WCPs) was looking at the symptoms, not the disease.

Cold-blooded and ruthless psychopaths, the paedophiles and terrorists raping and killing under the pretence they are doing it for God/Allah, are men of the antichrist, not God. The term 'antichrist' is self-explanatory: it is not a fierce mythical beast as described in Revelations—again, this was brilliant symbolism meant to literally scare the hell out of early followers. The antichrist is not a single being, it is a collective term for people who are contemptuous of any form of faith and choose to ignore the snakes that now slither amongst us—psychopaths that are the most destructive element of modern life.

While 9/11 was the night the seeds for this book were planted, the separation from my third partner, a Catholic, turned my interest in religious white-collar psychopathy into a more serious commitment. The fact that we have a world where no one dares to speak out against the horrific corruption within religions became a personal driving force. As a society, we had disturbing apathy regarding increased numbers of paedophiles in the male-dominant Roman Catholic Church. Now we have what I call Sunni 'hadith Islam', which continues to support religious enslavement, gender apartheid and female oppression in the male dominant cult offshoot of true Islam—and so the apathy continues.

It appears virtually impossible for obscenely wealthy people, driven by greed rather than need, to reach the golden heights of eternal rest. I, therefore, found it interesting that Australia witnessed our wealthiest man, who temporarily 'died' on the operating table several times, while receiving a donated organ transplant, proudly proclaiming there was nothing but blackness in the afterlife. He had been a hard man, expecting very high standards of his son and, as frequently happens, his well-liked son had very public emotional stress issues as an adult. I hope that excessively wealthy man did become far more philanthropic before his death, and possibly did see 'golden light' when he finally did die.

Interestingly, by contrast, a young surfer in Western Australia, who had been attacked by a shark, also 'died' a couple of times in the ambulance. Later, when he was being interviewed in hospital, he mentioned the sensation of being drawn towards a 'golden light', but

11

because he had a partner and two children he dearly loved, he had fought against it, as he had felt a much greater urgency to stay. I remember thinking how lucky that surfer was, to know his young soul had already been judged in a positive light by whatever ethereal power had created this incredible planet. Although I support faith and the values of GOD, I sit on the fence regarding religion. Curiously, the more I researched corrupted religions, the more I questioned the *Theory of Evolution*. *Evolution* and *Intelligent Design* are still both theories, but for civilisation to grow and expand, one could not have survived without the other.

Steve Jobs, the chairman, CEO, and co-founder of Apple Inc., was an incredibly wealthy man, whose famous final words were, 'Oh wow. Oh wow. Oh wow.'[8] While dying of pancreatic cancer, he opened his eyes for the last time, looked at his sister Patty, then for a long time at his children, then at his life partner, Laurene and finally, over their shoulders past them. He then uttered those monosyllables, repeated three times, and closed his eyes for the last time. I suspect those joyous words were not from a man looking into looming darkness.

Born Abdul Latif Jandali, he was put up for adoption and adopted by wonderful Calvinist parents, Paul and Clara Jobs. The animosity between his grandparents, who were of opposing Catholic and Muslim religions, caused that sad start to Jobs' life. His biological mother had been persuaded to have her son adopted by her Catholic father who refused to approve of his daughter's marriage to a Muslim.[9]

Jobs' immense intelligence caused the usual problems of student acceptance in schools that could not cope with the rebelliousness that often comes when high IQ children become bored. There was a lot of hype and curiosity regarding the late Apple co-founders last words. People knew Steve Jobs for his creativity, innovation and inspiring quotes. He recognised the importance of treasuring life and family before material things or success. I suspect because of the pain that the 'sins of the fathers' had forced on his innocent young life, his soul was being drawn by a far more caring spiritual 'Father' to the golden light of rest and healing—unlike many others of immense wealth who are driven by greed and were condemned by all three early prophets.

At least two men and one woman in the medical profession have experienced golden light in near-death experiences (NDE's) and have recorded these experiences. Dr Mary Neal, an orthopaedic surgeon, drowned in a kayak accident. While cascading down a waterfall, her kayak became pinned at the bottom and was completely submerged. Despite the rescue efforts, Mary was under water for nearly fifteen minutes and died as a result. Her book titled, *To Heaven and back,* tells the story.[10] Dr Eben Alexander, a highly trained neurosurgeon, developed a rare illness causing his brain to shut down completely. He lay in a coma for seven days and his doctors considered stopping treatment. Suddenly, he regained consciousness; his recovery was seen as a medical miracle. His book, *Proof of Heaven: A neurosurgeon's journey into the Afterlife,* is even more remarkable as Dr Alexander had previously believed NDE's were simply fantasies produced by brains under extreme stress.[11]

The mega-rich Dr Rajiv Parti trained as an anaesthesiologist in America. He had a 'hellish out-of-body experience' when he was having emergency surgery for complications after a cancer operation. He saw tunnels of dark hell before he saw golden light. It transformed his life. Now, every day, he tries to live a life of compassion. From the experience he realised certain truths: that there is life after death, that we all are connected to each other and that there is a supreme, loving entity. Dr Parti gave up his medical career. 'I used to put people to sleep,' he says. 'Now I wake them up.'[12]

I believe good souls do drift to a place of eternal comfort and reconciliation with loved ones, in the last moments of life. My life changed after my suicide attempt—I certainly saw no 'golden light'. I recall pitch black nothingness while in a coma, but I felt I had met my match. There were things I had to do before I was entitled to that 'eternal rest'.

In the Twentieth Century, doctors and psychologists compiled a short list of things that lead to longevity. Along with family, friendships and healthy diets, doctors noted that in times of serious illness it was the people who had strong faith and community support that often had better recovery rates. In addition, their recovery times were also shorter. The inner strength and courage gained by believing something, or someone, is watching your back has helped civilisation survive for centuries. It may be a placebo effect, but the enigma of golden light tilts more towards the fact that good souls do have value beyond this life.

Perhaps it is time for another religious reformation. The point of my book is to get people talking. I am simply a researcher—and a 'pot-stirrer'. Young people must learn from our mistakes, not continue to repeat them. However, before older readers put up counter-arguments to my essays, read some of the sites and books I have referenced. We need debates not denial, agreement not aggression. In the mid-twentieth century, when atheists started to drop the values of faith—morality, empathy, respect and conscience (MERC)—it allowed male-dominated, gender-apartheid religions to flourish unchecked, and evolution and civilisation took a backward step.

I recall, at the start of this process, looking towards the window from the desk at which I was working. I watched a beautiful, golden Monarch butterfly as it landed on a tall lavender spike. The stem arched over, and the butterfly hung in all its splendour, as it basked in the early spring sun. I paused from my writing just to savour the moment. Dozens of books, reference and fiction, lined my bookcase and lay on my desk, waiting to be read. I contemplated whether I really wanted to spend the hours of discipline and the hard slog of putting thousands of words down on paper, many of which have been written numerous times before and filled dozens of textbooks, but which the world seems not to notice, or even care about. Why didn't I just pack my bags and head off for distant places, back to Ireland, Paris, or Santorini, to continue the life of pleasure and comfort I worked so hard for, coming from such a dysfunctional start?

The butterfly fluttered away over the garden wall. I looked at the comforting, flickering flames of the fire on that fresh spring day and recalled the observation made by Tom Shadyac, while being interviewed about his thought-provoking documentary, *I am*.[13] He said that when you change one small act in your world, it has a ripple effect. I decided to push on, to ask questions of this world, to 'stir the pot', and to hope my words will cause a small ripple effect that will raise the conscience of governments, educational institutions—both academic and religious— and in younger people, who can question and make change.

~ 2 ~

Three courageous men of faith changed the world

'Hardship often prepares an ordinary person for an extraordinary destiny.'
— C.S. Lewis

Religion was the start of modern civilisation, earlier human species relied more on the kill-or-be-killed ethos of lower animal species. We were given brains that evolved from Neanderthal to scientific brilliance, but a moral compass did not automatically come with evolution. An incredible gift of insight and enlightenment was given to three chosen messengers who realised the value of moral integrity at times of appalling immorality and enslavement–that was the real miracle of their time on Earth. A moral compass had not been a requirement of early tribal groups.

Evolution and interaction with other cultures and communities did require far stronger emotional development (EQ)[1,] something entirely alien to tyrannical leaders. In circa 1400BC, came the first prophet Moses, whose heart and soul were guided by the values of GOD— Goodness, Order (including gender and cultural equality) and Decency. Moses, raised as a prince, recognised the shocking wealth disparity and the injustice and immorality of dictatorial control and sought change. The incredible bravery and enlightenment of this man, who risked his life in trying to introduce freedom in such a barbarous environment, has never really been satisfactorily explained by the hard science of evolution. The profound enlightenment of all three messengers, who laid the foundation of faith, has been linked with the alternative *Theory of Intelligent Design*.

The three major prophets, Moses, Jesus and Muhammad, were born centuries apart and all lived in times of extremely barbaric behaviour—of pagan worship and tribal oppression and spiralling immorality. Tribal dictators enforced enslavement, female subjugation and massive financial inequality. Faith was introduced by these three men, who tried to ingrain conscience, empathy and a moral compass into the fabric of society. Yet the powerful transformation initiated by these prophets has been minimised by many. Certain religions that formed after their deaths have allowed the male 'mine is bigger and better than yours' attitude to prevail, rather than perpetuating the unity which was the message of the three major prophets.

The messengers spoke with one voice to counter social injustice and to encourage moral integrity and a more caring communal life. While the prophets preached unity, it was male religious leaders that followed them that created immense disunity. They have torn apart the simple rules of faith, bending them to their own interests, and have created great divisions between the various forms of religion. Both Catholicism and Islam spurned female equality. The world has also witnessed horrific results of terrorism and crime because of these mentally skewed people who chose to distort the rules of faith for their own power. This state of affairs is the polar opposite to the unified message the three messengers attempted to spread, to change the immoral and barbarous behaviour so prolific in their eras.

Monotheist religions, characterised by the belief that there is only one God, have humanised the spiritual power and various titles have been used for the Creator, around which the monotheist faith developed. The titles Yahweh, Jehovah and Allah all represent the one God. Squabbles continue about the reality of Moses, Jesus and Muhammad and whose 'messenger' was best. Christianity even converted their messenger, Jesus, into a God, which was the eventual cause of his death, as this irreverence angered the first branch of the monotheist faith. Jewish men of faith saw the placing of an earthborn man as a substitute for God as a great sin. While the three major prophets walked this earth, the holy books show they strongly insisted they were only God's messengers and were not to be worshipped as gods, which would have turned them into pagan idols.

They were exceptionally valuable messengers as they promoted a more moral and law-abiding world, but to equate them with God defeats the purpose of monotheism.

What drove all three prophets to embrace a monotheist faith? That is the real mystery of life. It is also the reason why millions across the world still take comfort in that spiritual strength which drives cultural bonding and community. Sadly, with the increase in atheism and ungodly religious cult offshoots (which are by-and-large the fault of the Abrahamic religious fundamentalist dogma, created by men playing God), we have had a deterioration of faith. Earthborn men developed the three major monotheist religions, after the death of the prophets. 'God' has no religion; none of the three prophets demanded that their followers be Judaist, Christian or Islamic. They only asked that their followers believe in a single spiritual Creator, that they follow the ten basic *Commandments* and care for this Eden they have been given. The Twenty-First Century is failing on all counts.

Appropriately, humanity has given the title of God to that powerful spiritual strength and, interestingly, every letter stands for the values those messengers were trying to ingrain—Goodness, Order and Decency. The three major Abrahamic monotheist religions, Judaism, Christianity and Islam developed around men who appear to have been especially chosen 'sons' of the spiritual Creator. They were enlightened far above others of their eras, however, to judge one messenger better than the other is the action of dogmatic religious fundamentalists, not God. Catholics promoted Jesus as 'son of God' but we are all supposed to be children of the spiritual Father. Three were enlightened beyond people of their era, but a spiritual Father of all creation would not have chosen one of the three messengers as his favourite son—that is an earthly judgement that has torn apart religious unison. These three men's aim on earth was to develop more caring communities, turning killers into carers—religious disunity is the exact opposite of what they bravely struggled for.

Catholicism, the first major branch of the Christian faith, often ruled by bigoted, celibate men who practised gender apartheid, created the ultimate sacrilege by aligning the second messenger, Jesus, as equal to God. This action was condemned by all three prophets, who saw themselves as messengers, not God. By not treating women as equals, the gender now recognised (because of genes and hormones) as generally the more ethical gender, male religious clerics, over time, have subtly distorted the words and values of faith.

Being a messenger of God proved to be a very dangerous occupation. While the demise of the first prophet, Moses, is lost in the mists of time, the brutal murder of the second prophet, Jesus, and all but one of his twelve disciples, negatively impacted the entire Jewish community, who had not accepted him as a prophet and messenger, for centuries. A few wealthy men were not happy with the changes Jesus was trying to make, for instance challenging the money lenders' greed and the huge division of wealth, so they decided that he had to die. The second messenger was murdered at Calvary, not to pardon our sins but because of our sins. This was a male twist to sell the Christian faith, spread by serpents within the faith. The Catholic belief that baptism was given to take away any sins, inherited from Adam, is based on a symbolic parable. A parable completely mistranslated by men who could not recognise it was the symbolic serpent, a brilliant metaphor for pure evil, which had cast the sin.

The cold-blooded reptile, subtle, manipulative and incredibly deceptive is the action of psychopathy. It was the first warning of the corrupt persona neuroscience now recognises as psychopathy. Tragically, the action of one psychopath can impact negatively on thousands of innocent people. Criminals that are psychopathic have the widest range of victims, many more than non-psychopathic criminals.[2&3]

Roman Catholics wanted division, power and control over the other religions. The fact Jesus was born of Jewish parents is a fact that is pushed aside and ignored by this branch of the Christian faith. It was the Roman ruler, Pontius Pilate, who condemned Jesus to death, but many Jews who had despised the renewed fight for fiscal and gender equality, which both Jesus and later Muhammad fought for, supported the crucifixion of the second prophet.[4] A long shadow was cast over many innocent Jews for centuries because of a few corrupt individuals.

In their efforts to pull power from Judaism, the early church clerics of the first branch of Christianity, Catholicism, seemed deaf, dumb and blind to the sin of seeing their prophet and themselves as equal to God. To this day, they still adopt the role of God, taking confessions and giving absolution of sins. They are middle-men, making excuses for sinners they have forgiven in God's name, with little more than a few 'Hail Mary's' and the rattling of beads, and may, in the process, have condemned their own souls to purgatory. Of course, there is huge denial of this, but that is to be expected. Denial is the most dominant trait of psychopathy. Even when presented with indisputable facts and evidence, psychopaths are incapable of accepting they are wrong.[5] People of faith have been warned that the souls of those usurping the role of God will see the dark wrath of that spiritual force. The deceptive snake in the very first biblical parable was never forgiven, having to crawl on its belly for eternity.

Messengers of God were not God replacements; it appears that this ideology was driven by Catholics hundreds of years after the death of Jesus. The messengers were exceptional sons, their strong belief in the one God, a spiritual Father to turn to in times of need, gave people hope. All three messengers caused powerful change that has had continued benefits until current times.

The hundreds of religions that are offshoots, or corruptions, of the Abrahamic faith that was introduced simply to provide humanity with a moral compass, will have a lot to answer for, come judgement day. Earthborn rules of compulsion are the greatest desecration introduced into religion, as all three Holy Books forbid compulsion. However, atheism, also now disregards many of the *Ten Commandments* and ignores teaching their followers the values of GOD. Possibly the worst is the patriarchal heresy of Sunni 'hadith Islam', which insists that women are inferior and must obey or submit to men. Submission to earthborn men was never the rule of the three messengers. The prophets preached that men and women should obey and be submissive only to God, Women did not have to submit to men, who made themselves replacements of God in the women's world—that is appalling sacrilege.

Faith was about ingraining qualities that separate the humane from the inhumane, primarily conscience and empathy (C&E)—the qualities that divided the non-psychopath from the psychopath. Without C&E

humans suffered no guilt or remorse. The purpose of religion was to define the difference between good and evil, symbolised by God and Satan. All three major prophets strove for equality and concentrated on what they could give, while their enemies flourished on elitism and wealth inequality, pathological deception, greed and were content to devastate this Eden, for their own self-centred interests.

The prophets introduced qualities of emotional development that are essential for civilisation, morality, empathy, respect and conscience (MERC)—values atheists appear to have ignored when they discarded religion. One only has to look at the appalling dictatorial regimes of subjugation and enslavement, ruled by autocratic men who always tick boxes of psychopathy. The messengers fought to change the world by introducing freedom and equality and they did transform the world. The Christian world has evolved as a free world, a polar opposite to cultures that continued obscene dictatorial control. Evolution stagnated and died in the dark ages of godless, autocratic control and manipulation.

The three major prophets did not promote a particular religion, they were simply introducing a better quality of life, of freedom and hope, to a world ruled by cruel and godless men. Unfortunately, with the atheists' disregard for the values of faith across the world, we now have thousands of children growing up without a strong moral compass and without hope.

Hard science does not explain how a male, Moses, in circa 1400 BC, with absolutely no neuroscience training, so accurately described the most dangerous predator of the human species (the psychopathic persona), which is capable of destroying our small Garden of Eden, planet Earth. The subtle metaphorical snake-like deceiver whispered lies into the ears of the most vulnerable and paradise was lost.

As the banking system, the economic bedrock of society, is exposed as a haven for white-collar psychopaths, are we witnessing the arrival of the symbolic 'black horse', the third horse of the Horsemen of the Apocalypse? Its rider represented famine, pestilence, disease and earthquakes. That third horseman carried a pair of weighing scales, which suggested a continuing abundance of luxuries for the wealthy while staples for the poor, such as bread, were scarce.[6]

In the modern world, we are tragically seeing evidence of the gradual destruction of our Eden as once again we celebrate atheism and the drift away to more egocentric, narcissistic and self-serving values. We now celebrate successful WCPs that rise to CEO levels, particularly in financial institutions where vast amounts of money can be extracted for personal use and, as the last couple of years have shown, even to presidential levels. These deceptive, manipulative snakes were condemned as the lowest of all creatures, cursed to crawl in dust for all eternity. Yet now they stand amongst us unquestioned. Financial disparity eats away at civilisation like cancer, and white-collar psychopathic personas drive that disparity. Those early books of faith also gave warning of this peril (Matthew 19:24, Mark 10:25 & Quran 7:40). All verses relate to the statement: 'It is easier for a camel to pass through the eye of a needle than for a rich man to enter the kingdom of God' (Mark 10:25).

Peter Turchin, a Professor of Ecology and Evolution at the University of Connecticut, in the opening statement of his essay, *Return of the Oppressed*,[7] summed up the world problem when he wrote, 'From the Roman Empire to our own Gilded Age, inequality moves in cycles.' The wealth gap between the good and the greedy will never completely disappear, but people with a conscience must continue the battle to raise social awareness of these self-centred and avaricious individuals. Modern atheists once again need a few brave and enlightened people amongst them. Individuals, independent males and females, with integrity and innovation, who have the courage in politics, tax offices and law to rein in excessive and undeserved riches of the disproportionately wealthy.

The white-collar psychopaths (WCPs) with anaemic levels of C&E, who can afford to pay top accountants to reduce their taxes to almost zero, or hide money in tax havens, are the new-age felons, putting greed above need. As a result of our outdated tax system, the middle-class, nine-to-five workers, have to carry government funding in the modern world, where teenagers can now become millionaires. Individuals should be taxed on their actual worth. Individuals struggling to pay a huge mortgage on their one major asset, usually worth under a million dollars, with the added cost of educating children, should be at the very lowest end of the tax scale. It is they that should be paying the rate of companies like Netflix. Netflix Australia paid only $341,793 in tax for the 2018 calendar year despite reaping an estimated $600 million to $1 billion from local subscribers. Its tax bill for 2018 amounted to about 0.06 per cent of the lowest estimate of its Australian income, or 0.04 per cent at the upper end.[8]

Individuals, making more than the entire worth of the middle-class taxpayers in a day, a week, or a month, create the modern form of enslavement and crippling subjugation by the wealthy over the working class. Perhaps my favourite, symbolic, biblical verse is from Luke 16:19–31:

> There was a rich man who was clothed in purple and fine linen and who feasted sumptuously every day. And at his gate was laid a poor man named Lazarus, covered with sores, who desired to be fed with what fell from the rich man's table. Moreover, even the dogs came and licked his sores. The poor man died and was carried by the angels to Abraham's side. The rich man also died and was buried, and in Hades, being in torment, he lifted up his eyes and saw Abraham far off and Lazarus at his side.[9]

The powerful messages, which the three prophets brought to this world, initially redirected a world teetering between barbarianism and civilisation. The prophets, Jesus and Muhammad, tried to stimulate social conscience regarding poverty and the excesses of wealth. These two prophets were very concerned about social order and the wealth disparity, which continued to cause unrest and numerous civil wars.

In addition, the *Ten Commandments* in Exodus, also attributed to Moses who had no training in law, still stand as the bedrock of law within the Western world. If set that task today, it is hard to imagine the size of the report and the time and money it would take a modern day 'Royal Commission' to complete. Moreover, why did Moses decide to follow a monotheist religion? Why did all three key prophets settle on one God, when pagan gods added such a wide variety of options? The events of courage and personal empowerment far outweighed the mystical versions of how the exceptionally gifted baby Jesus, was conceived.

Equally, a fact also unexplained by evolution, was how a male without any training in palaeontology, meteorology or geology, provided the sequence of the evolution of life on this planet, with the same sequence modern science has provided? The biblical translation seven 'days' has often erroneously been interpreted as 24-hour days. In 1400 BC, seven periods of time were given; 24-hour time frames given when the word 'day' is used is obviously wrong, i.e. 'in the day of the steam engine', 'day' represents an age or era, not twenty-four hours.

Dogmatic religious fundamentalists that cling to theories created when people thought the world was flat, retard rather than advance the value of faith. Faith should be in accord with science, not stagnant and clinging to concepts introduced by creative and imaginative people of the past. While there is no scientific evidence regarding virgin births, there is evidence this concept was adopted from earlier pagan beliefs to empower the Christian faith and to win followers from the earlier faith of Judaism.[10]

My belief that there is some greater power that plays a role in our short lives on this planet makes me question the Christian interpretation of the birth of Jesus. If I did humanise God, as fundamentalists seem to do, I would question why, if God wanted a physical presence on earth, would a source with the power to create a universe, have taken such a time-consuming process of producing a son. It took nine months of gestation, a dozen years of happy childhood and several more years training as a carpenter with his father before he could realise his true vocation, introducing the values of GOD to the human race.

It is far more believable that Jesus was the biological son of Joseph and Mary. Mary was the mother of one of the three chosen messengers of God, not (as Catholics have been taught to believe) the mother of God. However, Jesus was certainly an incredible visionary who changed the world. An incredible gift set him apart from men of that era—which is a far more credible and impressive circumstance than the pagan virgin birth mythology pushed by early Christian clerics. Fortunately, Christianity continued the Judeo-Christian traditions of developing social integrity by trying to turn barbarous individuals into honourable and caring protectors of this planet.

To believe a female was formed from the rib bone of a male is also against scientific evidence. Research has shown the early hominoids, Neanderthals, evolved into modern homo sapiens—except possibly in rugby clubs. Neanderthal DNA seemed evident to rugby supporters long before scientific proof–in 2010 it was confirmed that up to four per cent of Neanderthal DNA still exists in modern man.[11] When one looks at the bulked-up bodies and hardly recognisable, mangled, facial features of some of these rugby players at the end of their careers, it must be to the despair of their mothers. Wear helmets!

Nor did the world of religious faith start with the third and last prophet, Muhammad, as Sunni 'hadith Islam' clerics deceptively suggest to their people. (Sunni 'hadith Islam' is the name I have given to the cult offshoot of Islam, introduced after the prophet's death, based on fabricated hadiths, which Muhammad had condemned). The earlier Judeo-Christian monotheist faith influenced Muhammad's adoption of faith, called Islam, which meant 'submission'—to Allah, not submission to man-made Sunnah rules, but to the same God to which the other two Abrahamic religions were also submissive. It followed the same path as Judaism and Christianity monotheism.

Muhammad always made it clear he was only the messenger of God. Both he and the second prophet, Jesus, strongly disagreed with people elevating them as equal to God. Muhammad respected the second prophet, but correctly (I believe) disagreed with followers, predominately the Catholic branch of Christianity, in elevating Jesus and his mother, Mary, to godly status.[12-13] Matthew 23:1–12 indicates Jesus was also offended by Jewish clerics using the religious title 'rabbi' (i.e. my master) and early Christian clerics answering to the term 'Father', religious titles he felt should be reserved for God.

After Muhammad's death, with no sons of his own to carry on the faith, enemy tribal men reintroduced the many barbaric pre-Islam tribal traditions Muhammad had tried to change. Many hadiths blatantly insult the world's last 'messenger'.[14&15] However, all hadiths additional to the Quran are a sin against Allah's word (Quran 6:112-113) and are contemptuous of the third prophet's warning. We know Muhammad in his last famous sermon pleaded for those hadiths already written by dictatorial tribal leaders to be destroyed.[16] The Quran confirms that followers of fabrications, created by earthborn men and added to the original holy books of faith, are the disbelievers amongst the 'People of the Scriptures'—the 'infidels' who will be in the 'fire of Hell':

> Quran 98:6, 'Indeed, they who disbelieved among the People of the Scripture and the polytheists will be in the fire of Hell, abiding eternally therein. Those are the worst of creatures.'(For more on Muhammad, Islam and Sharia law, see Essays 7 and 8.)

Harmony, compatibility and equality between partners who love and respect each other were the most important messages of the third prophet, Muhammad. He was married to the love of his life and remained faithful until the day she died, twenty-five years after their marriage. 'Hadith Islam' has become the greatest offender of these values, as it practices gender apartheid and inequality. Males of this cult have an unjustified sense of superiority because they blatantly place themselves as false gods, forcing total submission from women. They have been heinously bolstered by this illegal and false religious empowerment given to the male gender in the godless cult offshoot of Islam, Sunni 'hadith Islam'.

Even before his death, Muhammad realised the danger the false hadiths would create. Dictatorial Muslim tribal leaders reverted almost immediately to barbaric tribal traditions when he died. Their contempt for human life and the environment was completely sacrilegious; actions of the antichrist, not God-fearing people. In the present day it is very evident in the thuggish behaviour of men raised without respect for women and the incredible arrogance of men moulded to believe they are a superior gender or race.

The world has already witnessed this behaviour by another dictator who attempted to spread his beliefs in racial 'purity' and the superiority of the 'Germanic race'—those he called the Aryan 'master race'. Hitler, a Catholic, was anti-Semitic and tried to exterminate all Jews. Now we have men, moulded by the corrupted form of Islam, who (it appears) not only want to exterminate Jews, but also Christians and everyone not of their religion. Did Sunni 'hadith Islamic' clerics go out into the world as missionaries to convert people to faith in God, as the well-intentioned Christian missionaries of the past did? No, they did not, they took the option to kill people they could not force to remain in their religion by adopting the apostasy death cult two years after Muhammad's death![16-19]

The psychopathic men who cause world wars force good men to stand and defend. Do we have to face a repeat of this insanity with 'hadith Islam' terrorists? Terrorists are men filled with pure hatred; they are not men of God. Arrogance, narcissism, self-obsession and hatred are the world of the 'jinn devils'. Muhammad was an honest and enlightened man who brought monotheist faith where formerly there was polytheism and paganism. To imply Muhammad would support the murder of other followers of God is the sacrilegious misconception that dishonest members of this faith tell their trusting followers.

Muslims have been deliberately misled into believing Christians worship three Gods, because of the Holy Trinity: Father, Son and Holy Spirit, and are therefore polytheists. Yet numerous books of Sunnah and hadiths, deceptively based on Muhammad's personal conversations and actions, have made a deity of their prophet, which is the same polytheism they accuse Christians of by making Jesus a divine, god-like presence.

Some self-serving clerics in the Jewish religion rejected Muhammad, as did some Christian clerics, exactly as self-serving men in 'hadith Islam' now reject all other religions. These corrupt men rejected each other's religion because of the egocentric, godless, male attitude of clerics that believed their religion was the chosen religion and their prophet was the more superior. While the values of GOD (Goodness, Order and Decency) were the foundation of faith and the unified message spread by all three messengers, it was the religions that followed (created entirely by earthborn males), which have created great disunity. There are only two options in God's criteria: the choice of good or evil. Choice of religion, gender or colour has no bearing on God's final judgement. The Quran reminds us of this fact:

Quran 3:99, 'O People of the Scripture, why do you hinder from God's path those who believe, seeking to distort it, even though you are witnesses? God is not unaware of what you do.'

Muhammad was speaking as a messenger of the same God as the first two prophets. He did not reject the earlier two Abrahamic religions;

he did not 'hinder from God's path' the Jews and Christians, yet the Sunni 'hadith Islam' cult promoted slaughter of them. All three faiths have had clerics who committed *shirk* (aligning themselves, or their words, as equal to God and his words),[20] but all three holy books, the old and new Testaments and the Quran, have stated God is aware of what they do. Jews turned against Jesus, who was the Jewish son of Jewish parents, because he saw corruption by his people and tried to change it. It was the same for the third prophet, whose own people turned against him, reintroducing godless tribal traditions only a few years after his death. He was against female servitude and dictatorial oppression, yet both have now been accepted under Sunni 'hadith Islam'.

The messengers should not be judged by the religions that followed them, as some of those have failed humanity enormously. The only Christian Gospel that was accepted by Muslims as accurate, authentic and saved from distortion is that of St. Barnabas, a Cypriot companion of St. Paul (originally Saul). This was not canonised by the Council of Nicaea of 325 AD, where the 'Trinity' was incorporated into the Christian beliefs.[21] This happened in the Fourth Century and was dictated by clerics of the Catholic faith, giving preference to rules created by men, not God. This created considerable dissention among the religions that had formed around the three major prophets. The doctrine of the Trinity was that there was one God, who was Father, Son and the Holy Spirit. The Trinity should have been God, all three chosen messengers and the Holy Spirit.

I believe the Holy Spirit is the invisible emotional strength and sense of hope that we seem to have, when we have been raised in a monotheist faith. For almost 400 years, many Christians had not even heard of the Trinity. The Nicaea Conference was to settle the disputes among various Christian sects about what constituted Christianity and what did not, but it is said the Conference created more problems than it solved. It was boycotted by several non-Catholic Christian Protestant sects that did not endorse its resolutions.[22]

Moral and respectful Muslims may not recognise the term 'Holy Spirit', but they have it within them. It is the soul, the conscience and empathy, that separates them from evil, the godly from the godless. It appears apparent that the third part of the Trinity is simply the invisible strength, the internal steel that seems to slide into believers when prayers are sent, or in times of great stress and crisis. It encompasses the important emotional qualities which divide those with souls from those that are soulless. The prophets recognised the problem of evil people destroying good people, thousands of years ago. Modern neuroscientists are still trying to work out the same problem, the 'how and why' of psychopathic personas, who develop without C&E.

The Judeo-Christian faith has also been weakened by erroneous biblical translations, which are a result of bigoted or misogynist men not prepared to accept science. I have remained a believer in both natural evolution and a spiritual presence because of the unexplainable parallels within the Bible and science—particularly neuroscience. People who had no weighty tomes of academic research, or the high-tech equipment now used in scientific research, were coming up with the same answers in their attempts to recognise and change evil behaviour.

Interpretation of the Holy Scriptures separates evil from good. Evil people will always adapt the verses to suit their evil intent. Judeo-Christians have always struggled between the narrow, fundamentalist, literal interpretation of verses and the clever symbolism of the enlightened prophets who created them. Those early prophets provided accurate predictions of the damage that can result when evil people are ignored, which is now evidenced by the increase of WCPs in modern society—individuals who are guilty of excessive greed and driven by profit, rather than people.

Neuroscience has estimated that approximately one to two per cent of the general population are psychopaths–individuals who are unable to register the essential emotions that are the foundation of humanity.[23] One in a hundred may not seem enough to raise concerns but considering the fact that their crimes impact about ten times more individuals than those of the non-psychopathic criminal (i.e. one per cent of the world population multiplied by, on average, sixty victims) indicates many of us will be directly, or indirectly, affected by these monsters, albeit white-collar or heinous.

The most evolutionary advanced species on this earth was given incredible power: the ability to protect and nurture this Garden of Eden or completely destroy it. We were the first species that were given the choice to be good or evil. Other innocent species kill for food and survival and never require conscience or empathy. In addition, almost all other living forms have a predatory species that keeps their numbers in check, but not humans. Humans, destined to be the apex predator, kill for power and control and, in the case of psychopathic personas, for pleasure.

The values of GOD spread by the three major prophets transformed the world. One only has to look at godless dictatorships and the reduced quality-of-life in these less evolved cultures, which still cling to subjugation and gender inequality of much darker and less educated times. I believe there is a spiritual force that created the three messengers. They were exceptionally good and honourable men who strove to bring liars and charlatans to their knees and were dedicated to introducing a better world. Men who had an extraordinary social conscience and, at a particular time in their adult lives, realised they had to make change.

The thing that hard science cannot explain satisfactorily is the why and how of emotional intelligence (EQ). Social conscience is a learned process it is not innate; it appears it did not evolve from chemical elements in the 'Big Bang' billions of years ago. Yet we have a planet where good souls regardless of colour or creed, stand shoulder to shoulder to support others in times of disaster, or great need, and who continue to confront and fight evil. The three messengers were aware that the complex human brain could choose between goodness and wickedness, but from what driving force did they recognise that without the early emotional development, which faith provided, badly behaved, greedy and malicious people are formed?

I had to go back in history to uncover the roots of psychopathy, first described in the Garden of Eden parable metaphorically as the serpent. Today, they are still our most dangerous predator, threatening the survival of this planet. The cold-blooded, manipulative and pathologically deceptive serpent, whispering lies into the ears of the most vulnerable and trusting of the garden's residents, was a perfect description of this subset. The three major prophets, recognised as messengers of God, identified these serpents centuries before modern neuroscience had even given them a name.

In the mid-20[th]century, identifying the disorder of psychopathy was not a high priority. Psychopaths were considered more of a rarity: ruthless people, generally uneducated, and with lower IQs. After capital punishment was stopped, they were given life sentences with no hope of parole, and were forgotten. This perception has changed dramatically. We now have 'successful' psychopaths (WCPs) that can appear completely normal. However, these conmen and women are just as dangerous, emotionally and financially, as the old-fashioned image of uneducated, violent offenders. Researchers such as Hervey Cleckley and Dr Hare now recognise the evil behind the 'mask of sanity' and their work must not be ignored.

We are all familiar with the overworked term, 'fake news', used by a president who ticks all the boxes of the successful white-collar psychopath. When we read media articles, we now question the validity of the content. When I read the Holy Books, in my early life, I did so with the same cynical eyes. However, I recognised clever symbolism and very wise parables. They were words written long before science decided the living cell and all life evolved from dust—from the Big Bang.

Supporters of the *Theory of Evolution* have decided the *Theory of Intelligent Design*, upon which faith is based, has no legitimacy. Intelligent design, presented by its proponents as the religious argument for the existence of God, has been discredited as pseudoscience. I had a leaning towards science and did study the 'soft' science of psychology, so I recognised the value of both theories. One could not have evolved without the other. The forewarning of pure evil, the psychopathic personas that slither invisibly amongst us, was first given circa 1400 BC, by Moses, in Genesis, the first book of the Bible. The serpent was used as a metaphor to warn of these evil 'silver-tongued' con men and occasionally women, in that first symbolic parable about the Garden of Eden.

Psychopaths have been recognised by world leaders in neuroscience research as the most dangerous predator of the 'apex' predator, humans.[24&25] MRI scans can now reveal these deceptive and manipulative individuals, who have brains that do not register C&E and are still deceiving the most vulnerable and trusting of people. We have heinous psychopaths—serial killers and rapists, dictators who start wars, and WCPs driven by greed, not need—continuing to destroy our Eden at a horrifying rate.

Psychopaths lack both guilt and remorse and are the group of humans who choose the path of evil. The world is now witnessing the rise of psychopathic persons, from excessively wealthy WCPs to the most heinous serial criminals who kill for excitement. Credit Suisse reports:

> While the bottom half of adults collectively owns less than 1 per cent of total wealth, the richest decile (top 10 per cent of adults) owns 85 per cent of global wealth, and the top percentile alone accounts for almost half of all household wealth (47 per cent).[26]

These facts display skin-crawling financial greed; they are the new social 'bank-robbers' that reveal the total inadequacy of our outdated form of taxation, which was based on individuals working in nine-to-five jobs. The middle-class working group is now by far the most heavily taxed when based on total personal worth. Most people spend a lifetime paying off one house, while the fast-profit earners usually own several in the multimillion-dollar category—individuals who can afford teams of accountants that know every loophole for avoiding, hiding, or dispersing money to other family members, making them accessories to this financial corruption.

It was brave people who began to recognise that, unchallenged, male domination was damaging what should have been simple faith in a 'Creator' of life and was undermining the institutions of religious learning. The spiritual Father was a role model for goodness, providing support and hope for people, not some monstrous angry ogre who condoned hatred and brutality. Hence, Christians broke away from the deceptions fed by the world of Catholicism and started other Protestant, monotheist, Christian faiths.

The splendour of the Vatican reflects how far Catholicism has removed itself from the basic concepts of religious faith. The hugely wealthy Catholic kingdom appears to have little guilt regarding the

Catholic countries, where the faithful are living in abject poverty because of the shocking over-breeding forced on them by the Church. Like 'hadith Islam', this has resulted in much higher levels of criminal activity. Muslims, women in particular, should be aware of the damage caused when misogynist, sexist and corrupt men take control of religion—it never improves when earthborn men make themselves into God substitutes.

Religions that continue to allow male-domination, segregation, loss of freedom and terrorist fear, are farce, not faith. They are led by self-serving men who use followers as foot soldiers to gain power and control. They are the religious clerics who assume omnipotence and see themselves as gods in their own realms of power. They have not a care if the men who trust them and die for them go to heaven or hell.

Religions that infer they are the chosen faith are talking nonsense. God, or Allah, would not show favouritism—that is a petty earthborn trait. This belief has been the undoing of male-dominated faiths. It is written in the Holy Scriptures (Matthew 7:1-6), 'Judge not, that you be not judged,' yet we have dozens of church clerics judging one monotheist Abrahamic faith against the other. It certainly appears those who negatively judge will not be positively judged when their 'judgement day' comes. Following the path of goodness, rather than evil, is not going to be judged by which religion we follow. Bragging rights of the school of religious instruction one attended would have about as much credibility in the 'here-after', as the school one attended in the here-and-now.

Keeping modern faith at the level of early tribal behaviour defeats the purpose of religion. Holding people to evolutionary infancy is to retard the gift of life. Aligning Scriptures with science is far more exciting and credible than the pagan mysticism that unimaginative fundamentalists would have us believe in. The spiritual presence to which we pray will remain a mystery, as enigmatic as the soul within us, which separates us from the cruel and barbarous. Faith remains a strength, which has empowered and given hope to millions for centuries.

Albert Einstein made the comment, 'All religions, arts and sciences are branches of the same tree.'[27] This view aligns with the very first parable in the Bible, the biblical 'tree of life' in the Garden of Eden, these disciplines always were 'branches of the same tree'. The symbolic tree did not bear edible fruit. It was placed in the heart of Eden, the wonderful 'garden' representing planet Earth. It was the tree of 'the knowledge of good and evil'. That knowledge is the solid trunk, the core around which the branches of civilisation have grown. Unlike animals, which do not require this knowledge of good and evil, the most complex of all animal species, humans, were given the ability to choose between the two. It is a choice that divides the good from the predatory psychopathic personas.

To this day, psychopaths are judged as the 'bad, not mad' criminals: they are not insane, but plan their crimes against humanity with cold-blooded discipline. The deceptive, cold-blooded serpent was a very apt metaphor for these soulless creatures. The emotionally undeveloped serial killers and rapists, through to our white-collar psychopaths, remain our worst predator in modern times. With MRI scanning, neuroscience can now look into the brain of the psychopath and confirm these evil individuals do not register the essential emotional qualities required for caring, humane behaviour. They are a human subset who chooses to be the most deviant of lawbreakers. It took about three thousand years for science to catch up to those first warnings—we need to get better at recognising these dangerous people.

Corrupt clerics, as warned against by all three prophets (Moses, Jesus and Muhammad), have made rules that suited themselves rather than God, such as: celibacy, subservience of women, polygamy, banning any form of contraception and early abortion and keeping 'confessional secrets' against state secular laws. The appalling failure of religions that are driven by self-serving men has failed the world and the three great messengers of God. Society has reverted to the problems that brought these three separate enlightened men into prominence, the world is rife with financial disparity and the numbers of psychopathic personas are spiralling in the business world, even children are growing up with reduced moral integrity.

Einstein was a leading scientist, yet he observed, 'Science without religion is lame, religion without science is blind.'[28-30] Clerics who are dogmatic fundamentalists should take note. While God may remain a mystery, there is a very strong distinction between humans with kind and caring souls that I see as godly, and the ego-driven, soulless people who lack C&E. It is the welcoming, smiling faces that I have met in my travels around the world, and the brave and kind actions from ordinary people, which has held me to faith in the human spirit and that mysterious source to which we attribute the division between good and evil.

The 'why and how' of human life is a mystery, but I would not exchange the feeling of having someone watching my back 24/7, for the atheist belief in nothingness. I could not imagine a life where I could not send a prayer into the mystery of space, when I was frightened or needed strength to calm stress. It has been a need of the human psyche for centuries, a form of meditation, even before yoga enthusiasts recognised the value of that process. We can now witness people globally bind together at times of great danger, with that invisible cord of care, bravery and generosity. I would rather believe in a divine spiritual force that drives that, than the destructive godless evil that creates criminal, warlike barbarism, or obsessive greed that causes great discontent.

The spiritual force that drove the three messengers has no religion; the human species will be judged by its behaviour, not their choice of religion. The worthiness of the soul is dependent on the moral compass those three early messengers tried to ingrain. We will be judged on how we adhere to these values. It is male arrogance to believe their brand of monotheist (one God) religion is superior. The spiritual Father, who people of faith believe is the power behind the *Theory of Intelligent Design*, will not care which school of religious instruction you attended as long as the key values of morality, empathy, respect and conscience (MERC) have been learned.

~ 3 ~

Psychopathy - genetic and inappropriate early nurture

'The eyes of a psychopath will deceive you, they will destroy you. They will take from you, your innocence, your pride and eventually your soul. Behind these eyes, one finds only blackness, the absence of light.'

— **Dr Samuel Loomis**

What is a psychopath? Psychopathy has a genetic component and psychopaths will always remain the most terrifying predator of the 'apex predator', the human race. They range from the spiralling numbers of white-collar psychopaths (WCPs) in the business world, to the most heinous serial killers and rapists.[1] MRI scanning has shown this subset of humanity is incapable of registering—or has very anaemic levels of—conscience and empathy (C&E), the two qualities that separate a non-psychopath from a psychopath.

In early times, the cruel people in this subset were called satanic, antichrist and 'jinn devils', but MRI imaging has finally enabled neuroscientists to view the brain activity of these cold-hearted and ruthless people. Research has shown that this phenomenon is a combination of nature and lack of appropriate nurture. Psychopaths' brains show little or no activity in the areas which should be registering the key emotional qualities that make humans humane, namely conscience and empathy. Lacking the moral integrity usually learned at an early age, they are not individuals guided by a strong moral compass.

Research has shown that poor early environments can leave lasting effects on the brain. The study done by James Balm, *The subway of the brain – Why white matter matters,*[2] reveals how early stress can cause real cognitive damage, seriously retarding white matter development. Researchers investigated the long-term impact of parental mistreatment and came up with startling results. An increase in stress hormones can lead to long-term effects on white matter. These structural changes have been linked with social aggression, poor visual processing and emotional regulation, which contributed towards general anxiety disorder. It appears stress, by reducing the production of oxytocin, can affect brain white matter, even during pregnancy, and this damage has been linked to molecular autism—even vascular dementia and Alzheimer's.

MRI imaging has shown psychopaths have virtually no activity in the areas of the brain that are essential for emotional processing.[3] They were born with the complex brain of humans, which separates us from our most closely related animal species, the pigmy chimps (which share 98.4 per cent of our DNA[4]), but why didn't they develop the ability to process the bonding emotions which the chimps exhibit quite naturally?

Research has shown bad early environments create psychopaths and sociopaths. However, the evidence is showing that unlike sociopathy, psychopathy has a genetic component. Individuals with the genetic psychopathic brain inactivity can be sociable or antisocial depending on early childhood environments and positive male role models. When raised in a stable, loving nuclear family where strong guidelines have been established in early childhood, this genetic glitch can be overridden; happy early environments can turn a child with the genetic makeup of a psychopath (more commonly males), into productive and emotionally healthy adults.[5&6]

Dr Hare's research suggested that psychopaths can choose to behave badly, even when there has been no early trauma, as psychopaths have a malfunctioning limbic system.[7] The limbic system has been conceptualised as the 'feeling and reacting brain' and is important for conditioned emotional reactions. The hypothalamus, which is linked to this system, produces the essential bonding hormone, oxytocin, which is then transported to the pituitary where it is stored for later release.

Laughter sparks the release of oxytocin; if the early environment of children is inappropriate or harsh and lacking in unconditional love, children can suffer long-term damage caused by inactivity of positive emotional responses within the limbic system.[8&9]

Memory storage, also a part of this area, can carry deeply ingrained emotional scars, resulting in very angry adolescents and adults who take their anger out on a society and a social system that didn't care. Hence, we are seeing a huge rise in domestic violence as these males reach adulthood. A brilliant article by Joel Stein on humour in the workplace, *Humour Is Serious Business*,[10] is a recommended read, especially for dour parents and humourless single mothers who are moulding men and women of the future.

Oxytocin is the miracle hormone that softens and moderates parental behavioural patterns. It is the bonding and happiness hormone, which ensures the offspring of mammalian species have a far better chance of survival. Natural childbirth floods the mother with oxytocin with every stretch of the cervix, however, production of this hormone also increases in fathers as they grow closer to their children.[11&12]

Research has shown C-section mothers, who do not receive the essential flood of oxytocin required by both mother and baby, have reduced reaction time to infants crying and often have problems with breastfeeding.[13] Hence, C-section may also contribute to the postnatal depression some mothers experience after childbirth, if oxytocin levels are not checked. However, as breastfeeding also stimulates oxytocin production, these mothers generally do catch up after several months.[14] Sadly, many adoptive parents and infants have struggled seriously because doctors did not ensure that the adoptive mothers, who never received the oxytocin 'hit' of natural childbirth, had adequate levels to ensure strong positive bonding.

The major role of childbirth oxytocin is to counter the massive pressure in the early days of babies' lives, which can be hell for mothers. It is the hell of crying at all hours, constant nappy changing, the lack of sleep, which can and has resulted in aggressive behaviour, without this real miracle of birth. As Royal Commissions have shown, orphan children raised in Catholic orphanages, by celibate men and women who had never received the bottomless cup of this natural childbirth hormone, have had some of the worst records of child abuse.

There appears to be a link between reduced oxytocin production and decreased levels of brain white matter, moreover, drugs and alcohol reduce the production of oxytocin, the happiness and bonding hormone. When we read reports such as that from Jeffrey H. Meyer et al. (2006), *Elevated Monoamine Oxidase A Levels in the Brain: An explanation for the imbalance of Major Depression – an explanation for the Monoamine Imbalance*,[15] should we be concerned that serotonin, norepinephrine, and dopamine get a mention but oxytocin, and related white brain matter, is not even considered?

Why do we know so little about oxytocin levels and requirements? Pharmaceutical companies have shown little interest in researching this amazing hormone, not only for C-section mothers but also for depression. Why are oxytocin levels not checked regularly, in the same way iron levels and other hormone imbalances are? Do we have the power and greed of Big Pharma to thank for the lack of research on this vital hormone? Research has revealed levels required for iron, vitamins and minerals, genetic levels of progesterone, testosterone, even dopamine, serotonin and norepinephrine levels, but oxytocin rarely gets a mention.

Is it because it cannot be given in the hugely profitable tablet form and, therefore, the appalling profit-driven Big Pharma is just not interested? As the digestive process does not absorb oxytocin, oxytocin must be given by injection or nasal sprays. There is no multimillions extraction from the public with those forms of medication. Pills are where they make their huge profits and while oxytocin breaks through the blood-brain barrier (BBB) and floods through the body from head to toe, it cannot be taken in pill form. Hence, for anti-depressants Big Pharma concentrates on the less free-flowing and possibly less effective serotonin and dopamine for the 'happiness' drugs. If oxytocin was found to be a far superior antidepressant it would cause a couple of these exceptionally greedy companies to lose mega-bucks and possibly go insolvent.

Through MRI imaging, we have seen how the reduction of oxytocin in the mother affects the foetus. As shown on the popular Dr Oz show, when several pre-birth scans where shown on screen after stress events, the little fists of the foetus tightened and the facial expressions looked more like *The Scream*, painted by Edvard Munch, than the gentle serenity of a happy infant-to-be. Oxytocin levels can be reduced by stress caused by alcohol consumption, nicotine, the mother's daily emotional stress, or overweight physical stress on the foetal sac. Confused, unhappy little infants with autism may curl into themselves, or go on the attack with hyper-activity, to protect them from the world that terrifies them because their brain development has not reached the point when it is safe to leave the nest and be thrust into childcare.

Do the more intelligent brains of some children, who become psychopaths, need more intense stimulation to activate the oxytocin flow at a much earlier age? Psychopathy can occur if a blow to the head damages the emotional centre of the brain, however, as Dr Hare's research has shown, it is the one mental disorder where choice is the option. Several of the infamous serial killers and rapists, with MENSA IQ's, were raised in dysfunctional or fatherless homes.[16&17] While two years is the recommended time for bonding with the primary care giver, higher IQ children whose brains take longer to complete cell development, may need up to a year extra with a competent primary caregiver. Personality and social skills can be lost if a child is pushed out of the nest too early into the hands of strangers. As their brains have millions more cell interactions forming, this can cause emotional and possibly intellectual damage, as we are now seeing the rise in autism and hyperactivity disorders in the modern two parent working society and in children from dysfunctional and single parent homes.

Research by psychologists, Drs Keith Witt and Christopher Badcock, has shown males inherit their intelligence mainly from their mother, on the X-chromosome of the unmatched XY-chromosome set. The report by Christopher Badcock expands on the complexity of this chromosome in the XY set that determines gender.[18&19] While there are more male geniuses, as many women still put parenting as a priority in their lives, male dominated cultures that do not educate females lag behind cultures where equality prevails.

The article on the XY set by Keith Witt also explains the ineffectiveness of the 'Genius' Sperm Banks set up in California in the

1980s and 1990s.[20] In the beginning, women had to be members of MENSA, so they were already passing on high IQs to their offspring of either sex via their X chromosome—as there is no evidence that the Y chromosome of the preserved sperm, which produced sons, is implicated in cognition. The only confirmed Nobel Prize-winning donor was William Shockley, and most donors are now known not to have been laureates at all.

It disproves the belief that Nobel Prize-winning talent might be inherited from the father, given the role of the X chromosome rather than the Y chromosome in providing intelligence. Hence, men who receive the 'intelligence gene', from a clever mother or paternal grandmother and then marry beauty instead of brains, should not be surprised if their sons are incredibly good looking but are less clever than their fathers.

Badcock's report also reveals the autism spectrum disorder appears to be X-linked and that males outnumber females in the Asperger's syndrome by at least ten to one. As males have only a single X in the XY set, they are much more vulnerable to any X-linked deficits than females, who have a second X chromosome to moderate and dilute the negative effects.

We should be pushing EQ as strongly as we push IQ development. If these clever children have inherited the aggressive low-activity MAOA (Monoamine Oxidase A) gene and grow up with a sense of abandonment from being kicked out of the nest far too early into childcare with strangers, in an unfamiliar place, they are starting life well behind the eight ball. Australian research has shown male infants have less early coping skills than female children when placed in childcare too early.[21] This is particularly the case when boys are raised in the confusing single-parent 'mother–child soul mate' relationship—an adult role a child should not be required to meet—which causes confusion and skewed perceptions in later years.[22-32]

It is the female that passes both the cognitive gene and the warrior gene (MAOA) to their sons on the X-chromosome, in the unmatched XY-set.[33] While twenty-two of the twenty-three sets line up similarly the Y-chromosome, in the 23rd set, has about 100-200 genes,[34] none of which seem to be involved with cognition—thinking, perception, reasoning, planning, most of which we associate with intelligence.

However, the X-chromosome has about 900 to 1,400 genes,[35] and it appears a significant proportion of genes associated with intelligence is passed on to the male offspring from the maternal side as the X-linked genes play a disproportionate role in the development of human intelligence.[36] Hence, a male has his higher IQ as a direct result of his clever mother's X-chromosome and/or his clever paternal grandmother's X-chromosome, passed via the father to the son, mixed and perhaps a little diluted on the Y-chromosome. If it is a family tradition to marry beauty rather than brains, it serves them right if they sire incompetent sons who run the family businesses into the ground.

The warrior gene (MAOA-L) has been linked to increased levels of aggression and violence—it also relates to depression, however, although women have a double hit of this gene, the chance of having two negative low-activity versions is less common. It appears one positive high-activity version of this aggression gene can moderate a second negative low-activity version. The study by Sohrabi that investigated behaviour in response to provocation confirmed that overall, MAOA-L (low activity MAOA) individuals showed higher levels of aggression than MAOA-H (high activity MAOA) subjects.[37]

In addition, women produce less testosterone and also have huge amounts of oxytocin produced with every stretch of the cervix, during natural childbirth and breastfeeding, which also moderates aggression. Oxytocin is the miraculous hormone that places women in 'la la land' after natural childbirth and ensures infant survival. C-sections, where women do not get this important bonding 'hit', may mean babies also suffer more anxiety from this loss of oxytocin production. Oxytocin appears to be a bottomless cup for many lucky women in parenthood.

If men get a negative low-activity version of the single MAOA gene, they start with a huge handicap, made worse by poor parenting. Oxytocin production, stimulated by lots of laughter and physical activity, is absolutely essential in the daily life of male children and teens. Sadly, as this input is usually provided by fathers of the children, this is often lacking in overworked, physically and emotionally stressed single parent homes.

Psychopathy and sociopathy are seen, by many psychologists, psychiatrists and criminologists, as interchangeable titles. However, Scott A. Bonn (Ph.D.), who writes the blog *Wicked Deeds*, argues there are clear and significant distinctions between them.[38] This has been confirmed by other researchers, led by Nigel Blackwood, based at King's College, London's Institute of Psychiatry. In the report, *Psychopathy linked to brain abnormalities*, Blackwood states that while cognitive and behavioural treatments may benefit sociopaths, where negative behaviours are learned from bad early environments, the same approach is unlikely to work in the case of psychopaths who have the genetic varient.[39] When examining MRI scans of their subjects' brains, the study showed that the psychopaths' brain had differences that distinguished them from criminals with other anti-social personality disorders (ASPD) and from mentally healthy non-offenders.

The study revealed that if the more aggressive, spontaneous rage of a sociopath (ASPD), a proven result of a dysfunctional childhood, does not have the psychopathic gene (ASPD+P), there is some chance of rehabilitation. The psychopathic brain abnormality is a lack of emotional development in key areas of their 'social brains'. MRI scans have shown no activity in the areas that should register genuine remorse and conscience. To date, there is no complete rehabilitation for the cold-blooded ruthless, but more organised, psychopathic personas. When recognised in early childhood, intervention programs can be useful in modifying the behavioural patterns of 'budding psychopaths', these programs need to deal not only with the child, but also with the family and social context in which the problem occurs.[40]

The study found that psychopaths 'displayed significantly reduced grey matter volumes in the anterior rostral prefrontal cortex and temporal poles, compared to ASPD offenders and non-psychopathic offenders.' These areas are important in understanding other people's emotions and intentions and are activated when people think about moral behaviour. Damage in these areas, either physically, or by emotionally damaging early environments, is associated with impaired empathising with other people, poor response to fear and distress and a lack of self-conscious emotions, such as guilt or embarrassment.

A report compiled by over a dozen of America's leading neuroscientists, which I found in the American FBI Law Enforcement Bulletin, indicates that the psychopath is an 'intraspecies' predator.[41] The video, *Intraspecies Predator: How a psychopath sees the world*, narrated by Dr Hare,[42] includes a SPECT (single-photon emission computerized tomography) study carried out in August 2007.[43] While imaging tests such as X-rays can show what the structures inside your body look like, a SPECT scan produces images that show how your organs work. For instance, a SPECT scan can show how blood flows to your heart, or what areas of your brain are active. It shows the clear colour variation between the lack of activity of the psychopathic brain compared to the non-psychopathic brain when being tested using Hare's diagnostic tool, the *Psychopathy Checklist* (PCL-R, see Essay 6 for more details). The tests show no activity in the psychopathic brain when negative words like cancer, murder, rape, or death are presented.

The psychopath cannot extract emotional information from such words; they invoke absolutely no reaction in the psychopath's brain. Hare reported they respond 'in a very superficial manner' to concepts that would usually cause an emotional and distressing reaction in the normal brain. They do not register emotional depth, thus allowing them to detach themselves from emotional events.[44] This lack of feeling and bonding to others allows psychopathic personas to have clarity in observing the behaviour of their prey. They are not hampered by the anxieties and emotions that other people experience in social situations, which allows the psychopath to prey ruthlessly on others, using charm, deceit, violence, or any other methods that allows them to get what they want.

As with Blackwood's research, Dr Fallon's research, shedding light on how psychopathic killers are made and perhaps prevented, has shown the psychopathic brain varies from those with anti-social personality disorders.[45] There is a much greater lack of activity in the psychopath's brain in the sections that should register ethics, conscience, impulse control, emotional processing and memories. In addition, psychopaths also have the high-risk, violence-related genes which include the negative version of the MAOA gene (the warrior gene). MAOA helps regulate serotonin, though some research has shown low-activity MAOA does not efficiently break down serotonin, allowing a build-up of this transmitter to occur, which, as reported by Sohrabi, can cause a person to act violently. Insufficient oxytocin receptors, resulting from an unhappy childhood, also adds to the problem.[46-49]

While psychopathy appears to have a DNA link and can come from any family background, sociopathy is formed from bad early environments, usually welfare poverty, over large families placed in impoverished circumstances, or single parent homes with no positive male role models,[50] hence, trying to rehabilitate adult male domestic violence offenders is treating the symptoms not the disease. Differences between the personality traits of the two disorders are quite marked. Psychopathic personas are typically cold-hearted, organised and unemotional, yet they are very competent at faking emotions, while sociopaths are less organised and more prone to anger and violence. The less organised and impulsive rage of ASPD sociopaths differs from the deceptive, callous, more scheming behaviour of psychopaths. As researchers at King's College, London, explained, 'We describe those without psychopathy as the 'hot-headed' group and those with psychopathy as the 'cold-hearted' group.'[51]

A percentage of children with conduct disorder will be diagnosed with ASPD as an adult.[52-53] Non-psychopathic killers and ASPD sociopathic killers are random rather than serial repeat killers. Serial rape and killing is the pattern of the psychopath (ASPD+P). Sociopaths are a reflection of incompetent parenting in the first—and most formative—decade of a child's life. Sociopaths are capable of empathy in some circumstances, however, their anaemic levels of conscience and empathy (C&E) do not stop them from committing violent crimes. The one redeeming quality for the sociopathy disorder, which appears to be learned rather than genetic, is that when young people are taken out of their damaging environments and love, counselling, care and positive male role models are provided, there is some chance of rehabilitation. They do not necessarily lack C&E—the learned traits which are absent from the psychopathic brain.

Both Dr Hare and the UK research, led by Dr Blackwood,

have shown sociopaths may benefit from cognitive and behavioural treatments, whereas psychopaths, due to the genetic component, remain beyond total rehabilitation.[54]Where there is no external damage to the brain (accidental physical damage) and choice is involved—as in the psychopathic 'bad not mad' offenders—there is a deadly addiction to the adrenaline rush experienced through violent crime. It appears that brains that lack normal activity and emotional development (EQ)[55] need the greater stimulation that extreme violence creates.

Kent Kiehl in his book, *The Psychopath Whisperer*,[56] noted that Hervey Cleckley had 'reported that psychopaths never experience grief, honesty, deep joy, or genuine despair.' He added that the psychopath never ruminates on anything. Rumination is a process of reflection or contemplation. The process of rumination is often associated with anxiety, or subjective feelings of concern, or worry. This can precipitate a change in the individual and, in order to reduce anxiety, these people go on to seek help. The psychopath experiences none of these emotions and, therefore, they do not initiate help from mental health clinicians, they choose not to make change. As discussed further in Essay 6, Kiehl's research observed that psychopaths do better in prison because they do not reflect on the crime that put them in prison, hence, they do not get depressed.

In Australia, we have a judiciary system, parole boards and the inappropriately skilled AAT (Australian Appeals Tribunal) that lag decades behind in psychopathy research (again, this is discussed further in Essay 6). They continue to release these dangerous anti-social predators back into society with little care for the general public.

Research has shown that psychopaths begin offending earlier, starting as early as eleven years, and have a greater number of offending behaviours.[57] They also respond less to treatment programs in adulthood compared to the sociopathic group. Dr Bonn in his article, *Psychopathic Criminals Cannot Be Cured,* notes that psychopaths and sociopaths share key traits including a disregard for laws and social mores, a disregard for the rights of others, a failure to feel deep remorse or guilt and a tendency to display violent behaviour.[58]

In addition to these commonalities, Bonn notes important

differences. Sociopaths are likely to be more uneducated and live on the fringes of society, unable to hold down a steady job or stay in one place for very long. Bonn indicates that, while it is difficult for sociopaths to form attachments with others, it is not impossible. Some sociopaths are capable of empathy, however, in the eyes of most, sociopaths will appear to be quite disturbed. Psychopaths do form relationships, but they are more often short term, as this group has very low boredom thresholds. Research has shown psychopaths' brains are wired differently and, as adults, psychopaths cannot be counselled into being non-psychopathic. The patient must want to change, but psychopaths are perfectly happy as they are, they genuinely do not see they have a problem.

If psychopathy is genetic, why are governments across the world not pouring mountains of money into studying this most socially damaging of brain disorders? There are certainly enough of them available as long-term test subjects currently filling our prisons. In addition, we now have huge numbers emerging from the Middle East, in death cults such as ISIL, Jihadists, and Al Qaeda. Evidence that psychopathy has a genetic component should be of added concern in cultures that encourage first-cousin marriages. It makes for a dangerous world when men and women breed prolifically, choosing close relatives as partners.

In addition, essential oxytocin production in gestation and childbirth would be dramatically reduced if a mother must endure the lust-driven sex of a psychopathic partner, like they do in cultures where domestic rape is accepted. Psychopathic males are incapable of long-term loving relationships; they cannot register the emotions of love, which normally follow the initial stages of oxytocin-driven lust. Love requires the qualities of C&E (caring and empathy), and both are alien to psychopathic personas.[59] Dominating, egocentric males, driven by libido and testosterone, do not move to love. In addition, some cultures force female genital mutilation (removal of the clitoris), which also stops oxytocin stimulation.[60] Oxytocin is stimulated in lovemaking, not rape. Children deprived of oxytocin stimulation will be emotionally damaged.

The psychopathic genome—more frequent in brutal, warlike cultures and encouraged in 'hadith Islam'—should be analysed and monitored from early childhood, as it is beyond rehabilitation by mid-teens. Psychopathy, shown to have a genetic connection, is increased by familial inbreeding and over-breeding, both factors in the Muslim culture.[61&62] With attentive and unconditional love provided by a stable, two-parent team providing strong boundaries in the child's first decade, this genetic anomaly can be redirected to turn male children (with the low-activity MAOA gene) into worthy, rather than unworthy, members of society.[63]

Young people who do not have normal temporal lobe development because they have been raised in a culture that has allowed hadith laws to stifle oxytocin-stimulating bonding activities such as music, dance, laughter and sport in the first decade of a child's life, is a recipe for disaster. 'Faulty' white matter connections result in a range of deficits from language ability to delayed memory and visuo-spatial construction. It also contributes to vascular dementia and even Alzheimer's. Young people who have reduced brain white matter and lack of frontal temporal lobe activity due to lack of bonding and joy in their early life, can be a serious threat to society.

Banning laughter and joy in a child's early years, as 'hadith Islam' does, is creating monsters: creatures of hate. It would be interesting to look at the MAOA genetic component and the oxytocin levels in these men. Male immigrant offenders from cultures that support 'hadith Islam' should be tested under the internationally recognised PCL-R (psychopathic testing process, introduced by Dr Hare). This testing should be carried out by specialists in the field of psychopathic research. It should be psychiatrists and psychologists who are thoroughly trained in MRI imaging and the Hare psychopathic testing procedure, not public servants asking inane questions about our history, interviewing our immigrants. Having the warrior gene (MAOA) does not automatically make them dangerous, but how they were raised determines their capacity to be monster or marvel.

How could men of the Islamic faith, formerly recognised as the 'religion of peace', become so corrupt? Children come into the world biologically pre-programmed to form attachments with others.[64&65] Even in the first six weeks, before the eye–brain recognition connection has really formed, babies smile. Smiling has international currency—it breaks down barriers, overriding racism and sexism. Yet some cultures continue to mask this wonderful gift, which in humans alone has evolved from a need to communicate.

In the first decade of their child's life, parents can create either joy, or repressed and internalised anger, form happy, trusting children or (if devoid of unconditional parental love) monsters. How did the Sunni tribe babies, born to smile from birth—the raw clay of humanity—become moulded into psychopathic serial killers and rapists? Why were conscience and empathy, the key qualities that separate good people from psychopaths, not taught by loving parents, by educational institutions, or a caring community and their religious faith?

Male-dominated, gender-apartheid religions have protected and moulded the very people they were created to recognise and reform. Psychopaths are an obscene subset of the human race, worse than any other animal species. One only has to read the article, by the American activist Phyllis Chesler, Ph.D., *What Is Justice For A Rape Victim?* to realise many are still in the dark ages of completely un-evolved animal rutting.[66] If they cannot be re-educated then full castration should be the sentence for these horrific acts against other human beings. Their toxic genes should not be passed on to future generations, de-sexing is the common practice for poor breeding stock, and this article has certainly revealed this is still a factor in the human species. Psychopaths, predominately males, are destroying the reputation of the many good and caring men who do walk this earth.

Chesler reported in Algeria, as in Iran, 'unveiled', educated, independent Algerian women became 'military targets' and were increasingly shot on sight. Attorney Karima Bennoune reported that from 1992 on, Algerian fundamentalist men have committed a series of 'terrorist atrocities' against Algerian women.[67] According to Bennoune, the men of Algeria are arming and the women of Algeria are veiling themselves. As one woman said, "Fear is stronger than our will to be free." Cult religions that fill people with terror are a violation of everything the original monotheist faith stood for and tried to change.

As adults, tragically, these cold-blooded, ruthless terrorists are beyond any form of rehabilitation because emotional development and learning (EQ) has been shut down from birth. Children raised without love and laughter and the values of true faith, morality, empathy, respect and conscience (MERC), who continue to treat women as inferior creatures can, and will, develop the traits that neuroscience has recognised as psychopathic and sociopathic. Faith was introduced to change these evil creatures. Murderous terrorists spit in the face of Allah and the prophet Muhammad, as they break every commandment the three major prophets tried to spread. If not recognised early by parents, or educational institutions, neuroscience has warned that their addiction to bad behaviour is beyond rehabilitation.

Psychopaths get an adrenalin rush when they successfully con their parent/s or friends, using devious manipulation which, as with any addiction, reinforces the behaviour, turning it into a habit that they have no wish to stop. When raised with limited boundaries, by part-time or absent parents, or a lack of positive male role models, they drift into the bullying behaviour of more vulnerable peers, who may also have been raised in bad early environments. If sociopathy is combined with the psychopathic lack of C&E, we get the most horrifying murderers we are now seeing at the frontline of religious terrorism—men who can behead others without a moment of remorse. These men, who have been moulded from birth to hate, lack the activity registering in the frontal temporal lobes that are the source for bonding and caring emotions.[68&69]

The world of neuroscience tells us how we treat animals is an indication of how mentally sound our society is, as prolonged cruelty to animals is the earliest and surest sign of psychopathy.[70&71] Anyone who has looked into the eyes of a rescued and happily rehoused dog after it has been horribly abused is looking into a world of gratitude beyond anything a human can register. Their unconditional love and loyalty have been a huge stimulator of empathy and oxytocin production for people of all ages.[72] Pets are important parts of the process of empathy development. However, psychopathic personas, because there is a genetic glitch, do not register empathy. They should not be allowed to own dogs or any animals, because their brains do not register guilt or remorse after hurting animals.

A video on TV showed a girl using a pink rubber sandal to repeatedly bash the face of a very good-natured and docile cream Labrador dog, as it lay on the stairs. It was seen as entertainment, however, as prolonged animal cruelty is the earliest sign of psychopathy in a young person, such children should be seeing psychiatrists, not school counsellors. Counsellors should be referring them to specialists in psychopathic recognition, where psychopathic testing (PCL-R) can be carried out. This testing would also assess whether the home environment is suitable for the child to remain, without intervention and serious parental training put in place—intervention supported by law.

In some states of America, animal protection agencies pass on names of people who are consistently cruel to animals, as it is a record of psychopathic behaviour and predictor of possible future crime and domestic violence offenders. Records show all serial killers had horrific incidences of cruelty to dogs, cats and other animals in their childhood years. However, sociopathy, which is created by lack of early parental nurture, may be helped, as dogs can provide sociopaths with the unconditional love they were robbed of from birth.

Psychopathy can be managed, to a degree, if caught early enough, but to date there is no complete cure once the psychopath reaches adulthood—rehabilitation cannot change DNA. This is like banning doctors from telling patients who have been diagnosed with an autoimmune disease that there is no cure. To date, the autoimmune disorder is incurable and there is no complete rehabilitation, as it also has a genetic component like the mental disorder of psychopathy. Both can be managed but both are beyond complete rehabilitation because science has not as yet come up with answers. However, psychopathy is the one mental disorder that has the advantage of choice—something autoimmune sufferers do not have.

The psychopathic criminal group chooses to behave badly because of the adrenaline 'high' their skewed brains receive. In addition, they genuinely believe their own lies and always see themselves as the victims. Psychopaths are a terrifying, unevolved subset of humanity and only highly trained professionals who specialised in psychopathy, genetic testing and MRI scanning can analyse this behaviour. Cultures with less advanced scientific and medical training do not have access to these resources, so the untreated in these countries can become society's worst predators. Moreover, as this disorder has a genetic link, the custom of first cousin marriage, practiced in many Asian cultures, dramatically increases the risk of this genetic disorder, substantially adding to the number born predisposed to psychopathy.

Psychopaths' brains are undeveloped in the area that should register emotions, and they often lack humour, another oxytocin stimulator. Psychopathic men and women appear 'soulless', as they are cold-hearted and are noticeably lacking in essential human qualities. They can be superficially very charming, but they are also exceptionally devious. As conscience and empathy are essential in loving, long-term relationships their relationships are generally a series of short-term commitments.

The world must recognise the difference between psychopathy and sociopathy. Genetics, oxytocin and the environment in which a child grows up, all contribute to whether they become a psychopath—a largely irreversible condition and society's greatest threat.

.

~ 4 ~

Sociopaths and psychopaths are not interchangeable titles

'We stopped looking for monsters under our bed when we realised they were inside us.'

—Charles Darwin

My research, which focused on documents from Dr Hare, led me to the American FBI Law Enforcement Bulletin, *Psychopathy - An Important Forensic Concept for the 21st Century,* which contained a report compiled by over a dozen of America's leading neuroscientists.[1] The report is essential reading as it makes an important contribution to our understanding of these cold-hearted and ruthless predators. The report defines the term psychopathy as:

> [A] personality disorder that includes a cluster of interpersonal, affective, lifestyle and antisocial traits and behaviours, including deception, manipulation, irresponsibility, impulsivity, stimulation-seeking, poor behavioural control, shallow affect, a lack of empathy, guilt or remorse, sexual promiscuity, a callous disregard for the rights of others, and a range of unethical and antisocial behaviours.[2]

Hollywood generally presents psychopaths as terrifying people who look threatening or have off-putting characteristics. In reality, while they can be strangers, psychopaths are like chameleons and a great many fall into the successful 'white-collar' group of psychopaths. They can be charming, good looking and well groomed, they can be your boss, your neighbour, your boyfriend, or your mother. They are what Dr Hare calls 'subcriminal' psychopaths individuals who leave a path of destruction and pain without a single pang of conscience.[3]

The report confirms psychopathy is the most threatening disorder of the twenty-first century, and the most dangerous of the personality disorders. It is not an illness or a disease that can be treated medically, as it is based on personal choice. While psychopathy has been shown to have a genetic component, neuroscience research has confirmed sociopathy is a result of poor parenting. While we can guide children with this genetic glitch to become very productive individuals, if they are in the hands of incompetent or uncaring parents, the result is growing numbers filling our juvenile court system. Statistics have shown male children without positive male role models are the most emotionally damaged.

The Fatherless Generation, an outstanding thesis written by an American student, Sabrina, gathered the shocking statistics reflecting the new age trend of raising children without fathers.[4] Sabrina herself was luckily adopted at eight months of age. Single parenting has been the most destructive element of the modern age. Her story should be read by every female contemplating this irresponsible act and by every male who carelessly creates this emotional child abuse.[5&6]

To understand this disorder, one must understand some fundamental principles about personality. Individuals' personalities represent who they are; they result from genetics and upbringing and reflect how individuals view the world and think the world views them. Personalities dictate how people interact with others and how they cope with problems, both real and imagined. Psychopathy has a specific cluster of traits and characteristics (for a visual representation, refer to table 1 in Essay 6).

The article by Frick and Marsee, *Psychopathy and Developmental Pathways to Antisocial Behaviour in Youth*, explains that these traits ultimately define adult psychopathy and begin to manifest themselves in early childhood.[7] The lifelong expression of this disorder is a product of complex interactions between biological and temperamental predispositions and social forces; the ways in which nature and parenting shape and define the individual.

Donald Lynam in his report, *Early Identification of Chronic Offenders: Who is the Fledgling Psychopath?* explains that psychopaths' brains register shallow emotions, they are unable to maintain close relationships, and lack empathy and anxiety.[8] As a result, many exhibit a profound lack of remorse for their aggressive actions, both violent and non-violent, along with a corresponding lack of sympathy for their victims. This central psychopathic concept enables them to act in a cold-blooded manner, using those around them as pawns to achieve goals and satisfy needs and desires, whether sexual, financial, physical, or emotional. Most psychopaths are grandiose, selfish sensation seekers who lack moral integrity and go through life taking what they want. They do not accept responsibility for their actions and find a way to shift the blame to someone, or something else.

In general, white-collar psychopaths (WCPs) are glib and charming, and they use these attributes to manipulate others into trusting them. This may lead to people giving them money, voting them into office, or possibly being murdered by them. Because of their interpersonal prowess, most psychopaths can present a favourable first impression, and many function successfully in society. However, to understand how psychopaths achieve their goals, it is important to see them as classic predators.[9-11] Psychopaths see others as either competitive predators, or prey, and are skilful at camouflaging their own predatory behaviour through deception and manipulation.

Many of the attitudes and behaviours of the more violent psychopaths have a distinct predatory quality to them—they are the serial offenders. However, stalking offences are more often related to sociopathic behaviour, rather than psychopathic behaviour, as stalking a victim is usually an inordinate desire to form close attachments, whereas, psychopathy is characterised by the lack of desire and the capacity to form close attachments.[12] As described by Jennifer Storey et al., in the article, *Psychopathy and Stalking*, the stalkers that do reveal psychopathic behaviour (ASPD+P), are individuals who do function without the restraints of conscience, and these individuals do present a high risk of serious physical or psychological harm to victims.[13]

As mentioned in Essay 2, neuroscience has estimated that approximately one to two per cent of the general population are psychopaths: unable to register the emotions that are the foundation of humanity, conscience and empathy (C&E). What is truly interesting though, is that while psychopathy has a genetic base, when the child is raised in a happy, oxytocin-stimulating environment with a stable and loving parental team that provides strong boundaries, good routines and positive male role models (particularly for boys), marvels rather than monsters can be formed. With the right early environment, individuals carrying this genetic anomaly can become exceptional. Research has shown the psychopathic brain pattern does not guarantee a life of crime.

Magnetic resonance imaging (MRI) proved that Dr Fallon, a leading neuroscientist, raised in a close and caring family, has the psychopathic genome.[14] Fallon attributes his success in lift to his exceptionally happy childhood. He had a very loving, financially secure, two-parent early home environment that had set firm boundaries, the strong boundaries between good and bad behaviour. His parents had been well educated and were from a higher socio-economic level than the incarcerated psychopaths he was studying. Most of them had suffered a lifetime of poverty, emotional and physical abuse and a 'fatherless' abandonment in early life.

Psychopaths are narcissistic, creative liars, ruthless and egocentric and they are the more organised risk-takers in crime. When that risk-taking, creativeness, confidence and drive is properly harnessed, some of our most promising individuals were formed, individuals who have been leaders in fields from defence to science. James Fallon is evidence of this; he was shocked to find he had the same temporal lobe inactivity in areas of emotional development as the psychopaths he was studying.[15] Dr Fallon, a Professor Emeritus of Anatomy and Neurobiology at the University of California, had included a scan of his own brain when studying psychopathy with the MRI scans of the prisoners being studied.

Psychopathy, because of genetic factors, can come from any socioeconomic group, however, being abused or 'dumbed-down' by incompetent parenting in the first decade is now recognised as a major contributing factor in moulding psychopathic behaviour in children and later adults. Fallon's potential had not been reduced by a lack of education or the reduction of the happiness and bonding hormone, oxytocin, which is stimulated to much higher levels in happy early environments.[16]

Modern parenting—particularly single parenting and primary caregivers discarding the parenting role, passing this responsibility to strangers in childcare, before the essential two-to-three-year bonding process has completed, is creating emotional disorders in numbers in children never before recorded.

Both Hare and Fallon's research has shown that without a happy early environment, repressed anger and hatred could be forming and exploding in teenage years. Fallon stated that, in addition to particular brain and genetic patterns, there is a 'third ingredient' involved in the development of a violent psychopath. Fallon's research revealed that the reduced empathy seen in psychopathy may be associated with the influence of both reduced oxytocin and vasopressin production. Both hormones appear to be essential for appropriate and beneficial social interactions.[17]

A child's early environment can determine whether violence-related genes and certain brain processes towards aggression are triggered. Specifically, Fallon believes that abuse—especially severe, early childhood sexual, physical or emotional abuse—is instrumental in this process. He also believes that the precise timing of when various factors come into play is critically important in determining whether one becomes a psychopath and, if so, exactly what type of psychopathological behaviour is exhibited.

Dr Fallon is a direct ancestor of the famous Cornell family. While Ezra Cornell was the founder of Cornell University, other ancestors were more sinister.[18&19] Thomas Cornell killed his mother and was hanged in 1673, the first case of matricide recorded in the new American colonies. Fallon's research into his family background found numerous murders committed by those within his father's family line, which included Lizzie Borden, who was controversially acquitted of killing her father and stepmother with an axe, in 1892.

Psychopaths can often have surprisingly high IQs.[20] People with the psychopathic brain pattern can be sociable, or antisocial, depending on early childhood or educational environments and the presence or lack of positive male role models. The world has seen famous serial killers who had MENSA IQs: Rodney Alcala (135), Ted Kaczynski (167), Charlene Gallego (160), Andrew Cunanan (147), Jeffrey Dahmer (145),

Ted Bundy (136) and Edmund Kemper (145) to name a few.[21] Ruthless and emotionless, their stories are chilling.

Scott Bonn in his article, *Wicked Deeds: Understanding What Drives Serial Killers*,[22] explains psychopaths kill because they want to kill. In many cases inappropriate parenting or emotional or physical abandonment in early childhood (as in single parenting) caused insecurity and a fear of rejection. They are transferring their ingrained pain and anger to entirely innocent people for a sense of control. Infamous serial killers who were raised in single parent homes include David Berkowitz, Ted Bundy and Joel Rifkin. Some serial killers, such as Edmund Kemper, were tormented, abused and even tortured by their birth mothers. Kemper, close to his father, was devastated when at age nine his parents divorced. He was raised by his domineering, alcoholic mother who would frequently belittle, humiliate and abuse him. His shocking life story and horrific serial killings are one of the worst examples of nature and inappropriate nurture.[23]

As discussed in Essay 3, psychopaths have a malfunctioning limbic system, meaning that ultimately, psychopathic personas have the mental ability to choose to be bad, while other brain disorders, sadly, do not have that mental control. The limbic system has several functions, but most have to do with the control of functions necessary for self-preservation and species preservation. Hence, the human subset of psychopathic personas that focuses entirely on self, lack activity in the areas which are the source of emotional responses. Conscience and empathy are learned behaviours, so when parents provide neither, do their children learn early to adopt the poker player's skill to mask emotional responses, which so frequently explodes in teenage years?

Is their lack of emotional intelligence (EQ) being shut down by parenting incompetence, or abuse? When life has taught them their physical and emotional cries for help are wasted on those around them, do they not learn appropriate responses? In his book, *Emotional intelligence: why it can matter more than IQ,* Daniel Goleman explains that EQ development is far more important for civilisation to survive than IQ development.[24]

James Fallon is not violent or a killer and this has enormous implications for governments wanting to detain people simply because they have the psychopathic brain pattern, even when they have not committed a crime. Some of our bravest fighters and intellectual men may have this brain pattern but, when raised in good homes, they do not go on to commit violent crimes. The world needs to know why it is that despite having so many biological markers for violence, people like Fallon can end up as scholars and real assets to society, while others become aggressive criminals and serial offenders.[25]

If readers read no other reference mentioned in my book, they should read the article written by Robert Hercz, *Psychopaths among us*.[26] It reveals the world of psychopaths and the struggle Dr Hare has had to face, even in his own country, Canada, in his attempts to alert the world about these predators. The article draws attention to our refusal to accept psychopathy, which, because of the genetic component, starts in the cradle. If that cradle is not rocked with care and maturity and the child is raised by incompetent parents, particularly in 'welfare' poverty, monsters will continue to be formed. Society and legal systems seem to prefer to bury their heads in the sand as these evil 'chameleons' slither invisibly amongst us.

As explained by Hercz, instead of enjoying retirement Hare had to become 'a man with a suitcase, a passport, and a PowerPoint presentation, a reluctant celebrity at gatherings of judges, attorneys, prison administrators, psychologists, and police.' The cost and time of psychopathy testing is still seen by many as the greatest negative of the testing procedure. In addition, Hare's findings were based on over twenty years of research on a 'captive group' of *male* psychopathic criminals. Far less incarcerated women are psychopathic, because of genetics and because oestrogen, rather than testosterone, dominates their lives.

If children are raised in abusive or inappropriate early environments, where early prolonged behaviour of animal cruelty and bullying of other children is not recognised and treated by specialists in the field of psychopathy, society will continue to see the increase of domestic and public violence from these emotionally damaged people, who get their 'highs' from harming, not helping. Unfortunately, group therapy programs, often part of prison and court- mandated treatment, has been shown to make psychopathic offenders worse.[27]

Serial killers virtually always have a record of brutally killing pets and animals in the first one and a half decades of life. Ashley Fruno's article, *Who's the animal? Stop domestic violence by punishing animal abusers,*[28] is a wakeup call to society about animal cruelty and its long-term impact on our community. The study by Dr John Clarke, a lecturer in psychology at the University of Sydney and consultant to the New South Wales Police Force, which by using police data revealed 61.5 per cent of convicted animal-abuse offenders, had also committed an assault and 17 per cent were guilty of sexual abuse. It is apparent that animal abuse was a better predictor of sexual assault than previous convictions for homicide, arson or firearms offences. Only 1 per cent of cruelty-to-animals offenders did not have other convictions.

If feminists are serious about domestic violence, they should be lobbying politicians to make it law that all forms of animal abuse must be reported to the police, by the public, teachers and animal protection facilities. These convictions should remain on a permanent police register, as psychopathy does not respond to rehabilitation. When further offences occur, the police and the law should ensure that psychopathic testing is carried out, using the internationally accepted *Psychopathy Checklist* (PCL-R) created by Dr Hare, the world leader in psychopathy research.[29] Offenders who score between 30-40 points will remain an extreme threat as psychopaths are the most recidivist of all criminals. This dangerous subset needs to be registered, prison is deserved punishment, but it can never cure this genetic disorder. Serial offenders should be transferred to high security psychiatric clinics, after completing their prison sentence, where they can be held for analysis and ongoing research. Neuroscientists need to get answers for this behaviour, as does the general public.

As noted by Fruno, researchers have known for decades that animal abuse is a precursor to violence against humans, and those who abuse animals often use more dangerous forms of violence and controlling behaviour towards their partners. The world's most notorious serial killers—including Jeffrey Dahmer, Dennis Rader, and Albert DeSalvo (better known as the Boston Strangler) have long documented histories of harming animals. In Australia, serial killer Paul Denyer Martin Bryant

(Port Arthur mass murderer), John Travers, Christopher Worrell and Ivan Milat brutally tortured and killed pets and other animals before turning to human victims.

Bullying is the behaviour that reveals a total lack of internal strength, strength which is moulded by basic goodness and kind-heartedness. This horrible type of behaviour has increased massively since the mid-twentieth century, because of the anonymity of cyber bullying and children now growing up with lesser levels of C&E. Such prolonged cruelty in children under the age of sixteen must not be ignored. Along with consistent lying, this can be a sign of future white-collar psychopathy, and occasionally even heinous psychopathy.[30]

Narcissism is another early sign of possible psychopathy. WCPs do form relationships but, as this group has low boredom thresholds, these relationships are more often short term.[31&32] They are often extremely narcissistic and tend to change their usually glamorous partners often— examples are all too easily found in headlines.

Surveys in American colleges showed that over 50 per cent of their college (uni) students were narcissistic—with the spread of pointless 'selfies' across the world, no surprise there.[33] Narcissism has skyrocketed since the mid-twentieth century, when I went to school. We rarely met people who would rate as narcissists, and they would have been too embarrassed to flaunt such excessive vanity and self-absorption. Numerous books have been written about narcissistic behaviour, as it is a quality closely linked to white-collar psychopathy.[34-42]

Narcissism is now recognised as a psychological disorder by the American Psychiatric Association DSM (Diagnostic and Statistical Manual: Mental Disorders), with nine specific traits:
1. Grandiosity
2. Preoccupation with success and power
3. Belief in being unique
4. Sense of entitlement to special treatment
5. Requires excessive admiration
6. Envious of others
7. Lack of empathy
8. Exploitative of others to achieve personal gain
9. Arrogant and domineering

Narcissism, like psychopathy, needs genes that predispose a person to these disorders. One is rated as a narcissist if one exhibits at least five of these traits. With parents, particularly single parents, placing children on pedestals, this behaviour is grooming them for narcissism. However, it is paradoxical that narcissism can also stem from insecurity, caused by childhood emotional trauma where there has been an extreme lack of unconditional love—single parenting is often a case of more conditional love as the child is required to fill the role of soul mate. Many modern parents find it easier to buy their children a 'Merc', than to teach them MERC (morality, empathy, respect and conscience).

Some parents, for various reasons, now abandon their infants to childcare at the earliest possible time. Early separation issues can retard personality development. Brilliant 'nerds' are often quite deficient in social interaction skills because they were separated from their primary caregiver before their much greater early neural activity had completely developed. Reports have shown prenatal trauma or stress for the mother—even when the foetus is in the womb—can also have lifetime effects.[43] Anything that reduces oxytocin can be of concern to mental health.

We are now living in a society that celebrates the 'Seven Deadly Sins'. Narcissism, obesity, alcoholism, drug addiction, poor manners, coarse language, poor speech patterns, deception and theft are all evidence of a lack of personal discipline and control in the new age of disregard for welfare and general atheism. Society tends to see the 'Seven Deadly Sins' as Seven Desirable Debaucheries, acceptable behaviours by many in society: lust, gluttony (excess in eating and drinking), greed (excessive desire for acquisitions and wealth), sloth (welfare laziness), wrath (strong vengeful anger), envy and/or pride (narcissism and excessive self-esteem).

Atheism has been known to have followers kneeling, usually in the vomiting position, to their god, Bacchus. As a result, we have increasing numbers of teens consuming copious amounts of alcohol, taking drugs and growing up without C&E. Lost children who are steering through life without a moral compass. In the USA, in 1971, they lowered the voting age to 18-years, so younger people could be sent off to Vietnam to be killed. Australia followed suit. The drinking age was also lowered, although twelve American states, wisely, kept the drinking age at 21-years. However, in the 1980s, due to the influence of MADDs (Mothers Against Drunk Driving), brave American women who were caring mothers, challenged male-dominated governments because they had great concern about the health and welfare of their young teens. They were able to get all American states to raise the alcohol purchase and legal drinking age to 21 years of age. This was partly to combat the high number of drunk-driving fatalities, as well as to prevent other serious long term health issues. [44-48] Sadly, UK and Australian mothers lack sufficient concern and continue to allow the extremely wealthy and powerful alcohol industry to dominate their children's lives.

It is now recognised that psychopathic personas, in the form of paedophiles and dictatorial leaders, are attracted to the security of male-dominated religions (greater than the estimated 1-2 per cent found in the general public). Parents deserve to know that the leading church and school clerics, who play such a large part in moulding essential EQ in the brains of our children, have met set standards of faith. As religious instruction is now abandoned in many schools and with the rise in atheism, perhaps non-denominational religious clerics should play a much greater part in social and emotional learning (SEL) classes, which have been implemented from childcare to tertiary levels in many states in America.[49]

Private and government academic administration bodies should employ graduates of theologian and religious studies, which have covered all three major religions, to organise these classes. Using people with theologian backgrounds to provide the SEL training would relieve academic teachers from having to extend their already busy schedules. Teaching manners and EQ development, which were meant to become the responsibility of parents when they dropped religious instruction in schools, should not be imposed on teachers providing academic skills.

Now that more working parents have discarded religion, greater numbers of atheist parents are not taking responsibility to teach their children the basics of civilised society. When atheists rejected faith as mystical nonsense, they completely ignored the fact that it was these religious institutions that also taught EQ, which is as vital as IQ development in a child. Why should teachers continue to carry the brunt of the stress, caused by disrespectful, rude children that torment both teachers and other students, for no extra pay? The reason parents of these children should be included in the retraining is that most teachers are aware it is often ill-mannered, foul-mouthed, bullying parents who have been the role models for these ill-mannered, foul-mouthed, bullying problem children.

I am glad I grew up in a world where I did not live in fear, where trust was not blatantly abused by individuals who did not have the values of GOD (Goodness, Order—including gender and cultural equality—and Decency) ingrained in their early lives—values which included MERC, which made up our moral compass. Centuries of 'faith' tried to introduce qualities that form emotional intelligence. As Goleman explained in his book on this subject, children require social and emotional learning (SEL). Without it, we are creating generations of narcissistic, self-centred young people. Teaching young children these qualities, which are not inborn, has improved civilisation over centuries. Humanity has moved from early barbaric, tribal adversaries to caring communities, based on equality and social conscience.

Sociopathy is undisputed evidence of bad parenting. Their horrific behaviour is destroying the lives of teachers and this profession has become one of the most stress laden careers, with Australia recording some of the worst student behaviour in its history.[50-53] Welfare suburbs are frequently featured on the news, with teens displaying bullying behaviour and handling automobiles in a way that is a danger to themselves, their passengers and the public.

Universities and governments should give far more priority and greater funding to professions related to teaching and caring for children in tertiary education as well as to theologian studies (i.e. developing EQ as well as IQ). Society needs teachers and specialists in child development, parental training and neuroscience research far more than it needs self-serving lawyers. Lawyers rake in vast amounts of money, yet teachers who are far more valuable for society, get nowhere near their worth.

We need to fix the downward spiral that inappropriate parenting is creating, in dysfunctional early environments. They are creating emotionally damaged teenagers, who are the future guaranteed income for the legal system. The exceptionally well-researched report by Rachel Tiede, *Trauma in the child welfare and public health systems,* reveals the horrific statistics of children raised in impoverished circumstances, by incompetent parents.[54] Children who have had sub-standard or no positive parental role models—particularly male role models—are in turn becoming inappropriate and incompetent parents and often domestically violent men.

Kids will not learn social skills while they remain with bad parents, or in detention centres, and they frequently go on to create the next generation of damaged children. It is the vicious cycle of the twenty-first century. Parenting is one of the most demanding careers on earth. Raising a child in this era is tough enough for two, but now we have 'children having children' and singles choosing to raise children alone. It appears no one cares about the negative statistics regarding single parenting that 'new-wave feminists' choose to ignore.

Stable and happy two-parent homes, with a positive male role model—particularly for sons who have a greater need for oxytocin stimulation—neutralise the more negative aspects of the genetic inheritance of psychopathy and mould better children.[55] With atheists failing in huge numbers, particularly in the welfare groups, to ingrain manners and social skills in the first important decade of a child's life, society is suffering immensely. I question why, when religion was abandoned, governments, education departments and atheist parents did not pay attention to the warning Daniel Goleman gave in 1995 and made SEL (Social & Emotional Learning) classes compulsory in all schools that had abandoned religious instruction.[56]

Phillip Cohen in his article, *Single moms can't be scapegoated for the murder rate anymore,* quoted from a study on homicide trends released in 1991, by the US Health and Human Services Secretary, Louis W. Sullivan. He declared:

The collapse of the American family in the past few decades is historically unprecedented in the U.S., and possibly in the world.

Nowhere is this trend more apparent than in the black community....
Some argue that the high rate of single parenthood has not adversely
affected our children. But, sadly, the research does not bear them
out... Study after study has shown that children from single-parent
families are five times more likely to be poor and twice as likely to
drop out of school... They are also more likely to be involved in
criminal activity, to abuse drugs and alcohol, to suffer ill health, and
to become trapped in welfare dependency.[57]

The English author, Theodore Dalrymple, in his book, *Life at the
bottom*, described similar conditions.[58] We now have second and third
generation welfare single parenting. Atheist parents have discarded the
two key institutions responsible for EQ training: religious education
and the nuclear family concept—children raised by a two-gender team
with wider familial and social contact, rather than single matriarchal
dependency.

Who is now teaching these qualities that are essential for healthy
and stable human development? Leading childhood clinicians have
recognised babies need a bonding period of two to three years with their
primary caregiver. Can busy working parents, not there to teach their
children the basic skills that mould their future lives, trust strangers to
instil the values of MERC? Some child clinicians have voiced concerns
about the essential primary caregivers divorcing themselves from
their under three-year-old children by placing them in childcare with
strangers.[59&60]

More worrying, infants with higher IQs, which research has
shown have considerably more neural activity occurring than those
with lower IQs, can be damaged by the stress of separation from the
primary caregiver, therefore, impacting on personality and behaviour
development to a greater degree. Hence, the higher the IQ, the greater
the need for longer bonding time with the primary caregiver.[61&62] The
infant's attachment to his or her caregiver is a fundamental principal
of human development. Therefore, emotional connection is one of
the most important obligations that a parent has to a child. By being
robbed too early of this connection, children have developed a range of
childhood disorders rarely seen a half a century ago.

Australian research has shown that boys are more negatively affected than girls. They tend to initially demonstrate more problem behaviour in a day-care setting than girls.[63] As there are about four times as many boys as girls who suffer from autism, this greater sensitivity to stress and abandonment issues may be a governing factor. However, 'mother smothering' (a child placed in the unnatural position of being a 'soul-mate' to a single mother) can cause skewed emotional issues in later teen and adult partnerships.[64] Domestic violence is spiralling, more frequently perpetrated by adults who, as children were been robbed of the valuable learning process of belonging to a stable family team and, particularly in the case of sons, of the essential male role model from which the male persona develops.[65] We are now seeing the feral behaviour of so many young teens thrown out of the nest far too early.

The criminal behaviour of more and more young people in Australia is revealing an increase in moral deficiency.[66-68] Who is providing a moral compass for the children removed from their family home and left with strangers in childcare—often within a year of their birth and before they are toilet trained—or born to less competent, young, single, female parents? The statistics for this group are shocking.[69] Sadly, parents without a moral compass and who lack social skills, are raising children who are virtually alien to moral integrity. Many children are born to welfare-dependent parents, and 'children having children' are not taught these values, because the parents have never learned them.[70]

IQ is a genetic given, but EQ (emotional intelligence)—which includes self-control, zeal, persistence and the ability to motivate oneself—is a skill that must be learned. The first seven years have the most impact on a child's future life.[71-73] EQ skills are not inborn, they must be taught to children to give them a better chance to use whatever intellectual potential they have inherited.[74] When atheists and 'new wave feminists' discarded religious instruction and dual parenting, bullying became rampant when it became solely parental responsibility to teach these values. It has never been the responsibility of academia to teach EQ, and schools are now seeing children with a shocking lack of manners and respect. Many are so badly behaved they are already ticking boxes of sociopathy and psychopathy by the time they reach their teens—by which time rehabilitation may no longer be possible.

I agree with Daniel Goleman that the principles of social integrity and basic goodness unravel at increasing speed the further we distance ourselves from MERC. Goleman states that those who are at the mercy of impulse and who lack self-control are suffering a moral deficiency.

As atheism and the lack of EQ have become widespread, we now have a society where selfishness, financial greed and meanness of spirit are increasing. Unfortunately, many of these people are now parenting our young. Faith, and following the *Ten Commandments*, was seen to be a brilliant concept which helped to serve the greater good for thousands of years. Stressed teachers, police and medical staff are now trying to control young people raised in atheist and godless homes where MERC was not taught. We have children as young as five attacking teachers and youths who are alcoholics by the time they are in their twenties, popping drugs like candy.

When children assault teachers, administrative staff at these schools should report the child and parents to appropriate professionals specialising in sociopathic and psychopathic disorders.[75&76] In addition, with the increase of fatherless children robbed of male role models, it has become essential that there should be increased numbers of male teachers, preferably those who are parents and, hence, have higher levels of the bonding hormone, oxytocin.

Early detection and analysis are vital to counteract extreme behaviours of bullying and cruelty towards more vulnerable students or animals. Assessing behaviour for this group is beyond school counsellors' skill. Only professionals who specialised in psychopathy, genetic testing and MRI scanning can analyse this behaviour, where poor parenting or early emotional child abuse may have added damage to young brains genetically predisposed to psychopathic behaviour. If requests to attend counselling or analysis are ignored by parents, the threat of criminal law regarding children's rights should be an option, as the worst parents are moulding sad and bad young people.

Australia has some of the worst parenting because we have continuous welfare payments for every child born, which strongly supports single, never married parenting. Hence, the least competent, welfare-dependent females take advantage of the system, pumping out numerous children to qualify for welfare benefits to support their lifestyle—21st Century child labour. Coulter, in her book, *Guilty*, revealed the horrific statistics of single, never-married mothers in the US.[77] In Australia, our welfare system has also created increasing numbers of emotionally damaged, angry, self-absorbed children and teens. The welfare generations are more often uncouth, foul-mouthed, with no respect for seniors and exceptionally bad mannered. If the parent has always been on welfare and possibly never learned these values herself, where do these children learn EQ values in those vital first seven years?[78&79] Even private schools have their share of beastly children—they just have better accents when they abuse teachers. They are the new generation of WCPs and sociopaths.

Many infants are left in childcare far too early because working parents now make parenting—one of the most time-consuming and challenging jobs on earth (if done properly)—a part-time job alongside their nine-to-five working careers. Some prefer a huge house and mortgage to a smaller, more affordable first home and bonding with their children in the most important first two to three years, but most are trapped in nine-to-five jobs paying high taxes to feed, house and educate the children of the welfare world.

When I was employed by the federal government, it was obvious that it was the taxpayers who were restricting their family numbers to one to three children, numbers they could afford. Welfare recipients, who in reality could not afford to raise a single child, were frequently having four-to-seven children, simply as a means of support. Single teenagers were the largest offenders. As school dropouts they could never earn the money they could get on welfare. At the time, Australia had dozens of support programs for the welfare, whereas New Zealand had a better system with only about six programs.

When the public looks at the weekly dole payments and cry poverty, they forget that amount is tax free. In addition to welfare, they get reduced power costs, reduced water bills, travel reductions, reduced medical bills and numerous other concessions. With the large chunk of benefits they receive for each child, if they have enough children, their overall worth becomes basically the same as the lower paid 'blue-collar' workers. For this 'blue-collar' group, working nine-to-five, at the lower end of the salary scale, their take-home pay after tax and after bills are paid (for which they receive no concessions), did not leave them funds to spend on gambling, alcohol and cigarettes in their spare time, which was common practise with the long-term welfare dependent during my time working in this field.

If politicians were asked to introduce a plan to change the behaviour of these wayward kids, as religion once did, even if they formed a Royal Commission (at the usual huge public cost), they would have nowhere near the same success as those three early messengers when they introduced the moral compass to civilisation, now discarded by so many driven by financial greed. Even with neuroscience and our wealth of information, to find an 'atheist way' of recognising and converting individuals whose brains do not register C&E, is a task that appears beyond basic parenting skills. Australia should take America's lead, as mentioned in Goleman's book, and SEL (Social and Emotional Learning) classes should be compulsory for all schools, from childcare to tertiary, to help counter inadequate parenting.

Along with compulsory SEL classes, children—in all religious and non-religious schools—should have access to psychotherapists or psychologists specialising in psychopathy and sociopathy, rather than just counsellors, if they are exhibiting early signs of these disorders. These include prolonged cruelty to animals, frequent bullying of others, and deception. Even pre-school children are now showing emotional problems not seen in the mid-twentieth century, when most children at least had the 'trickle-down' effect of two-parent families and grandparents raised in some form of faith.

Teaching EQ to children from a young age is essential because Hare has revealed normal counselling and rehabilitation courses cannot restore a psychopath's emotionally disabled brain after they reach adulthood.[80&81] DNA research is advancing, but bad parenting is not improving as rapidly. These damaged individuals need to be placed under specialist care 24/7. Much greater funding should be poured into this research—neuroscience needs to find a way of reactivating emotionally inactive brains. We need less support for lawyers in tertiary education, who pick up these young people after they have passed through the gates to adulthood, but much more support for neuroscientists to assist young people before they reach that gate.

Parents should be forced to take much more responsibility in raising future generations. Having a child is not a single female's 'right', it is a responsibility which includes providing a child with its biological right: a parental team rather than maternal ownership and control.[82] This feminist-supported change has resulted in a shocking increase in juvenile crime, homelessness, alcoholic and drug addiction and teenage suicide.[83&84] The very detailed report by Kent Kiehl and Morris Hoffman, *The criminal psychopath: history, neuroscience, treatment, and economics*, should be read by all concerned about this mental disorder.[85]

The adrenaline 'high' psychopaths get when outsmarting others is such a powerful addiction it is the reason they cannot be successfully rehabilitated once they reach adulthood. If infants who carry the low-activity MAOA gene are assessed early and removed from bad parental situations, with compulsory parenting training provided for incompetent parents, there is a chance of reform.[86] However, as our society and the law continues to ignore the problem, thinking a child will 'grow out of it', refusing to accept that the first decade forms the future life of the psychopathic persona, the problem increases. Combining this with teenage and underage casual sex, the future of thousands of people born to incompetent and often 'dumbed-down' young girls, will continue to be destroyed—and the whole of society will continue to suffer.

The production of oxytocin in the body is shut down by anger, stress, alcohol and drugs, which are so often factors of these poorer and, in the case of single parents, self-inflicted, bad early environments. Fortunately, children harbouring sociopathic, internalised rage are more inclined to respond to care than psychopaths, because it is anger driving them, not genetics; they have a greater chance of rehabilitation when removed from the incompetent parents that moulded them.[87]

As explained in Essay 3, females carry the double hit of the MAOA warrior gene (carried on the X-chromosome of the unmatched XY set).[88] Carrying two copies, it appears one high-activity version moderates the more aggressive low-activity version, even without the large oxytocin hormone 'hit' mothers receive during natural childbirth. Men are not so lucky, as they have only one copy of the MAOA gene passed to them by their mothers, meaning they have a 50/50 chance of inheriting the aggressive low-activity version. When aggression is not moderated by childbirth oxytocin, or oxytocin receptors are not stimulated in children, by happy early home environments, this may partly explain the psychopathy ratio of 80 per cent men, 20 per cent women.

The fact that they only have one copy of the MAOA gene is the reason a male child has the greater need for oxytocin stimulation, both in childbirth and the first decade of life. Research has shown more boys than girls are affected by being placed into childcare too early. Darcia Narvaez' article in Psychology Today, *Be worried about boys especially baby boys,*[89] which refers to Allan Schore's research called, *All our sons: the developmental neurobiology and neuroendocrinology of boys at risk,*[90] should be read to reveal the damage that can be done to sons in early development.

Boys suffer more emotional problems when they are forced to leave the family 'nest' and are placed in childcare with strangers before the essential bonding with the primary caregiver is completed. Child clinicians have stated this bonding requirement is preferably two years, but higher IQ children may require a year longer, as they have millions more neural synapses forming. To shut down this production could well be the cause of the increase in childhood disorders such as autism and hyperactivity.

We are seeing children with mental disorders rarely seen in earlier times, possibly because many parents are now passing on the primary caregiver role to strangers at a much earlier age. Is this the reason some of our most intelligent children, if they have the more non-aggressive, high-activity version of the MAOA gene, mentally curl into the foetal position and close down internally from fear, into autistic behaviour, to shut out the world they are not ready to face? Do others become hyperactive to fight the strange new world they have been thrust into before they are mentally and physically able to cope with abandonment?

It appears those with the low-activity MAOA genotype (MAOA-L), paired with maltreatment in childhood, or single parenting with no positive male role models, were correctly predicted to commit crime.[91&92] Single parenting has been catastrophic for boys as it is usually the male gender, the father, who initiates humour and the uninhibited, oxytocin-producing fun and games that are so necessary for sons. Many male children, deprived of oxytocin in that first decade, are growing up with huge internal emotional damage.

A growing concern, in the era of single parenting, is that the lack of a father's unconditional love, and the strong self-esteem that bonding provides for sons and daughters, makes young people far more vulnerable to persuasion. We now see that men, who tick boxes of psychopathy, have infiltrated male-dominated religions, sabotaging faith and the emotional learning it provided, for their own personal power and domination.[93] Hence, deceptive, thuggish terrorists, masquerading under the original Islamic faith, appear to offer personal empowerment, which young men may not have received at home. It makes the 'fatherless' group far more easily seduced into radical terrorism.[94]

Psychopathic personas are more calculating, and their crimes are generally more organised than sociopathic criminals.[95] They continue to be the most dominant predator of the human species. With overpopulation, guns and equipment, it is now possible for humans to wipe every other animal species into extinction—and we are doing so at a terrifying rate.[96] Psychopathic personas generally start or force wars, however, until we find ways to control the rapidly spiralling human over-breeding, wars or pandemics, killing millions of people, will probably remain the 'necessary evil' this planet requires to survive the global warming and environmental damage caused by ever expanding population numbers.

Most countries have already reached population 'plague' proportions.[97] Today, more than 80 per cent of the world's population lives in countries that are running ecological deficits, using more resources than what their ecosystems can renew. In 1961 we used a little more than half of the Earth's biocapacity; in 2006 we used 44 per cent more than was available.[98] While Australia, Canada and Scandinavian countries are among the countries where their biocapacity, fortunately, exceeds the 'ecological footprint', the large majority of countries have biocapacity deficits (i.e. the demand for the goods and services that its land and seas can provide—fruits and vegetables, meat, fish, wood, cotton for clothing, and carbon dioxide absorption—exceeds what the region's ecosystems can renew).[99]

As early as 1994, the National Research Institute on Food and Nutrition (INRAN), in their study *Food, Land, Population and the U.S. Economy* had warned, 'to achieve a sustainable economy and avert disaster, the United States must reduce its population by at least one-third, and world population will have to be reduced by two-thirds.'[100] Were we really surprised when Italy, with very high Catholic population numbers, was absolutely devastated when the coronavirus (COVID-19) struck? The Catholic and Islamic religions that discourage contraception are choosing to remain in total denial about the destruction that overpopulation and overcrowding cause. We have the over-breeding 'Eve's' of the world destroying the planet. Afraid to make families more accountable, governments are acting like irresponsible teenagers, who put a public party invitation on the internet and are then totally surprised when the house gets trashed, because 500 people turned up to a house than can only take fifty guests. Infinite breeding in a world of finite resources and limited arable land now makes humans the deadliest plague on the planet.

IRA terrorists were formed in the overcrowded and large impoverished Catholic families in Ireland, while the Mafia and similar criminal groups formed in Italy and South America, largely because of the poverty caused by the appalling Catholic rule, which denounces contraception. The negative impact of this rule on thousands of children was ignored, because it substantially increased the Catholic numbers and power. Muslim clerics, who also encourage mass breeding, radically increasing their numbers and power, have moulded men who are seemingly incapable of registering emotional and caring responses, and who are carrying out horrific crimes against humanity.

Are they the threat of a future war, coming at a time when humans have allowed irresponsible breeding to create such a strain on natural resources, with unparalleled levels of consumerism and the dumping of massive amounts of plastic waste? After all, wars have been tragically effective in reducing population numbers. Bullets and bombs do not distinguish between rich and poor, young or old. Nuclear war is even more destructive, causing cancer and genetic mutations to carry through following generations.

MRI scans of adult psychopathic brains have revealed a lack of brain development and substantially reduced grey matter in the areas responsible for emotions.[101] Toxic parenting and bad early environments that puts stress on the child can retard the development of grey matter in the frontal temporal lobes.[102] If happiness is constantly blighted, internalised anger is slowly growing. The shutdown of oxytocin (the bonding chemical) due to stress (in any part of the child's life, from the day of conception to at least the age of six),[103] may be the contributing factor that makes the difference between adults who are outrageous and those who are outstanding.[104]

Nature versus nurture is still being debated, but slowly neuroscience is revealing there appears to be a genetic component. However, research is hampered because who is examining the brains and doing longitudinal studies on one-to-sixteen-year-olds in dysfunctional homes? Both the homes of excessively wealthy and homes of welfare poverty have produced horrifying psychopathic personas who, if not raised with strong parental bonds, positive male role models, set routines, moral boundaries and unconditional love, can murder friends and family.

Radical Sunni 'hadith Islam', which is the corruption of true Islam based on hadith fabrications that contort the word of Allah and Muhammad, disrupts the creation of the bonding hormone, oxytocin, which is essential for healthy child development. It bans music, dancing and behaviours that produce this essential hormone.[105-6] (Readers must note that the laws shown in the *Islam and Question and Answer* site are not from the Quran, but are fabrications and mistranslations of the Quran made by tribal autocrats). This retards intellectual and emotional development, as it reduces the formation of essential grey and white brain matter. A recent report told of two women in India who were killed by 'hadith Islamic' males for laughing and dancing at a wedding.[107-8] Friendly greetings stimulate oxytocin, yet the smiles of Islamic women are now being masked in greater numbers.[109] 'Hadith Islam', quite by chance, has given us the answer to how psychopathic personas are moulded.

Trying to understand these evil men, I questioned what their childhoods must have been like. One only has to read the report *Marriage practices in North India* by Marian MacDorman, to realise how women are treated as second grade citizens.[110] Were they born into a loveless arranged marriage where rape is accepted as the wife's duty? Was the mother they loved imprisoned in a burqa when they walked together, her smile hidden in public? Did they always confront faceless women in the streets who never smiled at them? Did wild and unkempt black beards, surrounding stern unsmiling faces so confronting for small children, always surround them? I have seen little ones scream with fear when they were first introduced to Father Christmas, who is always smiling and has a far less scary white beard.

I wondered what horrors their lives might have contained. Did they witness, as described in Phyllis Chesler's book, *The death of feminism*,[111] 18-year-old Zarife being shot dead in Holland, by her father, in 2003, for 'going out with Dutch girls and without her scarf'; or in Jordan in 1999, when a brother put four bullets into his sister's head in the living room because her rape had dishonoured the family. Perhaps they witnessed their father gouge out both eyes and cut off the nose and ears of their mother, as happened to Zahida Perveen in 2001, in Pakistan, because he wrongly suspected her of adultery. What message would a son have taken from that, when the male relatives shook that psychopathic monster's hand and congratulated him as he was being arrested, making the comments, 'she must have deserved it' and 'a husband has to do what a man has to do'. (I further explore 'hadith Islam' and the psychopathic, godless men it creates in Essays 7 and 8.)

People must recognise that it is the quality, or lack of quality, of parenting that creates marvels or monsters. Parenting is a huge responsibility, it is not simply a female's right. We have female groups that have no guilt in returning to feral or stockyard animal breeding—casual rutting with a male stud, or IVF, then raising the offspring alone, robbing a child of it biological right of unconditional love and support of a father. Increasing numbers of sons, who have no positive male role models in their first decade, is creating a new lost generation. Are we really surprised if these children lapse into feral behaviour as an adult?

Statistics show that children with the psychopathic genetic link, particularly male children, if raised in an inappropriate early environment, are the most emotionally damaged and are by far the larger number of criminal offenders.[112-114]

~ 5 ~

Religion above the law has allowed gender apartheid

'The Lord God said to the serpent, "Because you have done this, cursed are you above all cattle, and above all wild animals; upon your belly you shall go, and dust you shall eat all the days of your life."'
— **Genesis 3:14**

In the 21st century, a world of science and technology, the parallels between the Bible and science are more fascinating than the outdated world of religious magic and miracles. Religion was the first educational institution that taught essential emotional development (EQ). We now live in a world where many have lost their moral compass, where there is massive financial disparity. Our children are too sophisticated to believe laying on hands or speaking in tongues is reality. However, they live in a world of spiralling psychopathy and it is this evil subset of humanity that the three major religious messengers first warned us against as early as circa 1400 BC. We need children to once again learn the values of morality, empathy, respect and conscience (MERC) because they are the generation that can and must stop the destruction of our Eden by these evil predators, psychopaths, both white-collar and heinous.

The atheist modern world now celebrates 'white-collar' psychopathy: men lacking in moral integrity who get a warped sense of fulfilment and achievement from breaking dreams by siphoning money and emptying the bank accounts of their clients to feed their own appalling financial greed. Psychopaths are always in the realm of atheism, their lack of moral integrity, cowardice and deception are the perfect example of godlessness. Although fake, this quote (originally linked with Trump), 'Being an atheist gives me an edge in every deal. Christians are too moral for business', is a rather accurate summary of atheism.[1] People that tick boxes for psychopathy do not have a moral compass and do not recognise their lack of morality.

People are not born with a moral compass: it is a learned quality. Before faith, the early toxic world of enslavement, deception, female subjugation and financial disparity needed change. Was evolution alone capable of doing an about-turn? Rising like a phoenix from the ashes of a morally bankrupt, battle-scarred society, came the first messenger, Moses. Records show that he transcribed the book of Genesis from patriarchal records written on clay tablets, via the line of Seth, Noah, Shem, Abraham, Isaac and Jacob.[2]

His parable, telling of the birth of Adam and Eve, was a mythical example of the commencement of human life, but the Garden of Eden parable was a very clever prophesy. It was a symbolic parable told to show the cunning deception of predatory creatures that choose the path of evil rather than of goodness. The metaphorical serpent, a cold-blooded and emotionless reptile, used to define the most deceptive of all God's creatures, was an inspirational choice to describe cruel and more dictatorial individuals with a psychopathic lack of emotional development (EQ). It was not reality as many religious clerics would have us believe—people no more spoke with snakes in those days than they do now. However, the accuracy of that symbolic prediction is quite remarkable.

Moses' description of the behaviour of the serpent was a brief, but very precise, summary of the psychopathic persona described in Dr Hare's book two thousand years later: dishonest and insensitive creatures that would blatantly lie to their prey (the vulnerable and trusting), causing great loss by creating financial or emotional pain.[3] An uncanny, long-term prediction from an early human, who was born thousands of years before the word neuroscience, or psychopath, even existed. This egocentric subgroup, driven by profit and greed, do not have a care about the wellbeing of this planet. As predicted, they have the power and potential to destroy the Eden we are lucky enough to inhabit.

Misogynist male clerics blamed Eve, the victim, for committing the 'original sin'. Yet her only sin was that of trusting a liar. From that early ignorance in interpreting symbolism, choosing to read the text of Holy Scriptures literally rather than metaphorically, religious 'gender-apartheid' was formed, retarding civilisation for centuries. Deliberately, or through ignorance, this mistranslation by religious fundamentalists created the most inexcusable treatment of women from that time. Gender apartheid in cultures dominated by male tyrants and dictators has reduced the quality of life for both genders.

When females, considered to be the more nurturing gender, are subjugated and degraded in the eyes of men, some of the most horrendous men are formed—something the world is now witnessing from cultures steeped in misogyny. However, not being able to recognise the evil of these often good-looking but pathologically deceptive men is something to which women still consistently fall victim. Too many women still remain the most gullible and vulnerable conquests for these superficially charming social predators, the conmen and women in the modern age.

Psychopaths constitute on average one per cent of the population, however, CEO positions in businesses, where money can be unfairly siphoned from clients in excessive fees and bonuses, attract by far the highest number of psychopaths. Australian and American surveys have shown that on average 21 per cent of CEOs in these areas are white-collar psychopaths (WCPs),[4] with even higher numbers in property development and sales. These are the real criminals of the modern age. Other careers with the highest proportion WCPs listed in the top ten group include branches of law, which attracts three per cent, with politics and religion also included in this group.[5]

They absorb the knowledge of good and evil but reject the values early religions tried to teach. Preferring to choose the path of evil—they remain alien to, or have extremely anaemic quantities of C&E and lack moral integrity. Once called Lucifer, Satan, Beelzebub, 'jinn devils', or the antichrist, these evil people are now recognised by modern neuroscience as psychopathic personas. Psychopaths continue to be recognised as the 'bad not mad' criminals, as this group alone has the ability to choose the path they take.[6] Victims of other brain disorders do not have the benefit of choice.

These subtle snakes have slithered into religious teaching institutions, as the trusting congregations are the most vulnerable and always the prey for this subset of humanity. Over time, many religions, placed above the law, have given unrestricted access to predatory dictatorial men who target such people. These snakes are the very people religions were formed to recognise and convert, yet they have infiltrated male-dominated religious institutions—in above-average numbers.

Monotheism, introduced by the three major prophets, was about unity—faith in one spiritual Father. The three Abrahamic faiths that followed, Judaism, Christianity and Islam, were created by earthborn men, not God, and have generated great disunity in the world. Male-dominated religious education institutions, unlike academic institutions that have recognised standards across the world, often compete against each other in the most godless manner of compulsion and deception. Many religious leaders are more interested in personal power than in their roles as religious educators providing civilisation with moral integrity, gender and cultural equality and by restraining massive financial inequality. As they are above the law, many religious clerics have become exceptionally judgemental, which is a sin in itself.

Homosexuality caused by skewed maternal hormones in gestation

We have seen some religions cruelly judge homosexual children, when research has shown it is skewed hormonal balances of the pregnant mother in the first few weeks of pregnancy that sets the brain pattern of the child—brain wiring which is irreversible. This information has been shut down as much by feminists and the 'motherhood mafia' who avoid any negative statistics against them, as it was the industries that were pumping female hormones into everything they could.

The book, *Brainsex: The real difference between men and women,*[7] by English geneticist Anne Moir and David Jessel, should be essential reading for religions and other people with their heads still firmly planted in the sand, regarding homosexuality, because it revealed excessive oestrogen, in the first trimester of pregnancy, affects the sexual orientation of the male foetus. Corporate bodies wanted to conceal this fact because they were adding oestrogen into everything and, like thalidomide, there had been inadequate research of side effects. As a result it quadrupled the numbers of homosexual males, above what occurred naturally with skewed hormones in early pregnancy, for decades. It gives valuable information revealing the inadequacies of male-dominated religions ignorant of biological research. By trying to stop the publication of the book, the more narrow-minded 'feminists'—the motherhood group who wished to retain traditional values of marriage and childbearing—held back the acceptance of these victims of maternal hormonal imbalance for decades.

Feminists who concentrated on domestic and child-raising issues divorced themselves from both the Suffragettes and Women Liberation Movement, who had fought for equality worldwide, rather than accepting marital subjugation and domestic enslavement. Feminists did not want to accept that there were obvious emotional as well as physical gender differences in men and women.

As mentioned in Moir and Jessel's book, a male or female foetus has enough hormones to trigger the development of gender appropriate sex organs in the first six weeks, but if they do not receive sufficient gender appropriate hormones, because of an imbalance in the mother's hormone levels, it results in homosexual behaviour. When the mother's body is loaded with additional oestrogen, artificially introduced because of the common use of this hormone in food and the plastic containers that the food comes in, it is not surprising that (at the time this book was written) male homosexuality was four times greater than that of female homosexuality. Testing on animals showed that once the critical time of brain development was past, no amount of additional gender specific hormones added at a later time enabled the animals to regain their original gender identity.

Animal laboratory testing showed the brain pattern could not be changed by adding the required hormones after birth. In addition, the argument being pushed, primarily by feminists that both male and female babies are born with the same brain, was proven wrong by scientists and researchers into the subject. It is disclosed in Moir and Jessel's book that the potential social backlash caused some researchers to soften scientific facts and quietly shelve their findings. This fact retarded the acceptance of homosexuality for decades, allowing industry to continue pumping oestrogen into a large range of products and food industries.[8] It also allowed male-dominated religions to continue persecuting innocent offspring who were homosexual.

Stripped of its sexual machinery at the crucial time of brain development, the brain fails to produce the hormones that would return it to heterosexual behaviour. If religious leaders were to ban homosexuality, they would need to shut down industries supplying the female hormone and neuter unfortunate women who have natural hormonal imbalances during their pregnancies; a 'Catch-22' situation for the two key religions, as Catholicism and Islam have used women as breeding machines for centuries simply to increase numbers for their faith.

Religious education and counselling have been replaced by compulsory indoctrination in many faiths. Many Catholic clerics, living in the palatial splendour of the Vatican, appear to have no guilt about the immense poverty they forced upon the Irish and other Catholic-dominant countries, as a result of opposing contraception. Forcing women to breed continually, frequently beyond the numbers they can afford to raise, educate and house, is a practice continued to this very day, a godless practice also continued in the 'hadith Islam' branch of true Islam. Primarily, this practice's aim is to build religious numbers and power. This has resulted in the Catholic branch of the Christian faith and 'hadith Islam' moulding some of the most dangerous predators on earth.

Corrupt religious clerics tell outrageous lies to their followers, as did the serpent in the Garden of Eden. Killing and raping any of God's children would bring the same sense of anger from a spiritual Father as it would to any good and honourable father on this earth; it is only very mentally twisted men who would think this behaviour would please God. Surely, believers must realise that dreadful deception fed to them by deceptive religious clerics is destroying any chance of forgiveness? As warned in that early symbolic Garden of Eden parable, the serpent, used as a metaphor for pure evil, was never forgiven. Psychopaths are the one group that should not be forgiven by victims, or their families. This subset always convinces themselves that they are not guilty, that they are the victims and are justified in their actions, hence, forgiveness would only confirm this fantasy.

Catholic clerics, by providing absolution, have aligned themselves as equals to, rather than servants of, God. Man-made rules and religious hubris have made them accessories to crime. It was priests, not God, who introduced the two sacrilegious rules of confessionals and celibacy. They ordered the unnatural act of celibacy, which hid and possibly caused the appalling crime of paedophilia to flourish.

Continued apathy within the Catholic faith has led to disastrous consequences, which have shaken this faith to the core. This religion became a haven for some of the most monstrous deviates. Single, older men, with a cleric's white collar, could mingle unchallenged among young children, in plain sight, because of the presumed honesty and morality of the person wearing that collar. It became paedophile heaven.

The Catholic Church was very good at keeping secrets—secrets that had the potential to be used against people in high places. Paedophilia, which was kept hidden for decades until, finally, strong and dedicated legal action in a couple of States in the US revealed it to be one of the most criminal institutions in history. They found over 10,000 child victims whose lives had been horrifyingly damaged by these psychopathic personas.[9] Similar court actions in Australia and UK have started exposing these most odious of criminals. With very anaemic levels of C&E (conscience and empathy), the offenders suffered no real guilt. Their only concern was their continued livelihood and they relied on continued protection under the mantle of 'Catholic solidarity' to not expose their obscene transgressions.[10]

Celibacy is a man-made law that will continue to attract males with the psychopathic disorder, as they are invisible in this all-male domain. If the world cares for its children, it should force the Catholic Church to change the rule of celibacy or force celibate orders to remain in monasteries well away from children, as paedophiles are legally not allowed near children. Gender-apartheid religions, where males cannot have age-appropriate relationships, can retard sexual development. The inability to interact with adults sexually is the personality disorder of paedophiles, hence, they continue to seek out children for sexual release as they have much greater control over children. In addition, the rule of celibacy meant priests and nuns would not experience the miraculous life-changing flood of oxytocin, the bonding hormone that transforms parents into more patient and caring people around their children.

If priests genuinely see the need to be celibate, why do they not show total commitment by becoming eunuchs? It was the Roman culture that saw this as entirely acceptable, when Italy forced this on young male opera singers to retain their beautiful prepubescent voices. Let brave, married Catholic couples, true people of faith, take over positions formerly held by celibate church clerics. If the Catholic Church leaders try to stop married men, or women, applying for these positions, they should be liable for discrimination under secular state laws of sexism and gender bias.

Time may eventually heal the stigma celibacy has placed on Catholicism. It would be nice if the Vatican was filled with the laughter of children at schools and crèches, who were safe because they had Mum and Dad working there. The main aim of society should be a world free from corrupt, celibate serpents, who are currently invisible in the all-male environments and who will eventually, in the afterlife, be slithering on their bellies in the dust of the caverns of Hell for eternity (Genesis 3:14). In the biblical Garden of Eden parable, the Creator never forgave that subtle, deceptive serpent.

Inappropriately, priests answer to the title of 'Father', something they could never be in real life. While nuns answer to the term 'Sister', priests using the term 'Father', instead of 'Brother', are men blatantly equating themselves with the spiritual Father. It was a term which the second prophet, Jesus, condemned. He objected to churchmen answering to the forms of address of 'rabbi' (i.e. master) and 'Father', because doing so would signify that they were assuming the role of the divine entity to which all followers of the three Abrahamic monotheist faiths pay homage. As quoted in Matthew 23:9, 'And call no man [other than one's biological father] your father on earth, for you have one Father, who is in heaven.'[11] The Pope, head of the Catholic Church, is worshipped with pagan idolatry by followers and they have no wish to change or reform this display of high theatre.

Protestant faiths do not substitute their church ministers for the spiritual Father, they are usually addressed as Reverend, Minister, Pastor, Preacher or Bishop. Non-Catholic religions tend to start their prayers with, 'Our Father, which art in Heaven'. It is sadly not only an entirely inappropriate title for Catholic clerics, they also do not receive the markedly increased amounts of the parenting 'hit' of the bonding hormone, oxytocin, which mothers and fathers receive after their children are born. This lack may account for the harsher treatment, recorded by students, from childless men in the priesthood.

In earlier times, young school children at Catholic schools appeared to receive harsher punishments than their Protestant counterparts. Their beatings always seemed crueller than the ones we as Protestants had received from our teachers, usually married men and women. A male work colleague, born and educated in Scotland, told how the students at one Scottish all-male Catholic school were taken out to the school oval every morning by the childless priests, even in the freezing Scottish winters, and hit across the knuckles with a wooden ruler for some totally misguided reason. He, like a number of my Catholic friends, was a very heavy drinker by the time he was in his mid-twenties—and heading for alcoholic-dementia by his fifties.

Priests, because they are not allowed oxytocin-stimulating relationships with partners and who may have inherited (from their mother's X-chromosome) the more dangerous low-activity aggressive form of the MAOA gene and this awful genetic glitch was not moderated, may have been the reason for the higher rate of cruel behaviour in some child-caring institutions(more on the MAOA gene can be read in Essay 3). In a recent Royal Commission investigation in Australia, of the thousands of children that had been abused, two thirds (62 per cent) were from Catholic institutions.[12]

For priests to adopt the title of 'Father', then for some of those men to rape dozens of young boys and girls is the most horrific of all crimes against humanity. Sodomy and rape of children is the 'mortal sin' that dogmatic fundamentalists seem to ignore—while same-sex marriage, the sin they often choose to focus on, is an act of love between two consensual adults. Sodomy was common in the eras that the Holy Books were written. Females maintained their virginity until marriage, therefore, males driven by lust (and not love) would frequently use innocent children, including young boys, for sexual release. Even the act of masturbation was also forbidden by clerics, who wanted to increase numbers for their religions.

Paedophilia is now seen as a criminal act in both the biblical sense as well as legally and justly deserves condemnation. A Royal Commission investigation into child abuse within the Christian churches revealed horrific numbers of psychopathic paedophiles, predominantly in the male-dominated Catholic faith. The man-made rule of celibacy denies priests natural adult sexual relationships. A factor of paedophilia is that males do not learn or are incapable of mature social interaction with adult females. It is a psychopathic disorder, with control and manipulation dominant traits of this group, hence, children are their prime subjects. For centuries, thousands of victims whose innocence and childhoods were stolen from them, have endured intense pain. It is a disgrace that this will probably continue until major change is made to this godless religious rule and the unnatural practice is banned. But psychopathic personas are finally being held accountable for their gross moral and leadership failures.

Male-dominant religions originally forbade forms of contraception because they wanted women as breeding stock to increase numbers for their church—same-sex couples do not provide those numbers. Dogmatic fundamentalists do not realise it is the mother's skewed hormone levels in the first few weeks when the foetal brain is forming, which messes with the wiring of the brain, as covered in Moir and Jessel's book, *Brainsex*.[13] Excessive testosterone can create a lesbian brain in a female foetus, whereas excessive oestrogen creates homosexuality in the male embryo.

Industry has pumped oestrogen into food production—even certain plastic bottles have a compound that mimics oestrogen. It was why industry and feminists tried to shut down publication of Moir and Jessel's book. As lesbian numbers were more closely related to a genetic cause, it is also why there was, at time of publication, four times the number of homosexual males. Religions also would have hated the fact that they would have had to blame the mother's (their breeding machine) skewed hormone levels and not the innocent victims.

Religious laws, added by autocratic church clerics, were one of the reasons Martin Luther broke away from the corruption of the Roman Catholic hierarchy to form the Lutheran Church in Germany. The Catholic process of confessionals is secretive and frequently hides dishonesty and criminal acts.[14]

No middleman entirely unrelated to the crime can give another forgiveness for a sin that person has committed, especially when it should have been reported to the law. In faith, it is the role of God, not religious teachers, to give forgiveness. It must be earned, by months and years of repentance, not handed out for a few words repeated by rote, and the rattling of beads.

When Martin Luther and John Wesley broke away from the Catholic branch of dictatorial male domination and started Protestant branches, it brought religion back to the values of the monotheist (one God) faith, which the second chosen messenger, Jesus, had attempted to introduce.[15]

However, many religions and cults that formed after the death of the prophets have managed to put themselves above the law. Several have become cruel and corrupt institutions, run by manipulative and dishonest men. History has shown religious clerics have done themselves and spiritual faith no favours by clinging to fundamentalist dogma. The new godless cult of atheism was formed by disillusioned people turning away from religions that had lost their way.

It was a female politician in Australia, presumably an atheist, who pushed to drop the 114-year-old tradition of the opening prayer in federal parliament; she said it was 'insulting and irrelevant in the twenty-first century'. The Lord's Prayer was formed by the Abrahamic faith, on which all monotheist religions should be based. The foundation of politics, law and civilisation was the *Ten Commandments*, the moral compass introduced by the three major prophets that transformed humanity from godless tribal inhumanity to humane communities. Are we not allowed to risk letting faith interfere with the new world of atheism, cults masquerading as religions, and the horrendous spiralling numbers of white-collar psychopaths, a return to the godless world that lacked moral integrity? Must we continue to celebrate, not discourage, any change to the modern atheist addiction to those Seven Deadly Sins—pride, envy, gluttony, lust, anger, greed and sloth, along with the breaking of the commandments of adultery, murder, stealing and deception?

Half a century ago, we rarely had adults attempting suicide and almost never children—yet suicide attempts in this demographic has increased substantially in recent years.[16] Now in Australia 7.5 per cent of twelve-to-seventeen-year-olds were reported to have had thoughts about suicide and 5.2 per cent actually made plans, while in any twelve-month period, about 2.4 per cent (41,400 young people) will have made a suicide attempt.[17&18]

When society discarded religious training for their children, did females, still driven by their ovaries rather than their brains, expect their babies to be born with emotional development already formed, which would naturally flower as they grew older? As they discarded religious teachings, did they even consider the additional responsibility of developing a child's moral compass? The qualities of EQ, which make humans humane, must be learned, as they are not inborn. In the introduction to his book, *Without Conscience,* Dr Hare told of an experiment they had conducted where they had used a biomedical recorder to monitor electrical activity in the brains of several groups of adult men. The EEG's (electroencephalograms) were sent off to a scientific journal. When the editor returned their paper he apologised, he told them: "Frankly, we found some of the brain wave patterns depicted in the paper very odd. Those EEGs couldn't have come from real people." Hare stated they hadn't gathered them from aliens, they had obtained them from 'a class of individuals found in every race, culture, society, and walk of life.' He warned that everyone has met these people, often charming, but always dangerous, they have a clinical name: psychopaths.

This makes having a child one of the most demanding of all life choices, it is a 24/7 life sentence. To develop EQ, ingraining honesty, manners, respect, conscience and empathy in young children who are always testing the boundaries, adds an immense extra workload, especially for single young females raising children alone. The failure to do so has caused huge damage to societies across the world.

Unfortunately, the rigid, literal interpretation of the Bible by dogmatic, fundamentalist, religious clerics is as much to blame for the demise and corruption of faith. Male-dominated religious institutions created around man-made rules, without input from females, have severely damaged the respect religions should have maintained. While atheism has allowed the upsurge of narcissistic WCPs in the Western world, the corrupted Islamic faith in the Middle East and Africa is moulding some of the most heinous psychopaths. Islam has been corrupted to a far greater degree than the first two Abrahamic faiths. At least five books of Sunnah have overwritten well over 80 per cent of the original Quran and there is no real division of religion and state. Within fifty years of Muhammad's death, after the last of his loyal followers had died, tribal dictatorship regained its rule of total servitude—I explore this in detail in Essay 7.

Males moulded into psychopathic personas by barbarous tribal rules, introduced under the guise of religion, pose as 'religious terrorists'. This is an evil oxymoron, a tragic contradiction in terms. Religion, apart from introducing moral integrity, supports freedom from subjugation and peace on earth—whereas terrorists, driven by godless dictators, are intent on destroying it. The religious clerics of 'hadith Islam', the corrupted offshoot religion of true Islam, have moulded monstrous terrorist behaviour. They are the godless serpents still whispering lies into the ears of the vulnerable and trusting, as foretold in the Garden of Eden parable. They break almost every rule of genuine faith and are the group Allah warned will never be forgiven, destined to slither as the lowest of low.

By subjugating women, as 'hadith Islam' has done, morally corrupt individuals have been able to abandon the voice of reason to claim tyrannical, godless rule. Sharia law, based almost entirely on hadiths, supports and condones both female subjugation and paedophilia. Hence, we now witness individuals who rape and kill for pleasure, even children, without an atom of conscience or empathy. These men have so corrupted Muhammad's 'religion of peace' that they are not worthy to speak his name. 'Hadith Islam' clerics, like the serpents of which the first prophet warned, continue to seduce vulnerable people with lies and trickery—the psychopath's tools.

In this book, I have concentrated on the presence of the more dictatorial psychopathic personas found in religion, an area the world still treads too carefully around. Religions have been virtually untouchable by state laws. After centuries, only now are child abuse offenders in the Christian world being brought to justice. It is consistently the male-dominated religions that are the worst offenders; Sharia law in the 'hadith Islam' religious offshoot allows shocking female and child abuse, as do many other religious cults that have allowed white-collar psychopaths, the 'intra-species' predators, to slither to the upper echelons.

'Intra-species' predators prey on members of their own species and the human species is the greatest offender. There are very few lower animal species that do this—some fish, sand tiger sharks, tiger salamanders, polar bears and hamsters if they cannot get sufficient protein, while some others like meerkats kill to keep numbers in control. There are spiders that devour their mates and parasitoid wasps.[19] However, neuroscience has now recognised the subset of the human species that does this to fellow humans—they are the psychopaths. They range from white-collar to heinous, they do not kill for survival, like lesser species, they kill for power and control and, in the case of serial killers and rapists, for pleasure.[20&21]

Autocratic leaders, psychopathic 'intra-species predators' that start or cause wars, slaughter millions of humans. Tyrannical rulers, who expect total subservience to their despotic rule, have mown down innocent students with army tanks. People fighting to maintain personal freedom, as in Hong Kong, are being forced into the totalitarian rule of communism, which disallows the freedoms of democratic governments. Evolution appears to have failed cataclysmically, as the most intelligent of all species has become the most dangerous of 'intraspecies' predators.

The dictatorial personality is egocentric and narcissistic; they can never be men of God because they consider themselves omnipotent. They are not team players, which is why they run their countries as dictatorships rather than democracies. The fact that they do run their countries with dictatorial rule and disallow democracy is the strongest sign of skewed emotional development (EQ). Driven by greed for personal power and control, they are manipulative and generally extremely deceitful. Fraud resulting in immense personal wealth is very common, as many dictators rank as some of the wealthiest men on

Earth.[22] They rule by terror rather than social order.[23] Dictators generally lack moral integrity—they do whatever they want without any negative consequences. They were the reason faith was introduced to this planet by the first incredibly enlightened messenger, Moses.

Dictators kill people they dislike, without the legal repercussions that leaders of democratic countries would have to face. The Soviet Union even banned religion—communist states do not allow religious freedom.[24] Dictatorial personas expect their enslaved population to worship them like gods, with cowering sycophancy. If they do not, they are simply arrested and often killed.[25] This group of leaders lack moral integrity and are far removed from the values of GOD (Goodness, Order and Decency). They are the forewarned armies of the antichrist.

Cold wars are a state of political hostility between countries that are characterised by various measures that fall short of open warfare. It is generally dictatorships against democracies, and as long as we have dictatorial rulers abusing their population by this form of godless subjugation, there will never be world peace. Hostility, personal or political, is deep-seated ill-will and a completely pointless exercise. However, democracies should have the courage to give misogynist, controlling autocrats—particularly those who treat women as second-rate citizens—the more subtle political cold-shoulder.

Democracies should build an impenetrable wall of shame around these countries and block industry and trade until they allow political freedom for their people. Why do we continue to make countries that exploit their people with dictatorial rule, rich? Currently we are seeing political freedom being stolen from Hong Kong as the tyranny of Chinese dictatorial rule spreads its cancerous tentacles. Let us hope this is not a repeat of powerful Germany ruthlessly conquering the much smaller Poland in 1939, when the UK believed psychopathic personas would listen to reason.

Interesting articles written by Austin Cline, *Hitler, Nationalism, and Positive Christianity*[26] and *Was Hitler an Atheist*,[27] tell how Catholic churches helped identify Jews for extermination. Jews suffered horrendous crimes against them by the German dictator, Adolph Hitler, baptised as a

Catholic in 1889—he was never excommunicated, or in any other way officially censured by the Catholic Church. After the war, some Catholic leaders helped many former Nazis either get back into power or escape prosecution. However, the world has witnessed horrendous crimes against humanity by all three branches of the monotheist Abrahamic religion: Judaism, Christianity and Islam.

It appears Christians have very long memories. A few corrupt Jews had supported the murder of the second enlightened messenger, Jesus, and as a result millions of innocent Jewish people have endured terrible repercussions over time. German Protestants originally supported Nazism and produced a movement dedicated to blending Nazi ideology and Christian doctrine. However, Christian 'resistance' was mostly against efforts to exert greater control over church activities, not Nazi ideology.[28&29]

Autocratic dictators were psychopathic leaders and they needed 'soulless' people to fight their wars, so religion was banned in communist countries and countries with tyrannical leaders. Tribes like the Sunni did not want gentle, caring men—they wanted hardened killers that could win battles. This is to be seen in the Assad rule, in Syria, where his security forces have some of the most odious psychopathic sociopaths who are practising intolerable genocide and torture, beyond human imagination, as revealed in the brave Four Corners documentary in 2017, *Syria's Disappeared: The Case Against Assad*.[30]

Psychopathic personas can be extremely charming, along with cunning deception, it is one of their strongest attributes. They can turn, with incredible ease, from charming to ruthless in the blink of an eye. They always remain in total denial of any wrongs they commit. Without C&E, this terrifying sub-group never has the problem of post-traumatic stress disorder (PTSD). They are the creators of PTSD, not the sufferers. Dr Hare, in the Preface of his book, warned us in the late Twentieth Century of our most dangerous predators, but we appear remain blind, deaf and dumb to the psychopathic personas.[31]

We are now witnessing successful white-collar psychopaths, described as 'snakes in suits' by Drs Babiak and Hare:[32] individuals who hold glorified desk jobs yet pay themselves multimillion-dollar salaries, cunningly extracted from clients. Autocrats and dictators, who rule by fear, tick boxes of psychopathy, as do psychopathic terrorists moulded under the guise of religion, who are perhaps the greatest threat. Under tribal rule, certainly not the rule of God, this evil subset of serial killers and rapists kills other humans to gain power and control—the very antithesis of godliness.

Financial disparity is the death knell of civilisation

The apostles, Moses, Jesus and Muhammad, were born in different eras, but they all lived during times of horrendous financial disparity. The wealthy dictators of the Roman Empire imposed exorbitant taxes on ordinary people, which pushed most families into poverty. If taxes could not be paid, their property was confiscated. The tax collectors got rich and the farmers became their labourers. Jesus, the second messenger, saw the tax collectors as 'sick' (Luke 5:30–32).[33]

Jesus was murdered partly because of the anger of the gold merchants whose tables he had kicked over because they had set up shop in the holy temples. Muhammad, striving for a more egalitarian society, managed to ban usury, which caused violent battles with the wealthy elite back in the 7th Century.[34-36] The harsh and unfair taxes were continuing to increase the wealth of the wealthy and enslaving the poor. Usury was, of course, immediately brought back by godless tribal men after his death.

The prophets did not set themselves up as gods of their own worlds, they accepted their roles as merely messengers for a divine, spiritual presence—that inner voice that continues to pull at our conscience and social integrity. By attempting to bring down the wealthy elitists, who had no guilt or conscience, these good men knew they would be making many enemies, but continued to put their lives on the line. These individual men attempted to change the world into a better place, but they had, and continue to have, treacherous enemies.

Governments across the world *should* introduce a wealth tax for all with actual worth and assets over $30 million, based on the early religious tithe systems introduced to stop massive financial disparity. A flat 1% tithe tax based on actual personal assets, houses, cars, investment properties, yachts etc., which cannot be juggled by clever accountants. When religions introduced tithes many of the major education institutions and community buildings were funded by the wealthy of those earlier times. Modern age wealthy individuals without C&E have created financial anarchy. With the growth of these WCP's they are once again derailing the values of society. The difference between wealth and obscene wealth does not make people any happier, but poverty creates huge distress and internalised anger.[37-39]

Modern taxation has fallen into the same disgraceful pattern, with the wealthy paying less tax the more their personal wealth and accumulated assets spiral, with tax often in low single digits. The middle-income group pays a much higher percentage of tax, generally higher double digits, when compared with their much lower personal wealth and total assets.

The appalling levels of corporate financial greed, from wealthy white-collar psychopaths (WCPs) are far worse than the welfare mentality, many of whom also rob the real taxpayers. Both ends of the economic and social hierarchy unfairly siphon money away from the working middle-class. When taxes were introduced, the nine-to-five middle-class taxpayers, paying a fixed rate, had to start carrying the greater load. Welfare recipients were carried by taxpayers supporting them, and the wealthy got wealthier off the backs of the taxpayers that worked for them. Most of the former are paying less than the middle-class taxpayers because with clever accountants they can bring their tax down to virtually zero. The excessively rich can then squirrel away their massive profits in offshore places of investment—accomplices to this disgraceful fraud.

Two reports reveal the skin-crawling statistics of wealth disparity in the 21st Century: *Richest 1 per cent own half the world's wealth, study finds*[40] and *World's 26 richest people own as much as the poorest 50 per cent, says Oxfam.*[41] So why aren't the 99 per cent who are left with only half of the world's wealth storming their governments and their taxation offices across the world? The Oxfam report highlighted the mismanagement of the world's wealth, showing that the twenty-six richest billionaires own as many assets as the 3.8 billion people who make up the poorest half of the planet's population. Oxfam blamed rising inequality on aggressive wage restraint, tax dodging and the squeezing of producers by companies, adding that businesses were too focused on delivering ever-higher returns to wealthy owners and top executives.

Why do the poorest in the world not have greater power? Having the 26 wealthiest people in the world named and shamed and better financial equity by voters of the free world should be demanded. Voters of the world should be making them, and countries with super rich dictators as leaders, more accountable under international conventions—imposing penalties that would impact the autocrats, not the people.

Tragically, it is the wealthy that make the rules and, while some are extremely philanthropic, the majority are not. This massive wealth disparity between the super-rich and the poor has proved they do not have the required levels of conscience and empathy (C&E). It is the wealthy that should be carrying the greater load, not the middle-income workers—if they were, the tax paid by the nine to five workers could be halved.

Successful WCPs, more prevalent in executive positions dealing with large amounts of money, have also been exposed in the recent Banking Royal Commission. While the WCPs in areas such as casino and gambling venues, property development or Big Pharma, do not actually kill, they can destroy their clients' lives by charging exorbitant fees and commissions. They have been accessories to suicide deaths when people lost their houses or farming properties, or where seriously ill people died because of the appalling overpricing of prescription drugs.

Big Pharma is another area that is well due for international investigation into financial misconduct. Big Pharma can and does hold governments to ransom, with massive overpricing of their drugs—i.e. pay our price or let your people die. Some individuals are forced to pay thousands a week for medication for more serious illnesses, yet many of the executives in Big Pharma have personal wealth in the double-digit billionaire category.[42] It is very obvious that all the money is not being poured back into research, as people assume.

The welfare, particularly unemployed and poorly educated single parents, actually expect taxpayers, who are working hard to support their own children, to support the numerous infants they have, using them simply as an item to secure a regular income. Whoring oneself to welfare, expecting strangers to pay them money for doing nothing but producing fatherless babies, is a social disgrace. Social conscience and moral integrity appear to have spiralled down at about the same rate as religious faith.[43]

Angry, impoverished youths will follow ruthless gangs and faux religious leaders, who offer 'salvation'. We are seeing horrendous financial greed across the world from bank managers, CEOs in the financial world, Big Pharma, even singers, actors and sportsmen. If ever there was huge salary inequality, it is in the entertainment industry. Most of these stars would not shine if they did not have a great supporting group, yet it is the stars that cream off most of the profits. They should have stronger unions that spread the wealth around more evenly, encouraging the equally hardworking support players and bringing down costs for the viewing public.

In America, over 200 religious offshoots have been registered.[44] Many are little more than atheist paganism, registered for the money they can con out of people and the government rorts they can work because religion has put itself above the law. They do not have to pay tax, yet the Catholic religion is one of the wealthiest institutions in the world and cult religions, like Scientology, have also become massively wealthy. Registrations should be heavily policed to sort the cults from true religion. United religious administrative bodies should be formed, in all countries, to separate 'faith' from 'froth'. Tax should be paid by religions making excessive profits, money that is not being distributed to charitable causes, but is providing substantial wealth for the administrators.

Religious clerics, like academic teachers, should have recognised standards of theologian training. Only those who would, in effect, be helping with essential SEL (Social and Emotional Learning) training should be supported by governments in tax benefits.[45] Other religious cult offshoots are making a fortune in profits while genuine clerics of faith struggle. These greedy serpents should be crawling on their bellies in this life, long before the next—not living the high life.

Christianity still has serpents in its midst: WCPs (white-collar psychopaths) who flourish at the upper echelons. Holy 'freeloading' in religion is big business—and it pays really well. There are 33,000 distinct denominations in 238 countries, many genuine Christian groups along with many cult offshoots.[46] Scientology, a fringe belief system, has a tax-exempt status, however, according to Jeffrey Augustine, author of the blog *The Scientology Money Project*, the church has a book value of $1.75 billion, about $1.5 billion of which is tied up in real estate, mostly at its headquarters in Clearwater and in Hollywood, California.[47] The Church also owns property in Seattle, London, New York, and other places around the world.

If Scientology were to have its tax-exempt status revoked, there may still be no pressure by stakeholders to spend income efficiently. Even if the church were considered a for-profit organisation by the government, it is easy to see it continuing to funnel its money into real estate purchases and deduct that money in the form of capital depreciation over the years. Whatever might be left over after tax bills, may be spent on huge salaries. This is a huge profit-making business hiding under the guise of religious faith.

Many others have also put focus on profits rather than prophets.[48] Creflo A. Dollar, born Michael Smith, founder of World Changers Church, has an estimated net worth of $27 million US (his initials and adopted name should have been a give-away). His personal worth would appear to be an interesting use of religion used for personal benefit.[49] Benny Hinn, an Israeli televangelist, is worth about $42 million US. For years when people donated, it appeared he took the donation as something he earned. Religious donations are for charity and others who suffer poverty, only a pure narcissist could think the money is for his, or her, personal performance.[50] Even the squeaky clean tent revival pioneer, Billy Graham, had an estimated net worth of US$25 million, at the time of his death.[51] The late Eddie Long, a senior pastor of the American New Birth Missionary Baptist Church and suspected paedophile, had a bankroll in the millions.[52] It is time governments sorted the cons from the Christians. Those millions should help the needy—the real intent of faith—or be very heavily taxed, with that money retrieved by governments to go to the properly trained clerics and registered religious institutions that meet international standards.

Religions were introduced to mould individuals who are caring of others. It has been said if we did not have belief in God, we would have had to invent something else to give us hope, encourage compassion, and build internal strength and courage in the face of adversity. When we see youths under twenty years of age guzzling alcohol like water, one wonders just what have atheists contributed to replace this internal strength once provided by faith?

The prophets accepted the role of messenger for a divine spiritual presence—that inner voice which tugs at our conscience and social integrity (qualities that are quite alien to narcissistic, soulless and uncaring people) and has helped many to survive through very tough times. By attempting to bring down the wealthy elitists who had no guilt or conscience, these good men knew they would be making many enemies and putting their lives on the line. Where has that courage gone? Politicians, the law, feminists, educators, the apathy of the welfare mentality and religions are too afraid to confront the over-wealthy, the over-breeders, and the dictatorial rule of cultures still enforcing female subjugation.

The prime agenda of religion was to introduce people to the qualities of morality and social integrity, to encourage empathy and caring and to draw people away from greed and corruption. Alarmingly, some religions have failed to recognise the emergence of the one creature that all three messengers, wise beyond their time, warned us about: the evil predator that modern neuroscience now recognises as the psychopath.

When the prophet Jesus upended the tables of the gold merchants who were touting their trade in the temples, it was due to his anger at the hypocrisy of the godless people who were the embodiment of elitism and greed. Using the houses of God, where people of faith were trying to re-educate people away from this noxious godlessness, was extreme duplicity.

Do atheists really question why we needed the emotional learning of faith? We now have a world where atheism is on the rise. With it we see increasing numbers of WCPs (white-collar psychopaths), massive world financial disparity, rising crime rates and children growing up without

C&E. Children are now at risk: they cannot play freely as we did fifty years ago, yet we have stronger police forces and a judicial system that is supposed to protect us from these predators.

Lesser creatures never had to learn how to behave civilly as they can quite naturally live in harmony with other creatures and in union with their own species. Animals generally kill for sustenance and certainly not full-scale slaughter of their own kind, as humans do, in horrific wars. Only members of the human species, with the complex brain that separates us from lesser creatures, kill for pleasure, lie, cheat and choose to commit all forms of sin and corruption. Without a natural predator, we have become the worst plague this world has witnessed.

We were lucky that three brave and dedicated men divorced themselves from pagan mysticism and, with incredibly powerful spiritual force, introduced a vital part of human evolution: emotional development (EQ).[53] Each attempted to introduce a moral compass to men who were often tyrannical and ruthless. They sought to introduce MERC (morality, empathy, respect and conscience), striving for a more financially equal and unified community. When the lessons learned were forgotten and people reverted back to more self-centred, godlessness, mean-minded and deceitful ways, evolution once again started to devolve. With emerging atheism and celebration of the 'Seven Deadly Sins' the modern free world has again taken a backward step.

Hard science and evolution have never really explained how three basically uneducated (by modern-day standards) men realised that the brain's emotional development was of greater important for civilisation than the physical 'kill or be killed' mentality of earlier humanoid history. What unexplained spiritual strength united them in the monotheist faith? All three messengers should be rated equally, for any religion not to do so rather defeats the purpose of these enlightened and forward-thinking men. These men, born centuries apart, spoke as one, walking this earth to bring humane behaviour where inhumanity flourished. For the religions that followed to be in complete disunity—that is the failure of faith. The hubris of men, playing 'my prophet is better than yours', completely ignores the fact they are all accountable to the one spiritual Father.

If religion had not been 'above' the law, Catholicism, as a teaching institution, would probably have been shut down after investigations into its widespread paedophilia activity. A horrific crime, masked by celibacy, invisible behind the perpetrators' religious 'white-collars' and possibly formed because they were denied age-appropriate relationships (a symptom of paedophilic behaviour). Celibacy should not be allowed to continue: it has never been a rule of God, but a rule instituted by autocratic males, which has resulted in disguising the paedophile disorder.

Psychologists now recognise that people must want to change if real change is ever to occur. Psychopaths never voluntarily seek to change their behaviour.[54] Sadly, male-dominated religions are the last to learn this lesson. By placing themselves above the law, religions attracted psychopathic personas, serpents that preyed on the vulnerable who have slithered predominantly into these misogynist religions. As warned by Moses in 1400 BC, these evil men have slithered to the upper echelons of that symbolic 'tree of life'—the fruit being the knowledge of good versus evil. The Sunni tribe cult offshoot of Islam follows Sharia law, which is based on fabrications falsely created by dictators that followed Muhammad. The prophet in his last sermon warned of such deception and the Quran (6:112-113) specifically warned of this corruption. This corruption of Islam has a record of treating women as second-rate citizens and gender 'apartheid' is something the free world should not accept.[55]

Warning: This essay contains disturbing graphic violent content and should be read with caution.

~ 6 ~

Religious rules of compulsion have sabotaged faith

Jesus turned and said to Peter, 'Get behind me, Satan! You are a stumbling block to me; you do not have in mind the concerns of God, but merely human concerns.'
— **Matthew 16:23**

In 1980, Dr Robert Hare created the now internationally recognised diagnostic tool, the *Psychopathy Checklist*. His highly readable, but chilling book about psychopaths, *Without Conscience,* was published in 1993.[1] In 2001, Robert Hercz wrote a report, *Psychopaths among us,* in recognition of the enormous impact that Hare's work had worldwide. In the report, Hercz made the comment, "It was the first time in history that everyone who said 'psychopath' was saying the same thing. For research in the field, it was a starting gun".[2] These publications were virtually ignored by many in society who choose to ignore scientific evidence—but then came 9/11.

The Society for the Study of Psychopathy named their lifetime achievement award after Dr Hare, the brilliant Canadian psychologist. Yet, it appears, many still place his work in the mythological category and refuse to accept his thoroughly researched evidence, or choose to misinterpret it in entirely inappropriate ways. When Hare's book was published, the *Psychopathy Checklist,* as noted by Hercz, 'slipped the confines of academe'. The twenty key traits of psychopathy, now free from the textbook world of academia, had become available to the general public. A negative consequence was that the media, law, psychologists, counsellors, and the public were now judging individuals by using the list alone, forgetting that the checklist was only an introduction to the complete assessment of psychopathic behaviour.

Hare's valid concern was that the *Psychopathy Checklist* was being used in isolation by people who did not study the accompanying manual and who were not carrying out the intensive background checks from young age and the more intensive, time-consuming and costly MRI and genetic testing. In the US, a high score based on the key traits only, was being used to support the death penalty; in the UK, there was debate on whether such individuals should be detained, even if they had not committed a crime.

People were making premature judgements, from early findings that made correlations between alleles of certain genes and tendencies to antisocial or criminal behaviour. A report by Philip Hunter, *The psycho gene,*[3] told of the shocking decision by an Italian appeal court, in 2009, to reduce the sentence of a convicted murderer by one year on the grounds that he had a negative low activity version of the MAOA gene (Monoamine Oxidase A; for more information see Essay 3), which had been linked to aggression and violence. Most researchers in the field were appalled, as he was a confirmed psychopath the sentence should have been increased. Dr Hare's research has shown adult psychopaths will always be a danger. Although some get tired of spending time in prison or being in conflict with the law and do decrease in criminality, but this does not mean there has been a change in personality. Many psychopaths continue to commit offences well into their senior years.[4]

There is evidence people with particular alleles cannot be cured and that they will remain a risk to society if the signs of psychopathy are present. As stated by Dr Hare:

> Most of the children who end up as adult psychopaths come to the attention of teachers and counsellors at a very early age, and it is essential that these professionals understand the nature of the problem they are faced with. If intervention is to have any

chance of succeeding, it will have two occur in early childhood. By adolescence, the chances of changing the behaviour patterns of the budding psychopath are slim.[5]

Dr Hare has estimated that about one fifth (20 per cent) of the global prison population is psychopathic. Psychopaths have, on average, sixty victims in their lifetime, compared to the one-to-five that non-psychopathic offenders have on average. As stated in his book, *Without Conscience,* uninformed therapy may make psychopaths worse.[6] The Australian legal system has very limited recognition of this condition. Poor sentencing and parole board decisions indicate that the system is ill-equipped in recognising this most dangerous of personality disorders—as are many of our psychologists, who still think adult psychopaths can be rehabilitated by means of standard counselling courses. When I studied psychology, Dr Hare's book had not been written and psychopathy learning was limited to the very heinous subset. However, with substantially increased numbers of white-collar psychopaths (WCPs), his book should be on every university's essential reading list for psychology and psychiatric courses.

Hare's research has shown that recidivism increased substantially in psychopaths who attended counselling courses in prison. One of Hare's studies found psychopaths were 'almost four times more likely to commit a violent offense following release from a therapeutic community program', than other prisoners. Not only were the programs not effective, they may actually have made the attendees worse. Our judicial system releases high-level psychopaths back into society after their jail terms, exactly as they do non-psychopathic criminals.

Psychopathic predators are not cured by prison sentences: without conscience and empathy (C&E), they will always be predatory. High-security psychiatric clinics, constructed specifically for high-scoring psychopathic individuals, should be established where these offenders can be taken for ongoing psychiatric treatment after their jail sentence has been served. However, a study by Harris, Rice and Cormieron, violent recidivism rates has shown 77 per cent of the psychopaths (as defined by the *Psychopathy Checklist*) committed a violent offense in the ten-year follow-up period after release from a maximum-security psychiatric hospital.[7] Neuroscience research has confirmed the accuracy of Dr Hare's *Psychopathy Checklist*.[8&9] If ongoing research and treatment of their emotionally inactive brains are not successful, psychopaths should be detained for life.

Releasing these predatory individuals back into society is as dangerous as releasing a wild carnivorous animal onto the streets. This subset should be transferred to high security facilities, like Broadmoor in the UK,[10] after their jail sentence has been completed for permanent ongoing analysis and treatment, until faulty DNA and the wounds of poor parenting can be corrected.

The notion that genes play an important role in various diseases has been widely accepted, but many find it much harder to acknowledge a similar link with behaviour or predisposition to crime. Partly for this reason, the study of behavioural genetics remains a controversial topic, with disagreement not just over the science itself, but even more so about the therapeutic, societal and legal implications. Robert Hertz, in his exceptionally interesting and highly informative article, *Psychopaths among us,* reported that when he met with Hare, he had explained that after spending an entire day, going through the literature, people were often overwhelmed, Hare had said:

> There's still a lot of opposition—some criminologists, sociologists, and psychologists don't like psychopathy at all... a lot of people come out of there and say, 'So what? Psychopathy is a mythological construct.' They have political and social agendas: 'People are inherently good' they say. 'Just give them a hug, a puppy dog, and a musical instrument and they're all going to be okay.'[11]

Hertz had reported that Dr Hare had mentioned it was of great concern that specialists in the field are seriously ill-informed, regarding the brain variation of the adult psychopath, and do not understand the permanency of this disorder. The Correctional Service of Canada (CSC) ignored the psychopath treatment program Hare designed because there were personnel changes at the top of CSC. Hare's research has shown that some people behaved badly even when there had been no early trauma, however, the new team had a different agenda, which Hare summarised as, 'We don't believe in the badness of people.' His plan sank without a trace, which has impeded psychopathy research and treatment. People who are incapable of registering the basic emotions that separate psychopaths from non-psychopaths are quite capable of putting a knife into the back of a person, who hugs them, can brutally torture and kill a puppy dog, and can smash a musical instrument without remorse. They are not going to be 'okay' in a society that ignores their danger—and society is not going to be safe if it ignores them.

The world is now witnessing, almost daily, the result of this refusal to accept this 'bad not mad' group of criminals: the psychopathic personas. Hare had made the comment, 'The irony is that Canada could have had this all set up and they could have been leaders in the world. But they dropped the ball completely'—referring to the decade-old treatment proposal, sitting on a shelf somewhere within the Canadian Corrections Service.

Bureaucracy, psychologists and law should study the brains of cold-blooded psychopathic murderers and rapists, as well as the white-collar psychopaths who rort the welfare and financial systems, as Hare has done for twenty years, before discarding his research. Perhaps it is people concerned about losing their social service and welfare support positions, which in Australia are amongst the largest areas of government employment. DSS (Social Security) is in the large agency group (1001-10,000 employees) and Services Australia is in the extra-large category (10,000+).[12] Lawyers may also be concerned about losing their guaranteed 'cash flow' if a cure for the most criminally recidivistic of all brain disorders is found.

As reported by Hertz, Hare's research upset many people in the field of psychopathy and psychiatry, who were at that time not prepared to accept that because of nature or lack of nurture some people have problems registering basic caring emotions. Children born with imperfect limbs are not going to have them regrow, hence, children born with imperfect DNA are also not going to have it 'regrow' simply with rehabilitation counselling. Consequently, the concept of psychopathy is largely going unacknowledged because of political correctness.

If people with political and social agendas refuse to accept that young people can be genetically predisposed to psychopathy, with outcomes dependent on early parenting, it means society will continue to carry the burden of increased crime committed by psychopathic personas.[13-15] Research indicates that reduced grey matter in the right hemisphere of the male psychopath's brain, which is the source of these emotions, may be genetic,[16] but how children are raised in the first decade makes the difference between honourable and dishonourable adults if they are genetically predisposed to psychopathy.[17]

As discussed in detail in Essay 4, children, particularly sons, with this genetic pattern can be extremely emotionally damaged when raised in early environments that do not have a loving, caring father providing the essential male role model in the first decade. More damaging to the emotional health of the male child is the lack of humour in many inappropriate relationships. Humour is one of the greatest stimulators of the bonding hormone, oxytocin. Harsh male or humourless single female parents can be a disaster for the emotional development of male offspring.

Hence, testing for psychopathy is complex, as nurture as well as nature must be examined. The *Psychopathy Checklist* successfully assesses psychopathic or antisocial tendencies. It contains two parts: a semi-structured interview and a review of the subject's file records and history. During the evaluation, the clinician scores twenty items that measure central elements of the psychopathic character. The items cover the nature of the subject's interpersonal relationships, his or her affective or emotional involvement, responses to other people and to situations, and evidence of social deviance and lifestyle. The test allows for a maximum score of forty, a score of thirty designates someone as a psychopath. White-collar or corporate psychopaths will likely score lower, in the mid-twenties. Sexually deviant psychopaths will tend to score higher. People with no criminal backgrounds normally score around five or below.

The study by Paul Babiak et al., *Psychopathy - An Important Forensic Concept for the 21st Century*,[18] demonstrated it was possible to predict outcome with considerable accuracy, using combinations of childhood history, adult history, index offense and institutional program variables. However, it stated that the *Psychopathy Checklist* alone performed at least as well as any combination of variables, and also improved upon the prediction based on criminal history variables. Psychopaths continued to reoffend at a higher rate than non-psychopaths, even beyond forty years of age.

Table 1: The Traits and Characteristics of Psychopathy

Interpersonal relationships
- glib and superficial charm
- grandiose (exaggeratedly high) sense of self-worth
- pathological lying
- conning and manipulation

Affective or emotional involvement
- lack of remorse or guilt
- shallow affect (superficial emotional responsiveness)
- callous lack of empathy
- failure to accept responsibility for own actions

Lifestyle (responses to other people and situations)
- stimulation seeking
- impulsivity
- irresponsibility
- parasitic orientation
- lack of realistic goals
- sexual promiscuity
- many short-term marital relationships

Antisocial and social deviance
- poor behaviour controls
- early behaviour problems
- juvenile delinquency
- revocation of conditional release
- criminal versatility

Robert D. Hare, *Hare Psychopathy Checklist*-Revised, 2nd ed.

The *Psychopathy Checklist* has turned out to be the best single predictor of recidivism that has ever existed; an offender with a high PCL-R score is three or four times more likely to reoffend than someone with a low score. Our judiciary system and parole boards should recognise serial offenders with psychopathy assessment scores over thirty and move them to high-security clinics after their jail sentence. Until the emotional centres of their brain can be reactivated, these predators will always remain dangerous.

Furthermore, future victims should be able to take civil action against members of parole boards who did not include a specialist in psychopathy research and psychopathic testing when making recommendations for release of serial offenders. Only psychiatrists, or psychologists trained in MRI scanning, genetic testing and proficient in the *Psychopathy Checklist* testing process should be appointed on these boards.[19]

Hare realised the *Psychopathy Checklist* was being used in a way it was never intended. In places where it could do some good, such as in prison, the knowledge of psychopathy often goes unacknowledged. As mentioned in Essay 4, officials at the head of the Canadian Corrections Service (CCS), which had asked Hare to design a treatment program for psychopaths, decided it was politically incorrect to declare someone with psychopathy to be 'beyond rehabilitation'—something that Dr Hare could accurately predict, having worked for decades researching these ruthless predators. The cost and time of psychopathy testing is still seen by many as the greatest negative of the testing procedure. Isn't it worth it if it means we can discover psychopathic predispositions?

Dependent on their *Psychopathy Checklist* score, there are numerous levels of the psychopathic disorder. They range from heinous to 'white-collar', and include serial killers, rapists, dictators, terrorists, paedophiles, drug barons, members of organised crime, gang members, cult leaders, thieves, arsonists, swindlers, hype-prone stock promoters, unscrupulous businesspeople, arsonists, addicts and professional gamblers. White-collar psychopaths are able to blend very smoothly into society despite the danger they pose.

A major concern indicated in the report compiled by over a dozen of America's leading neuroscientists (which I found on the American FBI

Law Enforcement Bulletin), was the psychopath's ability to potentially manipulate authorities. The article within the report, *Psychopathy, Homicide, and the Courts: Working the System*, by Häkkänen-Nyholm and Hare indicate psychopaths more often see themselves as the victim and will deny charges brought against them.[20] They are the group most able to manipulate the criminal justice system to receive reduced sentences and appeal sentences to a higher court. Psychopathic sex offenders are 2.43 times more likely to be released than their non-psychopathic counterparts, while psychopathic offenders charged with other crimes are 2.79 times more likely to be released.

Psychopaths are about five times more likely than non-psychopaths to engage in recidivism within five years of release from prison. Despite their longer list of offenses and elevated risk, their 'acting ability' can enable them to frequently manipulate and persuade members of a parole board to release them approximately 2.5 times faster than other offenders up for parole.[21] Psychopaths continue to recidivate at a higher rate than non-psychopaths even beyond the age of forty years. With the absence of empathy or remorse, there is evidence that psychopaths derive gratification or enjoyment from their behaviour. Psychopaths can be adept at imitating emotions that they believe will mitigate their punishment.[22&23] Psychopaths generally acquire the affective deficits associated with psychopathy, such as grandiosity, lack of guilt or remorse and callousness, after experiencing long-term neglect or abuse in childhood. Research has shown emotional detachment to be spurred by disassociation and a more gradual blunting (or shutting down) of emotions during early life.[24]

The American FBI Law Enforcement Bulletin report revealed the risk that psychopathic offenders pose for society. Their ability to potentially manipulate the authorities should pose concern to all countries. Because of its relevance to law enforcement, corrections, the courts, and others working in related fields, the need to understand psychopathy cannot be overstated. This includes knowing how to identify psychopaths, the damage they can cause, and how to deal with them more effectively. The report's closing statement is of critical importance: 'The ease with which a psychopath can engage in violence holds significance for society and law enforcement.'[25]

Dr Hare has travelled widely; he has been invited to speak all over America, the UK, Europe, Jordan and many other countries. Yet in Australia, our schools of law, psychology and psychiatry presumably were not interested in the internationally accepted *Psychopathy Checklist* process he developed. He did speak at one Melbourne University, but it was in relation to the book co-written with Paul Babiak, 'Snakes in Suits' describing the WCPs attraction to the upper echelons of business.[26]

Psychopathy should become a specialisation in psychology, as there are specialisations in medicine, otherwise court assessments of the same individual done by different defence and prosecution experts can vary dramatically. Major differences are the result of bias or incompetence, as the internationally recognised *Psychopathy Checklist* has shown it has high reliability with consistent results when more than one qualified assessor assessed a subject.[27] The Australian public deserves better.

We have a legal system that relies on rehabilitation advice provided by therapists, who are still recommending group therapy for psychopaths when research has shown this does not work for this group. Psychopaths are clever and wily, and various studies have shown these courses actually provide psychopathic offenders with better ways of manipulating, deceiving and conning people.[28] Psychopaths are very competent at reading people. Many take counselling courses or use prison time to upgrade their education in psychology, sociology and criminology, which allows them to convince others that they have been rehabilitated. As revealed in Hare's book, in some jails in America, psychopathic inmates have been known to train non-psychopathic criminals on how to give the best answers and adopt the appropriate behaviour for early release.

Although many in the general public take these courses to enable them to better read people and consequently become more caring and humane, the key difference is that members of the public have conscience and empathy (C&E). These qualities, however, are alien to the psychopathic brain—they absorb this learning only to better con others. Only MRI scans can genuinely 'read' brains with complete accuracy, certainly not judges, parole board members, or counsellors.[29]

Kiehl, in *The Psychopathic Whisperer,* observed that unlike other inmates, psychopaths do not get distressed by being in prison.[30] Most inmates get depressed when they are imprisoned and find prison to be a stressful experience. Psychopaths fit into prison life better than non-psychopathic offenders as they do not suffer genuine anxiety or concern regarding their victims and all too frequently incompetent parole boards erroneously interpret this as 'good' behaviour. Kiehl observed that a hallmark feature of the psychopathic disorder is that they don't get bothered by much of anything. It is this behaviour that fools parole board members unschooled in the cunning manipulation of the psychopathic brain. Kiehl surmises that the difference between psychopaths and other inmates is that psychopaths do not reflect on the crime that put them in prison. Their problems revolve entirely around 'self'; things that happen to other people, no matter how awful, do not register in these cold-hearted people, they have only self-pity over being caught. The 'why me' attitude dominates psychopaths' minds because they genuinely believe that they are always the victim, even in the face of overwhelming evidence. This is picked up by forensic scientists who have specialised in psychopathy, finding that even the egocentric language patterns of the psychopath differ from the speech patterns of innocent people.[31]

Serial offenders who have been scored as psychopathic in the *Psychopathy Checklist* testing process (which should be compulsory for this group), should be kept separate from non-psychopathic offenders, even in prisons. Psychopaths, cold-blooded and controlling, tend to have very negative influences on others guilty of lesser crimes. Various documentaries on this subject worldwide have revealed jailed terrorists when not separated from non-psychopathic offenders, are radicalising these people in jails.

New South Wales is planning to set up maxi-jails for terrorists,[32] however, seeing as most of these would be psychopathic or sociopathic offenders, these institutions should become high-security psychiatric units. In the 21st century, we need more facilities like UK's Broadmoor Hospital, high-security psychiatric clinics specifically for psychopaths too dangerous to be released back into society after their jail term is completed. It is essential to build these clinics and to employ neuroscientists and staff specialised in psychopathy research with the skills and equipment for genetic testing and MRI scanning.

The legal system tries to use the psychopathy disorder as a loophole to get psychopathic murderers and rapists off with a lighter sentence, with a plea of insanity. However, the fact their serial actions have proved they are psychopathic should ensure these predators are kept incarcerated for life. Psychopaths plan with considerable cunning, whereas insane individuals with skewed mental capacity do not have this ability. After serving their prison sentence, psychopaths should be transferred to a psychiatric unit (a maxi-prison exclusively for psychopathic personas) until a cure for their brains that lack emotional development can be found—because (as discussed in Essay 4) normal counselling and rehabilitation courses cannot restore a psychopath's emotionally stunted brain once they reach adulthood. The public is not qualified to handle these predators. Releasing serial psychopathic criminals on parole is like releasing a tiger into the city streets.

Even hospitals and emergency medical departments have become dangerous areas because psychopathic patients—genetically or drug induced—are not immediately transported to high-security psychiatric clinics. These mentally skewed individuals cannot be allowed near genuinely sick and vulnerable patients or medical staff untrained in psychiatric care.

Psychopathy, unlike other mental disorders, is driven by personal choice. In a world that has rising numbers of atheists and godlessness, with increased numbers of parents not ingraining C&E in their children's early life, Royal Commissions investigations have shown a rise in psychopathic numbers. In Italy, young boys were castrated to retain falsetto voices; castrated males were used to guard and protect women in harems of the Muslim world; and in China, men who were in imperial service were also castrated, because the leaders wanted to protect their dictatorial control.[33] These were innocent men, yet our modern law allows serial psychopathic monsters to re-enter society after their prison sentences are served. Perhaps we should reconsider reintroducing the practice of castration, as these males drag down the reputation of good men and have lost the right to be part of the male gender.[34]

Many prefer the death sentence for serial murderers and rapists, but castration is more humane. Investigations of Korean eunuchs showed they lived up to two decades longer.[35] Studies suggest that testosterone may play a part in shortening men's lives—no testicles, no testosterone, longer life. There are mixed messages about testosterone and longevity as Italian opera castrati tended not have extended life spans. Possibly obesity may have played a vital role in the difference between the longevity of Korean eunuchs and Italian operatic castrati. Italians castrati tended to live only the average male lifespan because obesity was more common.[36] As women tend to live longer than men, some researchers consider the male sex hormones may in the long-term, weaken the immune system or damage the heart.[37&38] In addition, eunuchs could not get the cancers common in these areas of the male body if they were not there.

Good men who care for their mothers, wives and children should stand behind this move. Psychopaths are a subgroup of humanity that lack emotional development; they are alien to empathy and conscience and are serial offenders. They will always use their penis as a weapon of choice against women. The brutality of the serial offences should decide whether it is partial (testicles only) or full castration. It appears adrenal glands continue to produce sufficient testosterone for basic male function. Eunuchs live longer and healthier lives once their brains are no longer controlled by testosterone and their genitalia. So perhaps once the offending organs of the serial offenders are removed, they may be able to make some worthwhile contribution to society.[39]

Chemical castration is not effective with psychopaths, as they lack C&E, they will not continue taking the required medication. They do not think they have a problem, therefore, cannot be relied on to continue treatment. Of course, the literal interpretation of the biblical verse, an 'eye for an eye', in modern times is barbaric: we now have much more humane ways of dealing with wrongdoers. This outdated dogma requires a person who has injured another person to be hurt in the same way. In more civilised interpretations, the victim receives the estimated value of the injury, in financial compensation—and the offender is removed from society for a very long time. However, as there is a genetic component in psychopathy, full castration (penis and testicles) does have validity where men are addicted to rape, incest or paedophilia.

If it reduces the possibility of genetic deviation being passed on, reduces aggression and extends longevity, it should be a legal requirement. Men who have had this surgery (because of cancer) have commented that their appreciation for women as friends increases, once the sexual drive has been reduced. Appreciating females, for roles other than as an object of rape, should be something women should expect and demand from the judicial system and modern society. Full castration should become an accepted part of criminal justice when sentencing serial rapists.

Incarceration in high-security psychiatric clinics for life, after release from prison, should be compulsory, or the choice of full castration for 'serial' murderers or rapists, who register as psychopaths on the *Psychopathic Checklist*. Psychologists who are still giving standard self-testing questionnaires for psychopathic offenders to complete should be retrained or barred from assessing and treating psychopathic personas. Psychopaths are brilliant at deception as it is one of their greatest strengths.[40] Only those who are specialised in the disorder, or are in specialist training, should be working with this dangerous subset. Every aspect of their early lives must be studied and analysed. Research needs to be continued to find a way to restore psychopathic brains to more stable emotional activity.

The way this group of people have been nurtured must be closely examined. The reason I am writing this book is to alert parents to what creates these social 'time bombs'. To start managing this dangerous disorder, tertiary education funding should be directed away from schools of law to the more useful fields of neuroscience and clinicians specialising in childhood and parental training. We need to start looking far more intently at the first sixteen years of a child's life to stop them becoming legal fodder. This cycle must be stopped to ensure future generations suffering from incompetent parenting do not become incompetent parents.

While forgiveness is a big part of the religious belief, psychopaths never believe they are wrong, therefore, to grant forgiveness to this group encourages rather than discourages them. To be forgiven just confirms, in the psychopath's brain, that he/she too is the victim. Psychopaths always believe they are the victim, even against overwhelming evidence.

While they are victims of bad or broken parenting, when they *choose* the path of evil, they forego the right to be forgiven.

The victim, or those associated with a victim of a psychopath, has no need to forgive people with this skewed mentality and should not feel guilty for not forgiving them. Religions that push the idea that all must be forgiven appear to have individuals that are totally ignorant of the neuroscience research regarding psychopathic personas—or have psychopathic personas amongst their numbers. Psychopaths do not feel remorse, if they apologise it is usually because their lawyer advises it, or they are cunning enough to realise it gets them 'points'—it is a thoughtless question the media often asks victims. The answer should be, 'No! The offender *chooses* psychopathic behaviour. That never deserves forgiveness.' Forgiveness should also not be pushed in trauma counselling.[41]

Susan Forward, PhD, an internationally renowned therapist, lecturer, and author has said forgiveness does not necessarily ease emotional pain.[42&43] These tragic victims should learn to forgive themselves for natural human suffering—for feeling despair, great anger or hatred. They should make sure they live long enough to dance on the graves of the violent offenders who have died, hopefully, after spending all their remaining years in prison or a high-security psychiatric clinic. Many amazing victims and their families try to make a change to our unfair justice system, but the judicial system and over-confident parole board members continue to ignore this disorder, they appear to believe they can 'read' people better than specialists in the field of neuroscience.

Even top clinicians admit they can occasionally be fooled by this extremely wily group, hence, psychopaths, the serial offenders, are consistently released back into society by totally inept parole boards. Psychopathic testing and ongoing supervised treatment and research in high security psychiatric institutions, after they finish their prison sentence, is not even considered. If they test positive for this disorder, at least as patients in these institutions they would be of some worth as test subjects contributing to neuroscience advancement, instead of continuing to be a complete waste of space, slithering around somewhere, waiting for the next victim.

The world of neuroscience must find the cause of this social cancer. Does any baby, who smiles to win the hearts of people around it even before it recognises the parental connection, deserve to have stress, confusion, or fear moulded into its tiny body in those first early years that make marvel or monster?

The increasing numbers of atheists in once-Christian cultures should look at the abysmal juvenile criminal statistics over the last three decades. In addition to the spiralling rates of bullying in schools, self-centred, narcissistic, disrespectful and ill-mannered children are filling our juvenile detention centres. We now have young offenders raised without any form of early religious instruction or school SEL training, and who are no longer receiving these 'trickle-down' values from parents or grandparents who were raised with religious instruction.

Clerics within religious institutions were the early counsellors, tending to the psychological wellbeing of their followers. They listened to troubled people, as do modern psychologists. However, it has never been the role of counsellors or modern psychologists to forgive their clients. Early priests took on this role to empower themselves, but it was sacrilegiously placing God-like power in the hands of earthborn men.

Catholic priests making celibacy compulsory and giving absolution at confessionals went far beyond their role of counselling and guidance. To forgive a psychopathic persona is a dangerous act, as psychopaths do not register guilt or remorse and forgiveness only encourages their future criminal behaviour. Unless priests have studied neuroscience, it is way beyond their level of expertise.

The Garden of Eden verses (Genesis 3: 1-19) have been mistranslated by male-dominated religions to point the finger of blame at the female, Eve, rather than at the serpent. Catholic priests still believe and preach that God forgives all. In a recent interview with a priest, who had confessed to sodomising numerous young boys, he ended by saying that he will be forgiven by God. The significance of this first parable has been completely mistranslated, or deliberately ignored, by Catholic clerics. God never forgave the serpent. The symbolic parable clearly stated the snake, emblematic of the psychopathic persona, which had whispered lies to the vulnerable, would be cursed above all animals and to quote Genesis 3:14, 'upon your belly you shall go, and dust you shall eat all the days of your life.' There will be no future of 'golden light' for these monsters as they have been warned they will be crawling in dust in the black halls of hell for eternity.

Further, it does not give servants of God sole ownership of forgiveness to spread around as they please, as Catholic priests do in confessionals. Doing so is behaving as the serpent did: putting their words above the word of God. The serpent gave Eve permission to eat from the tree of life causing paradise to be lost. It puzzles me how priests explain to their own conscience the latter part of that verse. To 'retain the sins', by keeping them secret and not telling the appropriate legal bodies negates the forgiveness, as stated in John 20:23. To 'retain' unforgiveable acts as secrets means the offenders are *not* forgiven and the priests become accessories to that crime—and should be tried as such by the legal system. Going to confession, spilling out the wrongdoing, then coming away feeling good about the crime and escaping justice is a celebration of dishonesty.

Forgiveness should be earned, not given away indiscriminately by a third party, a religious cleric, who seemingly has the power to admit to wrongs and ask for forgiveness, from the victim, and for that victim to forgive (if the request is genuine) is a major part of social harmony. It is part of the essential emotional development (EQ) required by the human species. A church cleric should counsel the offender on how best to complete this task of asking for and earning forgiveness from the victim. It was never the role of church clerics to take that obligation away from the offender, by playing God, as the Catholic Church does by taking confessions.

Psychologically, nothing is learned by repeating a few rote words, with the knowledge their guilt will go no further than the confession box. Priests placing themselves as judge and jury are committing appalling blasphemy; they have aligned themselves as equal to God, the greatest of all sins. Even the Pope has been placed in a God-like role and continues to be worshipped almost as a God substitute by millions. God never forgave the serpent for its deception, condemning it to crawl in dust for eternity. The Bible aptly describes such people, 'they were like whitewashed tombs, beautiful on the outside, but full of dead men's bones' (Matt 23:27-28).

Churches and religious institutions were where people were taught not to commit sins; they were never places where mere mortals could absolve sins. The role of church clerics, as counsellors, was to give guidance to enable followers to improve their way of life. For a priest to take ownership of forgiveness, to forgive every misdeed, or crime, and give absolution is feeding the dictatorial persona. Psychopaths, to justify their behaviour, see themselves as victims, pushing the blame on the actual victims. Because of the secrecy of the confessional, getting away with crime becomes deeply ingrained in their psyche from early age. It is only the victim or family members that can choose to give forgiveness when asked by the offender. Church clerics should be training humans to settle arguments by asking for and earning forgiveness from the victims. A priest doling out meaningless forgiveness, to ease the guilt of the offender, is damaging farce.

Someone who has caused pain and asks a priest, not the victim, to forgive them is not showing genuine remorse or earning forgiveness from the victim. A spiritual Father would place no value on a middle-man offering excuses. Religious clerics are teachers and not God, hence they have no more of a right to forgive a sinner than an academic teacher would have, if a student came and confessed a sin. Members of the academic educational institution would rightly refer that person to the correct authorities, which is what all religious teachers should be doing—then offering counselling, not forgiveness.

Forgiving all sins given in confessions and not disclosing odious crimes to state law may have allowed subtle religious pressure, a form of blackmail, to possibly contribute to the enormous wealth of the Catholic Church, along with the payment for absolution in earlier times. It certainly enabled psychopathic personas to escape prosecution for the emotional and physical cruelty of paedophilia for decades. Both celibacy and the process of confession and forgiveness have brought this branch of Christian faith to its knees—and I do not mean in prayer.

On the Catholic Answers site,[44] the intent of the verse quoted (Matthew 9:6), 'the Son of man has authority on earth to forgive sins' simply indicates all children of men should have the power to forgive, as rage festers if forgiveness is not part of societal values. However, Catholicism, by narrowing this command to members of their Church, is adding insult to injury to victims and results in the substantial weakening of this lesson for followers.

Religious dogma on this site promotes, 'God had sent Jesus to forgive sins,' that is the duplicity church clerics have introduced. The second messenger walked this earth to teach *victims* to forgive, if the offenders are genuinely repentant for the sins they have committed. The messengers spread the values of GOD (Goodness, Order, which includes gender and cultural equity, and Decency) to ingrain moral integrity, which includes asking for forgiveness when pain and suffering has been caused and admitting guilt to the appropriate authorities, if serious crime has been committed. The Catholic Church, by placing itself above the law by keeping serious crime secret, has made thousands of priests accessories to the crimes.

History has shown that the male-dominated religions have strayed far from the path of faith and more towards personal power and control. The Protestant movement began because they disagreed with Catholic clerics placing themselves above the law and positioning themselves as God substitutes.

As kids raised in Protestant faiths, we rather envied Catholics as we thought it must be great to pop down to the church, tell the church cleric about the bad things we had done and come out without any guilt—which was quite apparent in some of the naughtier Catholic boys we mixed with. We walked around with the fear of being struck dead by lightening because we had a sense of being judged 24/7, by an all-seeing, divine presence. Unlike Catholics, we do not have a 'middle-man' acting as God, sacrilegiously smoothing things over, allowing some to get away with shocking crimes. Psychologically, the church confessional process and forgiveness by church clerics reduces the feelings of guilt and remorse, which is exceptionally bad for children with the psychopathic gene type—they always see themselves as the innocent victim, forgiveness just confirms that belief.

Confessions were not mandatory, but there was a certain expectation. This meant that young boys would frequently be very creative with small white lies, often done in jest, but which led to them developing the skill of bending the truth at a young age. The fact priests moved beyond a religious cleric's responsibility to counsel by 'absolving' them of their sins, failed growing young boys that needed firm boundaries. No earthborn man can absolve a sin. It is not surprising that the idea of having a man of the cloth, with no learning in psychology or psychiatry, siding with them and keeping crimes from the police, has created some of the worst criminals in the world.

A Catholic sub-culture of horrendous crime was largely a result of priests using John 20:23 to allow them to take confessions and forgive all sins: 'If you forgive the sins of any, their sins have been forgiven them; if you retain the sins of any, they have been retained.' As history has shown, Catholicism is the one branch of Christianity from which some of the most godless thuggish gangs have formed (e.g. Mafia, Cosa Nostra, the 'armies of the antichrist' in the drug cartels of South America, even the Irish IRA). If the Catholic Church had taken more responsibility for the massive poverty they had created by their perverse attitude towards contraception, the world may very possibly not have had the growth of these powerful gangs, as they have not formed to the same extent in other Christian faiths.

The Catholic interpretation of this verse is driven more by hubris than honour. Humans were given the choice to follow the *Ten Commandments*, the good souls that did were promised a world of eternal peace and reunion with loved ones. If, as we hope, there is a source of 'intelligent design', then failed souls, the faulty reproductions, would naturally be discarded into the inky black hole of nothingness.

The horrific Catholic-based criminal gangs across the world are thuggish men who have no real accountability and have learned cunning deception from an early age. Saying a few words of prayer or doing some trivial act of penance had no long-term impact on discontented children that were raised in over-large, impoverished families. Fascist and communist countries, which hold religion in contempt, do mould brutal men who lack C&E, but religions that cling to male-domination and the oppression of women have created equally brutal men and organised crime gangs. 'Hadith Islam' has created Jihadists, Al Qaeda, ISIL and many other murderous groups.

Believers in faith, which is based on the *Theory of Intelligent Design*, must always remember: it is how people interpret the holy words of warning that divide the good from bad.[45] For a form of religion that has indirectly created the underbelly of crime, as in the Mafia and ISIL, to not look at the negative outcomes of their religious training and not question where their interpretation of religious rules has failed (and make no attempt to make change), is a religion ruled by male hubris, not God. Male-dominated religions, that encouraged women to have as many babies as they could, to increase religions numbers, has created over-large families that put people into impoverished circumstances creating awful discontent and has ultimately caused immense environmental damage by overpopulation.

'Hadith Islam', which aligned subsequent tribal leaders with Muhammad and chose to follow tribal traditions rather than the rules of the Quran, continues to sabotage the third prophet's original Judeo-Christian influenced religion of peace. Paedophiles are now being exposed in the Christian faith, but they are still prevalent in the 'hadith Islam' cult offshoot.

The Catholic Answers site quotes John 8:1–11 where Jesus forgave the sins of a woman caught in adultery. This was in an era when men could act like sexual whores, but women were treated like second-rate citizens, stoned to death or brutally whipped for adultery. All three messengers walked this earth to help change female inequality. However, the world has witnessed the shocking corruption of Islam ('hadith Islam'), which is now ruled by godless dictatorial leaders who once again subjugate women. Sharia law, which was built entirely on the hadith fabrications which Muhammad and the Quran had strictly forbidden, still enforces this punishment for women to this very day. Like Catholic priests, their religious clerics continue to forgive the sinners rather than teach them the skill of forgiveness. Their jails are filled with women who have been raped or committed adultery, because rape under Sharia law is seen as the fault of women seducing men.

In Australia both sides of politics have rejected a separate stream of law for specific religious or ethnic communities, on the basis that Australia is a secular nation. Freedom of religion and worship is protected, but religion is to play no part in the formal legal system. Consequently, this position does raise challenges for Australian Muslims, whose acceptance and enslavement to their man-made rules, in preference to the rules of Allah in the original Quran, is a problem. They are from countries that do not have secular law, hence, their adherence to their dictatorial religious law, Sharia law, is a 'hadith Islamic' obligation and not a matter of personal preference, particularly in regard to family matters.[46] In their autocratic countries they would be killed or jailed if they dared to break away from the corrupt practices of their religion, as the Christians did from the dictatorial Catholic branch and created Protestant faiths, based on equality of men and women.

Religion was the foundation of democratic countries, and law in the free world respects the words of the messengers of God, but it does not allow religion to control politics and secular law as 'hadith Islam' has done. That is the world of dictators and tyrannical rulers who do not have this separation.

The three Abrahamic religions, which formed after the death of the prophets, were created to provide religious education, counselling, guidance and spiritual advice. Their role was never to be judge and jury, providing the sentencing for criminal behaviour. Democratic, judicial laws entirely separate from often false religious rules, should be universal, however, there seems to be no real division between state and religion in 'hadith Islam' cultures. Sharia law controls religion, law and politics and it has effectively sabotaged Muhammad's religion of peace.

Democracies recognised the abuse of privilege that could occur when there was no separation between church and state. Democratic secular law is now, finally, able to bring corrupt clerics who were psychopathic paedophiles to justice. These clerics have shown the horrendous corruption that can occur in male-dominated faiths when religion is placed above the law.

The Church is a teaching institution, not a justice system. Church clerics are not qualified lawyers; their role was always as counsellors, not judges—that is the dictatorial rule of autocracy, not faith. Police and the secular judiciary system have the role of keeping the law and punishing the criminals on this earth—the Church was, and is, responsible for saving people from the behaviour that puts them into law courts.

They are there to counsel and to teach morality, empathy, respect and conscience (MERC), the values of emotional development (EQ) that are more essential for social wellbeing than IQ development.[47]

The 'hadith Islam' cult offshoot now has religious clerics committing *shirk* (idolising anything other than God, Allah), stepping far above their role by acting as judge and jury, providing the sentencing for criminal behaviour. Democratic judicial law must remain detached from the often-false man-made religious rules, and entirely separate from religious institutions. When our justice systems were dominated by judges from Catholic religions, particularly in America, there were some awful failures of justice.[48] Justice McClellan said that for many years the prevailing wisdom of judges, whom he said "were all men", was that sexual assault victims could only be believed if they complained immediately. It is now understood that survivors, especially children, may not complain about an assault for years, sometimes decades after the event, he said.[49&50]

Secular law is now beginning to bring corrupt men, abhorrent paedophile priests, to justice. Sharia law, based on corrupt hadith fabrications, does not make religious clerics accountable for acting as judge and jury. Catholicism, through 'confessionals', forgave and kept the secrets of criminals from the police, while extremist 'hadith Islam' religious clerics judge all non-Muslims as 'infidels' and accepts murder and rape of innocent people of other faiths. This behaviour, carried out under the guise of religion, is sacrilegious. It is unfathomable how minds can become so skewed and antisocial in institutions created to stop this behaviour. Yet 'hadith Islam' followers continue to allow Sharia law, a legal system built on fabrications that were condemned in the Quran as words of the 'jinn devils', to dominate religious law—laws that continue to support paedophilia, polygamy and apostasy enslavement are never rules of faith. By allowing self-serving psychopathic individuals to constantly slide 'under the radar', not only does it affect entire world peace, it has sabotaged the third Abrahamic religion almost beyond repair.

Shockingly inadequate crime sentencing and early parole board releases in Australia have alerted the public to the fact our law students appear to be completely unaware of advances in psychopathy research and the psychopathy testing process (PCL-R).[51] While Dr Hare had been invited to countries all over the world Australian university schools of law were not interested. The judicial system appears to think they can read this subset of humanity, the psychopathic persona. Governments and the judicial system should start listening to neuroscientists and the warnings they are giving about these individuals. Compulsory testing of offenders for this disorder should be implemented, and many more high-security psychopathy clinics should be built across the world for adult psychopathic personas.

If you continue to believe this is not a serious current issue, read the examples below and think again.

Denmark

In 2008, Danish psychologist Nicolai Sennels was invited to be the first and only psychologist working in a Copenhagen youth prison. The fact that he was the only psychologist working in the prison appeared to be a rather astounding lapse in government mental care, as children with psychopathic problems need analysis and rehabilitation long before mid-teens. At that time, 70 per cent of the prison population in the Copenhagen youth prison consisted of young men of Muslim heritage.[52] Curiously, children from single-parent homes in America, Australia and the UK make up a similar ratio in their own juvenile detention centres, an interesting correlation between 'new wave' atheism and the abandonment of the true Islamic faith.[53]

Sennels' research showed the integration of Muslims into Western societies was not possible if the form of 'hadith Islam' segregation and female oppression remained unchanged. This statement was met with great resistance from Danish politicians.[54] Sennels was shocked because it was so patently clear that there was extremely disproportional anti-social and anti-democratic behaviour among Muslim youths—driven by the corruption of faith by early dictators, which discouraged integration, practiced gender apartheid and family first-cousin inbreeding.[55]

Muslims must accept that their tribal cultural influences and corrupt Sunnah rules have sabotaged the original Abrahamic monotheist faith, introduced by Muhammad, and created some of the most dangerous men on earth. 'Hadith Islam' continues to follow barbaric tribal laws and harsh traditions, which destroys any chance of integration. If they refuse to revert back to Muhammad's original faith and instead continue the offensive behaviour of segregation, subjugation and oppression(which modern 'hadith Islam' males practise), there is no place for them in the more advanced civilisations of the Western world. Democracies should never allow false politically based religious offshoots that force sacrilegious religious compulsion and enslavement. It is the world of fascists, dictators and communist rule.

Sennels published a book *Holy Wrath: Among criminal Muslims*.[56] In his book, Sennels shares a psychological perspective of Muslim culture, its relationship to anger, handling emotions and its religion.[57] He based his research on hundreds of hours of therapy with 150 young Muslim males in the Copenhagen youth jail. He voiced his concerns and was initially spurned for being so outspoken. Authorities tried to ban his book. Sennels was a professional, reporting on individual case studies, not a journalist—and yet, woolly-headed 'do-gooders' originally gave him short-shift.[58] According to the Copenhagen authorities, it was permitted to state that the serious problems among Muslims were caused by poverty, the media, the police, the Danes, politicians, etc., but two things that were definitely not allowed to be mentioned were the discussion of the 'significance of culture' and 'foreigners own responsibility for their integration' in Scandinavian society.

Unfortunately, lawyers are overrepresented in parliaments across the world—well above an acceptable ratio[59-61]—many lack a clear understanding of psychopathy. They appear not to comprehend the negative psychological impact that corrupt brutal male domination and the destructive influence of gender inequality have on healthy and happy integration.

It has been reported that the entire culture of Scandinavian countries is changing so rapidly that many fear that it has been damaged beyond repair. Sweden's population grew from 9 million to 9.5 million in 2004–2012, mainly due to immigration from countries such as Afghanistan, Iraq and Somalia.[62] The millions of newly naturalised citizens from the Middle East reproduced at a much faster rate than native Swedes.

It is a problem in all countries where this practice is encouraged by paying high levels of subsidies for every child born. 16 per cent of all newborns in Sweden had mothers born in non-Western countries and the unemployment rate among immigrants was 54 per cent.

It was nearly impossible for the country to integrate so many Islamic refugees and immigrants. Consequently, these outsiders have created their own settlements with corrupt 'hadith Islamic' values. Male-dominant, and gender-apartheid they paint all others outside of their sabotaged form of Islam as 'infidels'. They have no respect for the country's police force and, by 2014, police were in danger of being injured, or even killed, if they entered the fifty-five Muslim-dominated areas where thuggish, psychopathic, Sunni 'hadith Islam' Muslims had taken control.[63]

The Danish police and the Danish Bureau of Statistics reported that nearly three quarters of all crimes in the Danish capital were committed by Muslims. The Danish national bank published a report stating that Muslim foreigners, on average, cost more than 2 million Danish kroner ($468,970 AUD) annually in federal social assistance due to low participation in the workforce.[64] On top of this, they have had to add many additional types of social welfare benefits for people forced away from their own countries, and the cost is immense: expenses in connection with interpreters, special classes in school, increased one-to-one social work and extra police, to name but a few.

Due to the lack of integration, 64 per cent of schoolchildren with Muslim parents cannot read and write Danish properly, even after ten years in a Danish school.[65] The countries from which they are fleeing must be brought into the twenty-first century. The United Nations must force proper democracy or close the borders and let them squabble amongst themselves in the culture they refuse to change, where women remain uneducated, breeding machines. There will never be peace in a world where psychopathically skewed dictators rule. It is a huge failing of the UN to accept gender apartheid and cultures that subjugate their women and allow them to be treated as second-rate citizens.

Sweden

R.I.P. Alexandra Mezher

In Sweden, a migrant centre was banned from holding a memorial service for a Swedish social worker, Alexandra Mezher, who was stabbed to death by a Somali boy in January 2016 'in case it upsets refugee children'.[66] Alexandra was murdered when she tried to break up a fight between two teenage boys, at a home for unaccompanied minors, in Gothenburg. Every one of those children should have had trained psychologists counselling them after this appalling criminal act and the two teenage boys should have been placed in a psychiatric clinic immediately for assessment and intensive brain retraining, to restore the emotional retardation.

In another incident an immigrant gang, the night before New Year's Eve 2016, threw a powerful firecracker (known as a 'banger') into a stroller where a three-month-old infant was sleeping.[67] The father of the baby managed, at the last moment, to get hold of the firecracker and to throw it away before it exploded. Large gangs of immigrant youths rampaged across Sweden during the Christmas holiday of 2016, throwing firecrackers and shooting rockets at people, animals, buildings and police, in which Sweden described as a 'careless manner'.

At fifteen to sixteen years of age, children like this are already on the cusp of being beyond rehabilitation. Muslims should be ashamed and hugely embarrassed for allowing such degradation to occur in their faith. This ruin is due to apathy towards the blatant violation of true Islam and the acceptance of false hadiths added by evil old men who treat women just as breeding stock.

India

Only a male-dominated religious offshoot, spawned by the devil, could have created the demonic boys that raped and eventually caused the death of Jyoti Singh, in Delhi, on 16 December 2012.[68] The gang rape incident happened when 23-year-old female physiotherapy intern, Jyoti

Singh, was beaten and gang raped in a private bus in which she was travelling with a male friend. There were six others in the bus, including the driver, all of whom raped the girl and beat her friend senseless.[69]

Jyoti was returning home at about 9:30p.m., after she and her friend had gone to watch the film *Life of Pito,* to celebrate her graduation that day. Jyoti's friend became suspicious when the bus deviated from its normal route and its doors were shut. When he objected, the group of men already on board, including the driver, taunted the couple, asking what they were doing out at such a late hour.[70]

The friend was beaten, gagged and knocked unconscious with a rusty iron rod. The men then dragged Jyoti to the rear of the bus, beating her with the rod and raping her while the bus driver continued to drive. Medical reports later said that she suffered massive damage to her genitals, uterus and intestines due to the assault; doctors said that the damage indicated a rusty, L-shaped iron rod was used to pull the internal organs out of Jyoti's body. After the beatings and rape ended, the attackers threw both victims and the internal organs from the moving bus. Then the bus driver allegedly tried to drive the bus over Jyoti, but she was pulled aside by her male friend. One of the perpetrators later cleaned the vehicle to remove evidence.[71]

The partially clothed victims were found on the road by a passer-by at around 11p.m. (IST). The passer-by called the police, who took the couple to hospital where Jyoti was given emergency treatment and placed on mechanical ventilation. She had injury marks, including numerous bite marks, all over her body. According to reports, one of the accused men admitted to having seen a rope-like object, assumed to be her intestines, being pulled out of the woman by the others in the bus. She was gutted like an animal without anaesthetic, but this amazing girl, after eighty-four minutes of obscene brutality, managed to remain alive long enough to give evidence against her attackers.

Jyoti Singh's parents were from a small village; her father sold his agricultural land to educate his children and worked double shifts to continue to pay for schooling. In an interview, he related that as a youth, he had dreamed of becoming a schoolteacher, but at that time education was not considered important and girls were not even sent to school. He had vowed never to deny his children schooling. A true man of God, he said, 'It never entered our hearts to ever discriminate. How could I be happy if my son is happy and my daughter isn't?[72] The valued and much-loved Jyoti died at 4:45a.m. on 29 December 2012. After Jyoti's death, protests were staged all over India. Many of the mourners carried candles and wore black dress; some pasted black cloth across their mouths. Tragically, it was later reported that five years after the gang-rape and murder, nothing had changed.[73]

An Indian male, after one of the articles published about Jyoti, said, 'but we all know that woman is the greatest weakness of man, we cannot change the nature of man.' Well I say: full castration would![74] Creatures like this have lost the right to remain part of the male gender. Although there is a genetic component for psychopaths and it is generally the home environment that moulds them, they are the 'bad not mad' group of offenders—because they *choose* the path of evil rather than good.[75] Knowing they would be spending the rest of their lives as eunuchs would certainly have more of an effect on them than expensive forms of house arrest or expensive security ankle bracelets.

Australia

Australia had an incident of obscene gang-rape in Sydney when the psychopath, Bilal Skaf, organised a group of fourteen 'hadith Islam' thugs.[76] Young, with horrific, arrested brain emotional development, they were all eighteen or under. They selected Australian females and raped them repeatedly for hours at a time. Their corrupted form of religion referred to their victims as 'infidels'; these vicious boys referred to them as 'pigs' as they raped and physically assaulted them with kicking, biting and thumping, before robbing them—nothing is beyond bounds in these emotionally retarded brains.[77] They picked on weaker, more vulnerable people, as cowards always do. The third victim was raped by all fourteen of these sub-humans, forty-four times, over a four-hour period, permanently damaging her internally and emotionally.

Skaf showed signs of psychopathy in his early school years, as he was described as a 'loose cannon'. If the school had access to a psychologist trained in the recognition and testing for psychopathic behaviour, treatment could have started before he reached sixteen, beyond which there is no hope of complete rehabilitation. He has remained unrepentant. During his trial he claimed he was involved only in cases of consensual sex, laughed when his verdict was read and swore at the judge when he received his sentence.[78] He was originally sentenced to fifty-five years with a forty-year non-parole period, however, that was modified several times upon appeal by our appallingly inept Australian judiciary system. Ignorant of the psychopathic brain and decades behind research related to psychopathy, it was reduced to a thirty-one-year prison sentence, and he will be eligible for parole in 2033. He will only be fifty-two years of age. He destroyed the lives of numerous girls, his life should receive the same lifelong devastation.

The gang members alongside Skaf originally all received long sentences, but with the help of a female psychologist, who like many psychologists has not specialised in psychopathy research and treatment, secured early release. They are now breeding again—one with the female psychologist, who has converted to 'hadith Islam' and wears the full black robes of godless submission to tribal traditions and dictatorial men. Has this woman been living in a cave for the last couple of decades? God help the children born to this naïve woman. She is evidence of how ineffective many psychologists are when confronted with psychopathy.

When Skaf is released, it should be to a high-security psychiatric clinic where MRI scanning and psychopathy testing can be carried out to research ongoing treatment that may eventually discover how the brain activity and behaviour of this obscene subset of humanity can be retrained, if possible, to a normal state. As a product of 'hadith Islam' brainwashing, this may never occur and he will remain a threat to women for life. However, as a test subject he would at least being doing something useful with his waste-of-space life.

If the murder and sexual violence against these girls are not signs to the moderate Muslim world—and the rest of the world—that corrupt 'hadith Islam' must be reformed, then we all deserve whatever hell on earth these out-of-control, mentally skewed men are going to continue delivering. Godless individuals who commit terrorist acts of exceptionally dishonourable killing are seriously mentally and emotionally damaged. Prison and courses of rehabilitation cannot alter the adult psychopathic mindset.[79] Can society risk this being passed to future generations once they are released from prison?

Parole boards are failing modern society; they cannot possibly assess psychopaths, who have been known to fool even top specialists in the field of psychopathic research. The legal textbook-learned judiciary, with absolutely no knowledge of the psychopath's skill of pathological deception, are continuing to endanger the general public with early release of these 'charming' monsters. They refuse to accept MRI and psychopathy testing, even though there are now volumes of neuroscience research on this most dangerous disorder of the 21st century.

Psychologists, if not specialised in psychopathy and trained to interpret and use MRI imaging and the PCL-R (*Psychopathy Checklist*), should be, by law, restrained from counselling in prisons where there may be psychopaths. This should apply particularly for females, who are far more often seduced by the charm and charisma of the 'white-collar' psychopaths. Psychopaths are the most recidivist criminals and research has shown they are much more likely to reoffend after counselling.[80] This cunning group use what they learn to improve their criminal skills, to outsmart the judiciary system and to more effectively con innocent victims—who are predominantly women.

As the Garden of Eden parable warned, females will always be seduced by the subtle charm of these insidious 'snake-oil' salesmen. Heinous psychopaths should be released only to high-security psychiatric clinics, where they should remain until their emotionally inactive brains can be reactivated. These dangerous predators should be permanently quarantined away from society and should have their DNA placed on a world recording system because it reveals extreme psychopathic behaviour—adult psychopaths can never be completely rehabilitated. If release is allowed for serial offenders, it should only be if they agree to full castration. If they are de-sexed they cannot continue to breed—I deliberately use that veterinary term as these serial offenders have not graduated from less complex animal behaviour, they simply copulate when 'in heat'. We de-sex innocent animals if they have genetic problems or there is the potential to pass on faulty genetic characteristics to offspring.[81&82] And castration has additional physical health benefits as well as mental health benefits in humans.[83]

If psychopathy is genetic, as scientific research indicates it is, it would appear essential that this toxic DNA is not passed to future generations, particularly in a culture that prefers generational family inbreeding of first cousins.[84] Society must recognise psychopathy is a cancer within society, it is a disorder that should be eradicated as any other deadly disease—or the offenders kept incarcerated (in psychiatric units) until brain activity can be analysed and possibly, through research, restored. The world needs to study the emotionally undeveloped brains of psychopaths and sociopaths, examining every part of their lives from gestation to mid-teens, to find what caused the damage.

We need to know why their lives have taken such a horrifying departure from normal, humane behaviour.

~ 7 ~

Male domination in religion has moulded monsters

'The secret of freedom lies in educating people, whereas the secret of tyranny is in keeping them ignorant.'
— **Maximilien Robespierre**

Destined to become the apex predator, were humans a failure of evolution? Where one gender allows itself to be oppressed, the sense of superiority and self-importance in the other becomes horrifically skewed. Consider which faiths and communist-style governments have produced the most brutal men and the most horrific of criminal gangs: the Asian Triads, the Russian Mob, MS-13, the Aryan Brotherhood, Los Zetas, Jihadism and ISIL, to name a few. In 2017, male-led Russia reversed the law that made domestic violence illegal.[1]

Muhammad, who fought for a more egalitarian way of life in his short time on earth (twenty-two years from conversion), brought astounding changes to many of the barbaric tribal men of that era. The fact that many still do not consume excessive amounts of alcohol may be the one wonder of the Islamic world from which other cultures could benefit immensely. People of Judeo-Christian faiths drink in moderation, but in the new age of atheism, we see teenagers who are alcoholics and heavy drug users long before their mid-twenties, when their brains fully mature. The UK and Australia are amongst the worst offenders with many children starting alcohol consumption in early teens.[2&3] While Australia was not included in the European and American statistics, other statistics show Australia is in the top ten countries of highest alcohol consumption in the world, so our adolescents numbers would be high when compared with the teens surveyed in Europe, UK. Canada and North America.[4&5]

The horrific deceptions subsequent tribal men have spread about Muhammad, which the world has not questioned, mean many will never really know the truth from the fiction. I have included what my research has found in these essays to help people make their own decisions. Through spurious hadiths, tribal groups have brought numerous atrocities to the monotheist faith of Abraham, which had been introduced by the three faithful messengers, Moses, Jesus and Muhammad. The Sunni tribal offshoot of Islam, which I call 'hadith Islam', is now almost unrecognisable as faith in God, Allah. Due to Sharia law, it has become politically oppressive and submissive to the rules of autocratic men. The 'hadith Islam' religious offshoot has become opinionated, intolerant and a narrow-minded cult, closer to dictatorial communism than religious freedom, which was the original intent of Muhammad.

Religious institutions used to be responsible for introducing a moral compass, the ideology of unity, and promoting egalitarian communities by discouraging financial disparity. 'Hadith Islam', however, has buried Muhammad's attempts at reformation under an avalanche of corrupt and deceptive hadith fabrications. Democratic governments of the world should never accept the Sunni corruption of Islam, supported and driven by Sharia law. It is religious political dogma and as unacceptable as Stalin's communist laws of domination or the tyranny of Hitler.

Heretical, religious clerics, who have judged women as inferior because of the deliberate or misguided translation of the Garden of Eden parable, have seriously corrupted faith. Ignoring the metaphorical use of a serpent, the symbol of pure evil, they judged the vulnerable victim, Eve, as the sinner. The simple agenda of faith has been buried along with the prophets who tried to introduce moral integrity.

Earlier Scriptures (Revelations) stated the antichrist would destroy this earth. We are now witnessing 'hadith Islam' terrorists, moulded from the corruption of the translations of the Quran, in at least five books of Sunnah—the fabrications that were banned both in the Quran and by the third major prophet in his last sermon.[6] He pleaded that those already written by tribal men, who chose to corrupt the words of the original Quran to suit their more godless intent, be destroyed. However, after the prophet's death, self-serving tribal leaders under the guise of religion, reintroduced most of the cruel tribal traditions which Muhammad had tried to stop. The Islamic terrorists are the 'jinn devils' mentioned in these verses—servants of the antichrist, who are only interested in personal power and earthly control. They are the individuals Muhammad saw as the real 'infidels'.

Islam is the third Abrahamic religion, but the Sunni religious cult offshoot has no guilt about killing followers of the first two Abrahamic faiths, Judaists and Christians, as they consider them the 'infidels'. When apostasy was introduced, after Muhammad's death, they even began slaughtering their own people if they did not follow the hadith-corrupted form of Islam, which was created by tribal dictators a very short time after the prophet's death.[7] Muhammad foresaw these hadith fabrications had the potential to wreak havoc within true Islam, as forewarned in the Quran (6: 111-113). These corrupt laws, introduced under the guise of faith, were created by 'infidels', dictators who were not going to relinquish their former godless, autocratic rule. With Islamic extremist terrorists we are now witnessing the horror of which this man of God warned. The *Ashtiname of Muhammad* created by the prophet shows he did not reject these earlier faiths.[8]

Wars are generally started, or created, by cold-hearted, ruthless men who tick the boxes of psychopathy. Massive bloodshed and loss of life, not only for the Muslim culture but for the entire world, will occur unless Muslim men and women look very closely at their corrupted faith now moulding these monsters. Brutal terrorists are the 'spawn of Satan' and it is Muslim apathy and their adoption of hadiths which have allowed these angry and heartless individuals to form. The tens of thousands of fabrications (hadiths and Sunnah) sacrilegiously added after the prophet's death were substantially reduced after an immense effort by well-intentioned Muslims, but even one hadith, created by an earthborn man, is against the prophet's last pleas and is a sin against Allah, equivalent to *shirk* (accepting false gods or equating oneself, or ones words, as equal to God).[9] Deceptive, extremist Muslim clerics argue Allah is the personal name of the 'one true God', and that nothing else can be called Allah and the term has no plural or gender. They claim it shows its uniqueness when compared with the word 'god', which can be made plural or feminine ('gods' and 'goddess' respectively). However, moderate Muslims do use different names as much as Allah, for instance 'God' in English.[10] Whether or not *Allah* can be considered as the personal name of God has been disputed in contemporary scholarship.[11] In fact, it is simply the Arabic word for the anglicised title 'God'.

In English, when 'god' is spelled with an upper case 'G', it means the 'one true God' and it does make the title unique. None of the prophets spoke English, but English has become the common language and when the Bible was translated into English 'God' was used, rather than 'Allah', but it is the same God.

Moses spoke Hebrew and, for 'God', he would have used the words *Elohim*, *Yahuwah*, or *Yahweh*. It appears the first language of Jesus was Aramaic, but he may have understood both Hebrew and Greek. The Aramaic word for 'God', in the language of Assyrian Christians, is *'Ĕlāhā*, or *Alaha*. Arabic-speakers of the Abrahamic faiths, including early Christians and Jews, also used the word 'Allah' to mean 'God'.

To promote Allah as the only true God is a result of deceptive words pushed by monolingual men who have no concept of the English language, where capital letters define proper nouns. The deception that Allah is the only word that followers must use for God is offensive. It is inferring speaking any other language is a sin in God's eyes. Under Sharia law, anyone who does not use the Arabic word, Allah, for God can be condemned to death. Where in the Scriptures does it demand that we be dumbed down and only monolingual? 'hadith Islamic' terrorists using Allah as a battle cry when rushing to kill other humans, are using God's name in vain—and do they really not see a problem with that? Apart from breaking two key Commandments—'Thou shalt not kill,' and 'Thou shalt not use the Lord's name in vain'—killing any children of God is horrifying sacrilege and the most unholy genocide.

It is sheer lunacy if they cannot accept that words from other languages can mean the same thing. Beef in French is *du bœuf*, in German it is *rindfleisch* and in Arabic it can be *laHm al-baqr*, or *dajaj*, or *lahmbaqa*, but whatever language is used, the customers would all be getting the flesh of cattle. Greater education and becoming multilingual would be a good start in bringing people to accept that we are all, as faith tells us, equal in the eyes of God, i.e.Galatians 3:28, 'There is neither Jew nor Greek, there is neither slave nor free man, there is neither male nor female; for you are all one in Christ Jesus.'[12] Only psychopathic personas that choose evil over good will choose to be led down the path of godlessracism and sexism.

Muhammad was from the Quraysh tribe and had no surviving sons, but his daughter and stepchildren married people from the Sunni and Shia tribes. It appears that, because there was a connection by marriage to Muhammad, they saw themselves as the chosen tribes. However, a higher power moulds a prophet, the descendants carry no special privileges in the eyes of God. Individuals must earn their own worth in Allah's eyes. Sunni and Shia should refer to Quran 53:39, 'Every human being is responsible only for his own works.'

Corrupt Muslim clerics deliberately betray their followers with the most outrageous deception. They tell their people that the God of Judaism and Christianity is not the real God, implying that Muhammad created another God just for them. That is paganism, not monotheism. Muhammad respected the Holy Scriptures that were written before the Quran and respected the first two messengers of God, Moses and Jesus.[13] He always insisted he was only a messenger and did not infer his words were superior to those of the earlier two prophets, or that the Islamic faith should replace the other two Abrahamic faiths.[14] True Islam is derived from the Quran and not from the pre-Islamic traditions and cultures of Muslim people, which were reintroduced by the Sunni tribe.

Religious leaders were meant to be servants of God, not rulers in their own right, as appears in the Vatican and in the now corrupted Muslim faith, where dictators in the 'hadith Islam' offshoot of Islam have rewritten and seriously mistranslated the Quran. At least five books of Sunnah, compiled of hadith fabrications created by tribal men, not the prophet, are the basis of Sharia law and the ultimate corruption of Muhammad's 'religion of peace'. After the death of Muhammad, false hadiths were developed and godless tribal traditions were reintroduced, mainly by the Sunni tribe but also supported by the prophet's own tribe, Quraysh, and to a lesser degree, Shia tribal leaders. The Quran and Muhammad warned that hadith fabrications were fanciful words created by the 'enemies of the prophets' (6:112–113).

Early Catholic religious clerics and Muslim caliphs, in effect, usurped the role of the spiritual Father by adding their own words and religious rules to the Christian faith, thus committing *shirk*. '*Shirk*' is an Arabic word for worship that is equal to the worship of God, but is the exaltation of a messenger or caliphate to godly status.[15] It includes adding deceptive fabrications to equate with the words of the Holy Books and is the ultimate blasphemy in any religion. Sharia law and the tribal 'hadith Islam' offshoot of true Islam are controlled by religious clerics that are guilty of the crime of *shirk*.

Books of Sunnah are substitute books of faith, compiled of thousands of false hadiths, condemned by Muhammad. They were purportedly records of the sayings of Muhammad, but it has been estimated that over 99 per cent of what they consider holy verses are deceptive hadiths falsely attributed to the prophet.[16] Muhammad condemned hadith fabrications because they were condemned in the Quran. Alternative hadiths, created by tribal people, were placing words from earthborn men, above those of Allah which had been recorded by Muhammad in the Quran and, hence, they were a sin against God.

Hadiths and books of Sunnah added to Islam after Muhammad's death were created by the prophet's enemies. Most are related to pre-Islamic tribal traditions and bear little relationship to the values of true faith. Criminal actions such as murder, paedophilia, or rape show contempt for both the celestial Father and his messengers. Only mentally unstable people enslave and persecute others. Corrupt clerics are warned, in the very first parable of the first of the three Holy Scriptures (Old and New Testaments and the Quran), that they will have an afterlife of eternal damnation for deceiving the most vulnerable and trusting (Genesis 3:1–22). Even as a pantheist-Christian (belief that reality and nature combine with divinity) I do hope that slithering in hellish unrest is the final destination of all men who mislead followers—in any religion.

Tribal leaders have developed 'hadith Islam' and Sharia law more as a war against women than respect for a Holy Father.

Dictatorial mullahs, who choose to continue gender apartheid and treat women as second-rate citizens not worthy to pray as equals with men in houses of God, are among the serpents of which Allah first warned. They continue to lie to their vulnerable followers, destroying lives and freedoms by enforcing barbarous subjugation which Muhammad tried to change. However, as the very first holy parable warned and a fact which most religions choose to ignore, the serpent (a metaphor for pure evil) was never forgiven. Allah proclaimed the serpent would be cursed above all creatures and would slither in dust for all eternity.

To add even greater insult to God, deceptive mullahs convince their gullible male followers that the heavenly Father is a pimp, supplying them with dozens of innocent virgins to rape when they reach the golden world of eternal peace. That is so outstandingly sacrilegious it is beyond human understanding. For even one person to be fooled by this outrageous deception, shows the sickening result of corrupt religious indoctrination. For showing such contempt for the spiritual Father, godless tribal religious clerics must know they are condemning their followers to join them in the world of eternal mercilessness.

We are now seeing terrorists and corrupted men failing humanity's greatest test—to be carers of this planet, Earth. Only fools, or psychopaths, would think killing and raping fellow humans and caring not a jot for this environment are going to earn them a place in the afterlife. Do Islamic terrorists really think they will be compensated, by Allah, for trashing this world we live in? Muslim clerics should have taken a little more notice of the first prophet's warning in the Garden of Eden parable—of what happens to those that deceive. If there is a divine creator, as people of faith believe, the eternal life of the cold-blooded, deceptive serpent that was never forgiven would mean that instead of seventy-two virgins greeting rapists and murderous terrorists, it will be seventy-two hissing vipers, slithering on their bellies in the black halls of hell.

Killing anyone in the name of God is the most offensive of all transgressions of corrupt religious men—of any faith. Godless psychopathic men choose to kill, godly men do not. Raised in environments that teach disrespect for women and no self-discipline in areas of sexual control, even denied pet dogs because of hadith rules, many of these males are anti-social by their mid-teens. Religious clerics were supposed to lead humanity away from the path of bad behaviour, but this is not happening in Sunni 'hadith Islam' because of dictatorial rule, which every messenger from Moses to Muhammad fought against.

The Abrahamic faith was based on freedom of the people and equality for all. To fight for the souls of the unbelievers does not mean to slaughter them. Thuggish tribal men who see the word 'fight' in the Quran and interpret it as 'kill'. They lack the EQ (emotional intelligence) to comprehend that the fight to save the soul is not a physical act of cruelty, but a non-aggressive psychological act of caring and support. The conversion to faith was meant to turn people away from more decadent lifestyles, by examples of good and caring behaviour, not by fear and murderous terrorism. Killing seems easier for these men, but evil behaviour destroys any chance of forgiveness on judgement day.

Why has 'hadith Islam', the corruption of true Islam, been allowed to become so powerful? Their horrific murderous behaviour will continue if the subjugation and segregation of one gender, even within mosques, continues. Men, keeping young males separated from the more nurturing and empathetic gender will continue to groom young boys to a point where they will be impossible to rein in. It is the first decade of a child's life that moulds the man.[17-19]

Continuing female oppression is allowing 'hadith Islam' to continue feeding the innocent to the lions—the godless 'hadith Islam' cult leaders. It will cause the continued deterioration of the world of the moderate Muslims—and world contempt for this acceptance of religious corruption.

Martin Luther stopped the Catholic world from using only Latin in its services, which limited the understanding of Christian followers. He had the Bible published in their national language so followers could recognise any corruption of faith by religious leaders made to enhance their personal power and control.[20] Yet Sunni 'hadith Islam' still discourages the education of women. Sinister religious clerics have recognised the vulnerability of less-educated men and women and would be fully aware the uneducated are so much easier to brainwash and lead down the path of deception.

Physically or emotionally imprisoned victims learn to align with their persecutors as a way of extending lives when there is a threat of death. This state is recognised as the *Stockholm syndrome*.[21] It is a survival instinct. Rather than feeling like the perpetual victim, it is a way for victims to sustain ego and self-esteem. This was first recognised in 1973 when captives in a bank robbery in Stockholm were kept imprisoned and eventually ended up robbing banks with their captors. When isolated with the criminals, who could deceive and manipulate people into believing what they were doing was right, the victims— in fear of their lives—ended up doing what the captors demanded. Often charismatic but psychopathic men of evil mould the Stockholm syndrome. It is a bond formed between the tormenters and their victims. This brainwashing can also occur when men segregate women and ban them from education, as 'hadith Islam' does.

Failing to learn the lesson of equality between genders, Judaism, Catholicism, and 'hadith Islam' have violated and deceived their faithful followers in a way that falls foul of the godly, religious behaviour they are supposed to practise. Not educating females is possibly why many Muslim cultures now lag behind Western cultures in science and academic intellectual achievement.[22-24] Faith in one God should have common values but religions, created by males around their prophets, have become a far more conflict-ridden educational system than the academic system—as witnessed by the crime gangs (Mafia, Cosa Nostra) and Islamic terrorists that have grown from conflicting religious rules.

Corrupt men, under the pretext of faith, have perfected this with fear and terror. Dictatorial egomaniacs have placed themselves as the dominant gender and have no conscience about destroying, or breaking the will, of good people by annihilating self-esteem and their sense of personal control. 'Hadith Islam' rules enslave women, making them too afraid to complain for fear of beatings, rape and possible death, which are frequently the results of living with a psychopath. Women cower behind the sheets that these evil men command they wear so that people are discouraged from befriending Muslim women.

By covering the smile, which breaks through all language barriers, the women are forced to shun friendships with others, making them more dependent on and vulnerable to their controlling partners. This is the rule of the antichrist followers—not God. Only the most insecure and possessive men could have come up with the idea of reintroducing the burqa in modern days of peace.

It is incredibly sinister that early tribal men perfected the moulding of the *Stockholm syndrome* centuries before that city was even founded. There is a whole culture of women who have been enslaved to this horrifying 'trauma bond', which can be very difficult to break naturally.[25] Muslims have generations of women lost to this chilling female enslavement because they have allowed tyrannical males to treat them as second-grade citizens for centuries. However, even dictatorships where religion is not a dominating factor can have the entire populace locked into this terrifying form of control; China and North Korea are interesting case studies.

Fearful Muslim women would never have the courage to form women's groups like the Suffragettes, or the Women's Liberation movement, which have improved the quality of life for men, women and children in the Western world. It is not only out of fear for their own safety, but these cowardly men also often threaten reprisal against children and other family members.

Hugely damaging excessive breeding was encouraged by corrupted male-dominated religions, which discouraged contraception and abortion. They wanted to increase their religious numbers; they did not care an iota for the welfare of the thousands of children born in extreme poverty because of the disgraceful excessive numbers of children men and women were having—far above what they could afford to house and raise. The thuggish gangs that grew in countries ruled by the Islamic and Catholic churches are powerful evidence of this shocking male rule.

Compulsion is the rule of the dictatorial, psychopathic persona, alienated from the process of forgiving, or asking for forgiveness, dictators and autocrats are the very worst of the planets 'intraspecies'.[26] All three holy books, the Old and New Testaments and the Quran, reject any form of compulsion. The messengers all decried religious enslavement, and it is very clearly stated in the Quran, 2:256, to be an offence of true faith: 'There is no compulsion in faith.' The Catholic Church, as explored in Essay 6, introduced the man-made rules of compulsory celibacy and confessionals. 'Hadith Islam' corrupted the Islamic faith when dictatorial leaders added thousands of false hadiths (rules made by earthborn men), most driven by compulsion, after the third messenger's death.

Dictators rule by terror, not compassion. Autocratic leaders see themselves as the god their people must follow without question. Narcissistic, they want sycophantic adulation and complete control. They are manipulative controllers, consumed by greed, and are the reason faith was introduced—to give hope of freedom for people enslaved to this awful rule. In the Muslim world, freedom was shut down as soon as the apostasy rule of total religious enslavement was introduced, two years after the death of the third major prophet. That was the day Muhammad's 'religion of peace' died.[27&28]

The second messenger, Jesus, was crucified by tribal enemies: the cruellest and most humiliating of deaths. While the third messenger was not physically crucified, the sabotage of the faith after Muhammad's death, with corrupt fabrications, was verbal crucifixion. He had asked for all hadiths, other than those within the Quran, to be destroyed, so each one of the thousands that made up the books of the Sunnah is a nail in his flesh.

Muhammad died in 632 AD; the Ridda (apostasy) Wars that followed took many lives, killing many of the men who had memorised the original Quran.[29] The apostasy rule was introduced (circa 634 AD). Islam became compulsory and Muslims were condemned to death if one dared to leave the faith.[30] Many other corruptions of the Islamic faith were introduced by tribal enemies of the prophet.[31–32] There is a widespread belief that Islam was spread by the sword, but this is not the case.[33] Prophet Muhammad proclaimed that he would adhere to God's commandments and he was entirely opposed to forcing people to accept Islam.[34] The Quran quite clearly states that God explicitly prohibited forced conversion and that there should be no compulsion in faith (Quran 2:256). If people chose to revert to another faith, or relapse, it was—and still should be—individual choice. They are answerable to

God, not men who equate themselves with Allah. Hence, the clerics that enforced the apostasy death cult were the voices of the enemies of the prophets, 'jinn devils' as forewarned by Muhammad (Quran 6: 112–113). We are now beginning to witness the failure of the hadith-ridden sabotage of Muhammad's religion of peace.

At least six books of Sunnah have been written, which were shocking corruptions of the true Islamic faith. They allowed horrific traditions, subjugation and the devaluing of females and continued paedophilia with underage girls being sold as wives. This has moulded the very people Muhammad tried to change. Quraish Shihab, an Arabic Indonesian Muslim scholar in the sciences of the Quran, an author, a cleric, and former Minister of Religious Affairs in 1988,[35] wrote an article, *The Roots of Violence in Islam Today is originated from The Book of Hadith Muslim-Bukhari*. It was a powerful exposé on one of the false books of hadith fabrications, created by a dictatorial tribal leader in contempt of both the prophet's words and the Quran. However, it has now, unfortunately, been taken down (possibly by powerful 'hadith Islam' opposition), but if it can be reprinted it is worth reading.

We know Muhammad was not the psychopath tribal leaders painted him as (i.e. a paedophile and womaniser). As has been recorded, he suffered times of great depression.[36] Anxiety is not something psychopaths suffer; they do not have the emotional depth.[37&38] Muhammad loved his children and lost his first two sons in childhood and also a third young boy in his second marriage, a decade after the death of his first wife. Of course, he would have suffered great despair for those losses. Psychopathic personas do not suffer either depression or despair, even if they are caught out in their deception or crimes—they only feel sorry for themselves, not for their victims.[39]

Muhammad married for love, not lust, something men who practise polygamy would not understand. Hedonist men would have hated that. The adoption of 'hadith Islam', the tribal cult offshoot built on false hadith fabrications, has retarded the quality of life, particularly for women and female children, which is now so bad in many Muslim countries that millions are fleeing to other shores. If they are not prepared to discard false hadiths, the books of Sunnah and Sharia law (which has destroyed the cultures they are fleeing from), they have no right to bring down our culture of religious freedom by following those corrupt practices in democratic countries.

Muhammad introduced the Abrahamic monotheist faith and, like Jesus, attempted to introduce a more egalitarian lifestyle and greater equality between the genders. The Shia tribe was initially supportive of this ethos. However, Sunni and Quraysh tribes, run along more autocratic rules, did not support Muhammad's egalitarian views and strongly drove the return to the tribal pagan traditions of dictatorial political enslavement and the domination of females.[40] They chose to treat women as second-class citizens and, by reinstating corrupt usury practices which Muhammad had banned, they once again reintroduced financial disparity and social deprivation. Usury was the unethical and immoral monetary loans and profits that unfairly enriched the lender.

The Muslim world reintroduced horrific animal cruelty in the corrupt hadith-driven sacrificial form of animal slaughter.[41] Halal slaughter, which ironically is a corruption of Allah's name as well as his rules, is not mentioned in the Quran. The brutal form of killing is as corrupt as this tribal rule—it is as if someone has thrown the letters of God's name into the dirt and then used the order in which they have fallen to create this entirely godless law. The brutal throat slashing was an obscene way of desensitising young males to cruel throat slashing. This was a lesson well-learned by terrorists, but certainly nothing to do with faith in God. Halal was simply requesting thanks be given before eating, like saying grace before starting a meal. We will be judged in the afterlife as much by the way we treat animals as we treat humans.

In addition, they branded dogs as satanic and believed that they were to be killed—actions that develop early psychopathic behaviour. When children consistently practise animal cruelty, it is the earliest sign of psychopathic disorder.[42&43] By banning dogs, which stimulate oxytocin the bonding hormone, and forbidding other oxytocin-producing activities—such as singing, dancing, sporting activities and even public laughter—'hadith Islam' has turned the original 'religion of peace' into one of the most violent cult offshoots on earth. Through MRI scans, modern neuroscience has revealed that psychopathic brains do not register essential emotions—and history has shown if we allow wickedness to flourish, all will suffer the consequences.

Influenced by the earlier -prophets, Muhammad's version of Islam was more respectful than the irreverent religious offshoot of Sunni 'hadith Islam', which has become corrupted and overrun with misogynists and sexist men.[44] Hence, we are now seeing males who exhibit all the traits of men who have grown with the arrogance of thinking their gender is superior. This indicates psychopathic behaviour, not followers of faith. Tragically, through sheer ignorance (or possibly deliberately), in the tribal culture of 'kill or be killed' fighters, 'hadith Islam' has ticked almost every box on how to create the perfect psychopathic persona. Specifically, they forced gender-apartheid and the oppression of women, in halal killing they encourage prolonged cruelty of animals, thus desensitising children to horrific forms of killing and they introduced forms of compulsion and religious enslavement. Sharia law directs Muslims to engage in *Taqiyya*[45] and lie to non-Muslims to advance Islam, which encourage pathological lying, a strong indicator of psychopathy. Banning forms of entertainment such as dancing, singing, even laughing in public, and masking the smiles of women behind burqas are all actions that reduce oxytocin receptors in the brain. Oxytocin is essential for the emotional and mental health of young children, banning activities that stimulate this miraculous bonding hormone has produced many dour, humourless monsters.

Apart from the commendable continued abstinence from alcohol and drugs, many Muslims have reverted to the barbaric rules of the Middle Eastern pre-Islam culture. The world has now witnessed increasing numbers of terrorists who are emotionally bankrupt, with reduced activity in the area of the brain that should be producing empathy, remorse and guilt. They are our most dangerous predators.

The male-dominated religions have failed, to a far greater degree, than the Protestant faiths where women have greater equality. 'Hadith Islam' treats women little better than dogs, which were considered unclean and killed. Widowed females were also seen as unclean because they were no longer virgins. To cling to the Sunnah corruption of faith, shows complete contempt for the pleas made by Muhammad, indicates they relish the pre-Islamic lifestyle that includes polygamy, paedophilia, and female oppression. The accuracy of the prophets' warning, that the deceptive fabrications were created by 'jinn devils' and the 'enemies of the prophets', is being revealed. We are now seeing the real unbelievers, the 'infidels' who have rejected the Quranic laws to follow books of Sunnah and false hadiths, who slaughter innocent people without guilt or remorse.

As in World War II, the world is again being engulfed by brains bereft of EQ that align mass genocide with the simple act of swatting flies. Because of their lack of normal emotions, psychopaths never suffer PTSD, only self-pity when they are made to pay for their crimes. It is the good people who have to fight the psychopathic personas that suffer this emotionally crippling disorder. The 'hadith Islam' rule of terror and religious enslavement has subjugated good men and women of the true Islamic faith. However, moderate Muslims must recognise the evil that has been spread under the guise of Islamic faith and make changes to end this corruption.

Faith has always been about equality, freedom and hope—factors which are the antithesis of communist and dictatorial cultures. As autocratic leaders suppress equality, freedom and hope, religions are banned in many of the countries ruled by them. Sunni 'hadith Islam' has been formed outside of the values of GOD (standing for Goodness, Order and Decency), as it continues to practise appalling gender apartheid. Muslims who support the true Islamic faith should recognise that the cult offshoot of 'hadith Islam' could well be Allah's warning, given in the last book of the Bible, Revelations. The prophesy of the four Horsemen of the Apocalypse described the riders bringing destruction, through time, as people fell away from faith. The pale horse, the last horse symbolising Death, represented the people who were anti-Christ, the rise of religious deception and the destruction of this 'Eden' we have been given.

Unbelievers are described by Muhammad (in the Quran) as 'the vilest of animals' and 'losers'. Historians and writers must surely recognise that the harsh words in the Quran directed to unbelievers apply directly to followers of hadith fabrications—the false hadiths and books of Sunnah, added by tribal men after the prophet's death. Those who disobeyed the plea, given by Muhammad, to destroy these fabrications were the real unbelievers, deserving of these words of condemnation, they were the 'jinn devils', the real 'infidels' (6:112-113). Muhammad had stated that the unbelievers are those that do not follow the word of God, as written in the Holy Scriptures from the Torah (Old Testament) down to the Quran (5:44):

> Indeed, we revealed the Torah, containing guidance and light, by which the prophets, who submitted themselves to Allah, made judgments for Jews. So too did the rabbis and scholars judge according to Allah's Book, with which they were entrusted and of which they were made keepers. So do not fear the people; fear Me! Nor trade my revelations for a fleeting gain. And those who do not judge by what Allah has revealed are 'truly' the disbelievers.[46]

Yet Sunni 'hadith Islam' and Sharia law, based on at least five books of Sunnah, show complete contempt for many of the verses in the original Islamic book of faith. They contain heinous corruptions of the Quran. The evil that has formed over the decades is now seen in all its terrorist horror—and shows exactly how accurate Muhammad's prophesies were.

Religious clerics, guilty of following this corrupted form of Islam, brand people who have remained faithful to the Holy Scriptures of the earlier prophets (Judeo-Christians) as the 'infidels' Muhammad was referring to. They were not, as clearly stated in the verse above. Muhammad had already observed the damage these false hadiths were causing when he pleaded that they be burned and destroyed. The extreme hubris of these tribal men allowed them to divorce themselves from the words of rebuke in the Quran. They have twisted the words to imply Muhammad was directing them at everyone else, other than themselves. That is indicative of the psychopathic disorder, as individuals with this disorder always see themselves as victims and accuse others, even against the strongest of evidence.[47]

Muhammad was a man of God and believed the Quran was complete for his people. He did not reject earlier Holy Scriptures: he saw the Quran as an addition to them, not a replacement.[48] However, the books of hadiths, Sunnah, are corrupt tribal replacements introduced by tyrannical leaders.[49] 'Hadith Islam' clerics remain in denial and continue to feed deception to the masses—and no one questions it. No one has the courage to fight against the men whom Muhammad called 'jinn devils': corrupt individuals who are destroying the third major Abrahamic faith, Islam. Quran 3:95, 'God has spoken the truth, so follow the religion of Abraham the Monotheist; he was not a Pagan.'

The fact Muhammad mentioned former Scriptures with respect, and that many of the verses align with biblical verses, should have encouraged Muslims to also read these Holy Books, not treat them with contempt. He believed the Quran did not need any additions or amendments. Muhammad knew the followers of the earlier faiths, Judaism and Christianity, had remained loyal to their two books of faith: they had respected the words of their messengers. His last plea was for Muslims to do the same. He would suffer great grief if he knew how horrendously corrupted his 'religion of peace' has become because dictatorial tribal leaders ignored his final pleas.

The 'hadith Islam' offshoot is the reverse of Quranic Islam, creating hatred and harm, not striving for equality, egalitarian community and peace. The TROP (The Religion of Peace) article, *Is the Quran Hate Propaganda?*[50] is typical of narrow-minded critics who appear to have no concept of the appalling distortions of the holy books, most notably the Quran. Almost every verse has been mistranslated to suit the evil intent of brutal and dictatorial tribal men that Muhammad had fought against. After his death, they introduced hundreds of thousands of hadiths, replacing the original Quran with books of 'Sunnah'. One estimate was 200,000 hadith fabrications, which were eventually reduced to 7,000, however, as the Quran warned, every single fabrication included under the guise of religion is showing complete contempt for both Allah and his faithful messenger—who followed the same Abrahamic faith of the first two messengers.

The hadith cult offshoot of true Islam has been literally allowed to get away with murder. As the first prophet warned, these deceptive serpents will be crawling on their bellies in the dark halls of hell. Of all the followers of the major prophets, these have been the most disloyal—a disgrace to the third and final messenger of the spiritual Father. The books of Sunnah are from men who did not respect the words of the Quran or their prophet, and they should never be considered as references to support true Islam as the TROP article has done.

Both Moses and Jesus followed the religion of Abraham; their followers are not the 'infidels'. The 'hadith Islam' followers that accuse them of unfaithfulness are responsible for the greatest infidelity. Muhammad respected believers within the earlier two faiths, but was aware they also had 'jinn devils' in their midst—as any faith has: Quran 98:7, 'Indeed, they who have believed and have done righteous deeds— those are the best of creatures.'

Muhammad never endorsed slaughter of other believers in God. 'Righteous deeds' are driven by conscience and empathy (C&E), the traits that all true religions were created to ingrain into their followers. The Sunni 'hadith Islam' offshoot embeds hatred, as it teaches that the third branch of the Abrahamic faith, introduced by Muhammad, is superior to the other two Christian faiths and followers are inferior infidels. This is a sacrilegious bastardisation of true faith. Sharia law condones murder, rape and the subjugation of females, yet these are not righteous deeds— it is the behaviour of evil 'jinn devils'.

The threat of death, because of the apostasy rule, gave unjust and brutal Middle Eastern tribal men a strangle hold on their followers for centuries. Several tribes wanted to leave the religion once it became corrupted with spurious hadiths and return to their preferred religion, while other families fled to places like Abyssinia where they could safely continue the faith that followed the Quran.[51] In the conflict known as the Ridda (apostasy) Wars, they were slaughtered by the thousands in places recalled as the 'Garden of Death' and the 'Gully of Blood'.[52&53] This slaughter of innocents empowered dictators and tyrants. Muslims were enslaved by terror and torture, which was the death of Muhammad's 'religion of peace'.

These dictatorial religious leaders did not go out as men of peace and faith to spread the word of God, Allah. Most were murderous men of psychopathic godlessness who wanted complete power and control. They did this under the cunning disguise of religion. They were the 'jinn devils', evil men distorting the words of the Quran with false hadith whilst showing complete disregard for Muhammad and the original Commandments of God.

Tribal men, with the heinous, verbal character assassination of the third messenger, Muhammad, and their replacement of the Quran with hadith fabrications have, like the Jewish population who allowed the assassination of the second messenger,[54] also cast a long shadow over many innocent Muslims. Great distress and death appear to follow the assassination of a messenger, be it a physical or verbal character assassination, which tribal leaders did to Muhammad after his death. They ignored the fact Muhammad had followed the Abrahamic faith the first two messengers had introduced. This verbal assassination and the resulting fallout destroyed the 'religion of peace'. Now people, unaware of the appalling tribal corruption, are turning against peace-loving, moderate Muslims who have tried to adhere to the original Quranic faith.

History tells us that millions of innocent Jews have experienced immense suffering since the appalling decision to crucify the second messenger. This decision was driven, not only by a few wealthy Jewish gold vendors who had no wish to drop usury, but also by Pontius Pilate, the Roman procurator of Judea.[55] Sadly, the horror of that crucifixion turned many Christians against Jews and Judaism. Further devastation was caused centuries later by a German genocidal maniac, Hitler, who may have had a more personal reason for hating Jews, as there was some question about his own ancestry. His grandmother's illegitimate son, Hitler's father Alois Hitler, may have been fathered by a wealthy Jew.[56]

Hitler's psychotic behaviour turned the world against anyone and anything Germanic for decades. And yet we are again witnessing horrific genocidal maniacs, the Islamic State terrorists, who are causing the deaths of thousands of innocent people, including many of their own. Wikipedia has listed the number of Islamic attacks worldwide, between the 1970s and 2020 as around 300 with thousands killed and wounded.[57] It shows the horrifying spread of these psychotic individuals. They have been warring against the rest of the world for over five decades and this battle has nothing to do with faith. It indicates the horrific corruption of Muhammad's 'religion of peace' by Sunni tribal men wanting earthly domination. Once again, it is turning many people against an entire culture. Sadly, the one or two per cent of the populace that is psychopathic always creates a much greater number of victims than non-psychopathic offenders.[58] Psychopaths, white-collar and heinous, average about ten times more victims than non-psychopathic offenders, as they are the most recidivist of offenders. Many innocent Muslims are caught in the negative light these emotionally retarded individuals spread.

Christians may sacrilegiously worship Jesus as God, but they have never dragged down their prophet, as corrupt Sunni tribes have done. They chose to present Muhammad as a paedophile and degrader of women, by recording that he married the nine-year-old he fostered— when in fact he fostered her to protect her in a culture where females were seen as having no value. Arabia was a male-dominated society. Women had no status of any kind other than as sex objects, having a daughter was seen as a failure. The report, *Arabia before Islam,* relates the savage custom of the Arabs to bury their female infants alive.[59] Even if an Arab did not wish to bury his daughter alive, he often still had to uphold this 'honourable' tradition, being unable to resist social pressures.

One only has to read Spencer and Chesler's report, *The violent oppression of women in Islam,*[60] to realise why Muhammad also took widowed wives under his care, all of whom who had children. Governments of the world must rally to bring equality and freedom to these women and good Muslims should return to the values of true faith as introduced by Muhammad and cast aside the Sunni corruption of their faith. Muhammad's fight was for the protection of women and children, equality not subjugation.

Housing and caring for numerous widows were not the gathering of a harem, but an act of protection to save these widows from lust-driven men who saw it as their right to rape widows, as they were no longer virgins. This fact has been disgracefully misinterpreted by tribal men who had no more sexual control than rutting feral animals. They had no wish to change their pre-Islam custom of taking numerous virgin wives, which had been banned in the Quran. The third messenger did not deserve that character assassination by the corrupt tribal men who followed him, nor should followers of true Islam allow this lack of respect to continue.

The 'do as I say, not as I do' men fool people for a while, but they do not transform societies for the better, they are too self-centred. Many have witnessed self-centred men who take numerous wives and use them as nothing more than objects for sexual pleasure and for breeding their heirs. Only men who are incapable of forming loving, committed partnerships for decades, as Muhammad had done, could believe the deception that has been spread about this dedicated man. Sunni tribal men, who led the destruction of the 'religion of peace', were among the worst offenders who chose to believe these lies.

When brave people of the Christian faith began to make changes to the corruption of their faith by Catholic priests, huge numbers also died. There is great risk that history may repeat itself, but we must help protect those that want reform. Muslim women, in particular, must be braver. Tragically, they would be slaughtered in their own countries, but in democratic countries, they should follow the lead of our Suffragettes and Women's Liberation movement and demand equality within the church—and stop simply being breeders for increasing 'hadith Islam' numbers.

Moderate Muslims must take a long, hard look at their corrupted faith and make changes. They should have the courage to follow their prophet's example, not remain enslaved to the hadith fabrications added to Islam by the ungodly caliphates and irreligious clerics that followed him. The Christian faith had courageous people who created Protestant faiths that broke away from Catholicism to return to true faith and religious freedom—a faith in God, which was against female discrimination and fundamentalist dogma.

Muslims, once they are in democratically ruled countries, should have the courage to enforce equality, especially in houses of God. They should walk with their partners into houses of prayer as equals and sit in a refined manner, not grovel at the feet of religious clerics in disempowering positions—noses in the dust and rear ends pointed towards God. This rule was instituted by men desirous of the feeling of power and control over other men—it is earthborn men who desire sycophancy, not Allah.

Centuries of tribal corruption of Muhammad's original 'religion of peace' has moulded many godless men. Murderous psychopaths have grown up with brains that do not register conscience or empathy. While ISIL actually stands for the Islamic State of Iraq and the Levant, it is an appropriate acronym for 'In Sin I Live'—a very accurate title for followers of Sunni 'hadith Islam'. ISIL is a dictatorial branch that has moulded terrorists instead of men of God: serial killers and rapists who break almost all the rules of the Abrahamic faith that Muhammad introduced.

Dictators in Muslim cultures are now so powerful that ordinary people fear for their lives if they try to make any change. There appears to be no real division between religion and secular law. As with communism, it is autocratic political rule, not religious freedom as encouraged by Muhammad.

Muhammad had strongly opposed forcing people to accept Islam, but within two years of his death the 'religion of peace' was destroyed, when tribal tyrants introduced compulsory apostasy enslavement, a regime far worse than communist control. Communism was originally set up as a socioeconomic structure, a political ideology that promoted the establishment of an egalitarian, classless society based on common ownership of produce and property, whereas, apostasy enabled the most tyrannical rule of dictatorship. The leaders who came after Muhammad completely distorted the Abrahamic ethos to which he had converted. Dictators are psychopathic personalities, they are leaders that hold or abuse an extraordinary amount of power, they do not allow political elections and they force massive restrictions of civil liberties and have no guilt in deceiving their enslaved masses.[61]

False hadiths and the Sunni destruction of reputation continue to paint Muhammad in a negative light to the rest of the world. Harsh, uncaring, loveless men do not have long-term committed relationships, as Muhammad had; he was devoted to his wife and children in a monogamous marriage of 25 years, until Khadija's death. Always treated as equals, both wife and daughters deeply respected and loved him.[62] Fabricated hadiths that allow men to continue treating women as second-rate citizens fuel egotistical male self-righteousness, which is prevalent in the 'hadith Islam' cult offshoot of the Islamic faith. Consequently, this creates massive prejudice against Islam from people of other faiths and from people across the world that supports equality, the real message of faith.

The article in the New York Times, *ISIL Enshrines a Theology of Rape*,[63&64] revealed the grotesque sub-humans that have been moulded by the most monstrously corrupted cult that has been formed by godless dictators, masquerading under the guise of religious faith. To call them animals would be to insult innocent animals that never act in this way to their own species. These creatures need to be removed from civilisation to permanent high security psychiatric clinics or de-sexed, as are animals that are not good breeding stock. Their toxic genes should never be carried to the next generation. If countries do not have high security psychiatric clinics with medical staff specialised in neuroscience and psychiatric training, then full castration should be considered. Eunuchs live longer and healthier lives once their brains are no longer controlled by testosterone and their genitalia.[65-67]

Humans are supposed to have evolved from this bestial behaviour, yet ISIL and the corrupted form of Islam have enshrined the theology of rape. They are the antichrist of which the Holy Books warned. ISIL is practising religious genocide by slaughtering followers of other schools of faith, which is unjust not only because of deaths they cause, but also because of the horrific corruption of Islam, the third branch of the Abrahamic faith Muhammad tried to introduce to the barbarous tribes of his time.[68] Sunni 'hadith Islam' has been created almost entirely around rules made by autocratic males.[69&70] They show complete contempt for their God and their prophet's requests. The slaughter of Yazidis, Christians and Shiites and the kidnapping of thousands of women and children to be used as slaves and sex objects, is almost beyond human comprehension. It has been called the ISIS 'industry of rape'.[71&72] This slaughter of men, women and children makes Hitler's genocide look mild, these monsters continue to spread their toxic psychopathic genes far and wide.

The brains of psychopathic rapists have, for some yet undiscovered reason, stagnated at the procreation level of lesser species of animals—serial rapists are bestial males only interested in basic animal rutting. Under 'hadith Islam', men are raised to degrade women and to treat them as inferior. Hence, the terrorists that have been moulded by this behaviour perform in the same manner as feral animals servicing their 'harem-herds'. There is little emotional attachment, just sexual release.

With no bonding or care, there is no more attachment to the female body that they are raping than there is for the toilet. Females are just a convenient vehicle for dumping their possibly genetically impaired DNA waste.

ISIL sells kidnapped women and children to other sub-human fighting men, in the same manner that farmers sell actual breeding stock. They actually put price tags on their human victims when they are marketing them because they are simply another form of property.

There used to be a criminal code of retribution for anyone who would deliberately kill a child, as this was a step too far even in the underbelly of crime. The story of one of Australia's worst serial killers, Stewart John Regan, a highly successful drug dealer and brothel owner, was proof of that. When Regan killed a girlfriend's little boy and made his body 'disappear' like that of his other victims, it was the underworld that ended up killing him.[73] The underworld criminal cohorts could accept cold-blooded murder, rape, even pimping, but they put seven bullets into him, one for every murder he had committed (where he had managed to escaped justice) and one for the child. Killing an innocent child was unforgivable, even in the underworld, so why would 'hadith Islam' terrorists think a heavenly Father would accept this horror?

Moses and Muhammad both predicted that adding deceptive words to the words of God would cause destruction. The world is now witnessing the accuracy of those predictions as innocent Muslims are having their wives and children killed, and their homes being destroyed by murderous 'hadith Islam' terrorists. Killing innocent children is the most evil of all actions; the black souls of such terrorists are doomed to the blackest pits of hell.

Sociopathic psychopaths are sub-human, they have absolutely no bounds. We now see 'hadith Islam' extremists (who are essentially the Muslim criminal underworld) register a complete lack of moral restraint. Children count for nothing, they are slaughtered with no more concern than when these men kill women or the aged. Corrupt 'hadith Islam' clerics, leading young boys into this monstrous behaviour, are the epitome of the beast that people of faith call the antichrist—they have moulded the soldiers of Satan.

Pathological liars have the potential to destroy community and civilisation. 'Hadith Islam', to promote their form of religion, encourages lying (taqiyya). Deception is one of the most significant and deeply ingrained traits of psychopathy.[74] Psychopaths develop exceptional skills in lying and deception. A culture based on deception is like building a house on drifting sand: it will cause civilisation to degrade and crumble—ironic when considering the desert environments in which 'hadith Islam' has endured over the centuries.

The subtle tongue of evil deception, like cancer, spreads its deadly influence. The prophets (Moses, Jesus and Muhammad) served their time on earth well, but the words from psychopathic people, who epitomise the predicted antichrist, are still very strong. Atheists and many in the modern world now see the messages of those three enlightened prophets as worthless. Natural evolution moved on; finally, the new-age world of neuroscience gave us Dr Robert D Hare, who confirmed the presence of pure evil—the psychopathic persona.[75] However, many of us still prefer to bury our heads in our teacup worlds, hoping the problem will just disappear of its own accord. We ignore Dr Hare's words in much the same way many have ignored the words of the earlier prophets. Cancer does not disappear of its own accord, so why do we think pure evil will? It has been nearly three and a half millennia since the first messenger's warning (circa 1400 BC) and we are still waiting for people to take this skewed mental disorder seriously!

Muhammad encouraged religious freedom and respected the prophets before him, but 'hadith Islam' was formed after his death by men who ticked boxes of psychopathy. They had no intention of reducing human enslavement and dictatorial control and within a very short time had reintroduced every barbaric tradition. Psychopaths have high rat-cunning intelligence and they realised by including these barbaric practises as part of religion, which is above the law in most countries of the world, they could rule the world.

Gender segregation is as disgraceful as racial segregation, but it still continues in Islamic mosques. Governments of the world, and feminists, who accept this godless behaviour, should be ashamed. The Muslim world should separate all hadith and books of Sunnah from the Quranic Islam faith, while the rest of the world must recognise corruption and demand change. Religion should return to its original agenda, encouraging faith in God, Allah, and, more importantly, respect for life and all that is within this small planet. We are supposed to be the shepherds, not the wolves. Single-handedly, in a space of twenty-two years, Muhammad brought hope to Arabia and a new beacon for that world.

While many people may not believe in God, this phenomenon of true evil, which we see in Islamic terrorists, does make us believe there is a 'devil incarnate', a satanic force intent on destroying everything that is godly and good. The world cannot treat the symptoms by waging war on this barbarism, they must treat the disease, which is the corruption of male-dominated religions, which has moulded monstrous men.

Trusting the serpent was the shame of the Garden of Eden's residents, as it represented pure evil. That parable told the world that deceptive snakes (psychopaths) will always be slithering amongst us. With that ominous warning it appears behaviour would need to change well before judgement day. Terrorist suicide bombers have no hope of forgiveness as they have fallen victims to corrupt clerics that have distorted the true messages of Allah, for personal power and control.

The symbolic Garden of Eden residents were not the initiators of sin, but as they trusted the sinner, the serpent, who completely twisted the words that God had passed to them, they were guilty of sin. In the same way, followers of 'hadith Islam' are not the initiators of sin, but by following deceptive hadiths passed to them by Sunni 'hadith Islam' clerics who, like the serpent, have also twisted the words of God, passed to them in the Quran, they are also guilty of sin.

Of course, there can be no afterlife for serial murderers and rapists who break the most basic religious commandments of common decency. Surely, believers must realise that dreadful deception? They had better hope the Hindus have it right and wicked souls get recycled, possibly as the innocent creatures they have harmed. The place of eternal rest, which people of faith have been promised, would hardly allow access to murderers, rapists or wealthy financial 'whores' who are driven by greed, while millions suffer in poverty.

What is the point of life, if we do not learn the difference between good and evil, the most important lesson of all? If this life is about testing one's worth, then worthless souls who do not learn the lessons, which faith was introduced to teach, could not be rewarded. If souls do have an afterlife, just the thought of spending eternity with only depraved, failed souls is enough to make anyone have second thoughts about actions that may lose them 'points'. It does make one hope that Hinduism, which provides a fallback option of being reincarnated, to give one a chance of making amends second time around, is an option allowed by the spiritual Father of the monotheist faith.

~ 8 ~

Terrorists, murderers and rapists are soldiers of sin, not God

'Segregation is the adultery of an illicit intercourse between injustice and immorality.'
—**Martin Luther King, Jr.**

As Sharia law is tied to religion, religious clerics often act as God's judge and jury in Muslim cultures. Tyrannical men, who formed Sharia law, have made justice for women and children virtually unobtainable. This form of religious enslavement now favours men and condones mistreatment of women. Allowing this ungodly behaviour to continue, because it has been cunningly linked with religion, has allowed this corruption of faith to slide beneath the radar in the Western world where democracy, not dictatorial rule, is the government of the people. Governments and genuine followers of true Islam must separate corrupt practices that are barbarous tribal traditions and completely disallow rules of gender inequality, which break the laws of Western world democracies. These include:

- Religious, 'apostasy' enslavement, driven by dictators, not Allah.
- Segregation and female subjugation. Gender apartheid practised in houses of God, with female and male segregation at times of prayer, is male misogyny.
- The burqa is not Quranic law, dressing modestly is the rule in all Abrahamic faiths; full-covering is cruel male oppression of pre-Islamic times.
- Work-time allowances and separate rooms specifically created for hadith-driven compulsory and regimented forms of prayer. The Quran banned compulsion (2:256). Salat prayers are the rules of male domination—'subjugation' to tribal control, not 'submission' (i.e. Islam) to Allah. Prayers to Allah can quietly be given 24/7.
- Polygamy, allowed by Muslim clerics, is the retardation of human evolution, more closely linked to animal pack or herd behaviour—lesser animal species casually rut with females of their species with no long-term commitment. Polygamy has become illegal in most parts of the Western world because it is an example of gender apartheid and totally supports male control, the antithesis of equality. It is shocking sexism, it allows men to have numerous wives, but women are not allowed to have several husbands. Polygamy is seen as bigamy,[1] which is against the law in most countries. In addition, neuroscience and child clinicians have proved beyond doubt children, particularly male children, fare far better in stable monogamous marriages, or long-term de-facto relationships (see Essay 4). Even in situations where divorce has occurred and a second relationship has formed, it adds emotional stress to children. It is supported by males who are ruled by their genitals rather than their brains, who put self before long-term child welfare.

Psychology has a term for individuals who cannot graduate to love and long-term commitment from lust, they generally fall into the 'borderline personality disorder' (BPD) category.[2] Even in the first year of psychology at university, we learned that men or women who start professing and using terms of adoration in the first four weeks of a relationship are a 'red flag', often indicating the obsessive neediness of the borderline individual. Tragically, we now have TV shows like *Married at First Sight,* which should have a warning at the commencement of the show, 'This practise must be avoided in real life, as it does attract people who may be suffering from psychological borderline issues.'

Behaviour like this from humans indicates they have limited or damaged emotional development (EQ). Relationships can only survive if there is emotional development—polygamous men generally lack the ability to make deeper committed relationships. Cultures that encourage polygamy have remained more backward than those that have made monogamous relationships the law, largely because monogamy has a more positive impact on the intellectual and emotional development of children. Singapore, when it dramatically reduced population growth to virtually ZPG (zero population growth) levels, IQ levels moved to the some of the highest in the world.

The foundation of religious faith was to care for this world and all that is in it—to earn our place of 'eternal rest'. For a religious cult offshoot to treat half the population as second-rate citizens, supporting rapists, murderers, liars, child molesters and adulterous men (in the form of polygamous marriage) is disgraceful blasphemy. 'Hadith Islam' has, by force, made Muslims submissive to thousands of corrupt hadiths and has formed the terrorist armies, whom Allah has warned, will be cursed for eternity to slither on their bellies in dust.

Linking law with religions dominated by males, as in the case of Sharia law, has had horrific results. Sharia law is based on books of Sunnah, which (as mentioned in Essay 7) were tribal traditions, many of which Muhammad had fought against, as they included the subjugation of women, polygamy and the selling of young girls for wives. These inhumane traditions were reintroduced as false hadiths after the death of the prophet. These fabrications, the Sunnah books, are the false hadiths that Muhammad and the Quran (6: 111–113) reject as words of the 'jinn devils'.

Compulsion should play no part in religion as both the Bible and the Quran reject this form of dictatorial behaviour. To follow Sharia law built on fabrications, introduced by tribal men is to show contempt for God, Allah, the third prophet, Muhammad, and the rules of the Quran:

> Bible, 1 Peter 5:2, 'Shepherd the flock of God among you, exercising oversight not under compulsion, but voluntarily, according to the will of God; and not for sordid gain, but with eagerness.'[3]

> Quran 2:256, 'There is no compulsion in faith.'

In the Western world, the legal system does respect faith (the original *Ten Commandments* are the foundation of the legal system) but it is not controlled by religious clerics. Religion has always been an educational system, providing a moral compass—it was never supposed to be an institution of government or dictatorial rule. If 'hadith Islam' mullahs were successful in their teaching, their followers would not end up in the court system, or killers and rapists as part of grotesque terrorist groups. Dictatorial Sharia law is a bastardisation of the Abrahamic faith Muhammad tried to introduce and because it is so far removed from the Abrahamic faith, it should never be accepted in the Western world. It is basically the dictatorial control of women: they are treated as second rate individuals, with some misogynist Muslim men refusing to even shake a woman's hand.

No educational system, religious or academic, should ever be untouchable by civil law—it is too open to abuse. Male-dominated, communist countries that originally banned religions and Middle Eastern dictatorships that moulded religion to suit their male-dominant traditions, have reduced standards of life compared to democratic governments. In the free world, where educated women are included as equals in both religion and employment, there is far greater quality of life for men, women and children. People are not fleeing in the thousands from countries of the free world. Men and women of the Muslim faith must pull back the original value of equality and completely stop gender apartheid; they are not the rules of Allah, but the dictators that took over the rule of the Middle Eastern cultures after the prophet's death.

Muslims have not had religious freedom since 634 A.D. when apostasy was introduced two years after Muhammad's death. Religious clerics feeding deception are the sinners, but followers certainly should feel shame for allowing male domination and compulsion to continue, which is against the will of Allah and the prophets, who confirmed there must be no compulsion in faith. The prophets also warned that by listening to deceptive and manipulative individuals, hadith-corrupted mullahs and dictators who put themselves above God, would always destroy 'paradise'. Muslims are now witnessing the destruction of their villages and homes, their small gardens of Eden, by godless terrorists.

Apostasy was death if one dared to leave, or marry, outside of the religion. This has changed to long jail sentences in some countries ruled by Sharia law. Tribal leaders quickly reintroduced usury, which Muhammad had banned because they were excessive and unfair taxes creating financial disparity. They also returned to female subjugation, accepting paedophilia (because marrying children ensured their partners were virgins) and supported polygamist herd-animal relationships—these are rules of earthborn men, not Allah.

Polygamy and having numerous children are hadith rules, not the rules of Allah or his messenger. Muslims should be standing up for true Islam, not bending to the disgraceful fabrications introduced to faith by dictatorial tribal men. Remaining obedient to hadiths created by earthborn men is entirely sacrilegious and equates to paganism.

To support the reversal to pre-Islam traditions they had no wish to change, Sunni tribal men painted the third messenger as a sexual athlete and a paedophile, raping Aisha, a nine-year-old he took into care from six years of age. What they do not tell us is that, in an era of absolutely no forms of contraception, Muhammad had only two committed relationships that bore children, Khadija and Maria al-Qibtiyya, his second committed relationship, nearly a decade after Khadija's death.[4] Neither Aisha nor any of the widows had children in the many years they remained under Muhammad's care. The Sunni tribal men completely ignored he was monogamous entirely by choice and because of basic morality, for twenty-five years, until the death of his first wife. It has been recorded that he was in deep mourning for some years after Khadija's death.

The moral debasement of this good man by his tribal enemies, who aligned Muhammad's personal life with theirs, was outrageous—but they preferred to continue their immoral behaviour of taking child brides and practising polygamy with virgin brides. Islam, like Catholicism, has promoted complete lack of sexual control resulting in massive overpopulation, the most destructive environmental behaviour contributing massively to global warming. To claim that Muhammad, a messenger of God, would commit the crimes he was trying to reform and stop, is an indication of the psychopathic, dictatorial mindset of his enemies.

In western Sydney, cowardly veiled women—classic *Stockholm syndrome* females who are completely desensitised to normal social interaction (see Essay 7)—held a seminar to tell women that men are allowed to hit women.[5] They are now so brainwashed from years of oppression and subjugation that they think it is normal for women to be treated like lesser animal species. Thankfully, the evolved, free world of equality does not allow even dogs to be brutally hit these days. They had the audacity to lecture local Muslim women about how they should expect to endure a level of physical punishment at the hands of their husbands.

As followers of pathological deception fed to them by tribal clerics, these cowardly women said their husbands and their fathers are allowed to hit them if they step out of line. These foolish women have allowed themselves to be treated simply as property—vehicles for male sexual release and breeding machines to increase religious numbers. They are part of the reason 'hadith Islam' has moulded monstrous men: narcissistic, self-centred, godless men who demand complete control and intolerable domination.

These women should pull their heads out of their all-encompassing burqas and research the life of the amazing wife of Muhammad, Khadija, who was an educated, competent businesswoman, caring and strongly independent. While women were forced to cover themselves completely, by insecure, controlling men who were extremely possessive of their 'property', Khadija was an equal to men in the transport business she had inherited from her father and she did not cower behind sheets of fabric.

Khadija was a symbol of everything tribal men disliked in women.

She was also a widow and, therefore, seen as 'unclean'. This was the reason they virtually denied her existence, telling the world Muhammad was raping the nine-year-old Aisha, whom he had adopted from age six— as he had earlier adopted Khadija's first three daughters.[6] Even to this day, as shown in the Wikipedia site mentioned, Sunni still argues that Muhammad fathered all of Khadija's children, but their ages made a lie of that statement.

Deceitful religious clerics claim to this very day that his preferred wife was the child he had fostered, to save her from the horror her future life held when young girls were seen as worthless and sold simply as instruments for sexual use and abuse. They continue to spread horrific lies about raping this young girl he had taken into care from the age of nine. Aisha, his foster child, was never his preferred wife. Muhammad was a monogamous man and it is documented that he never really recovered from the death of Khadija, his wife of twenty-five years.

Muhammad and his wife Khadija, a successful career woman, fought as equals for the protection of women, particularly women who had been widowed and their female children who were seen as nothing but chattels to be sold to the highest bidder. Early tribal men saw women who had been married and widowed as 'unclean'. As Khadija had been twice widowed and had three children before she married Muhammad, tribal dictators (primarily members of the Sunni tribe) told outrageous lies to Islam followers, saying she was a virgin when she married the prophet and that all her children were the biological children of Muhammad. Khadija was forty years old when she married Muhammad, even in modern medicine older primigravida (women having their first baby over the age of thirty-five) have difficulties, for Khadija to have a further three children, making a total of six is monstrous deception.

When women lost their husbands in the many tribal battles that occurred, they and their children were often pushed onto the streets and employed in the filthiest of jobs, such as sweeping up animal manure from the streets. They were seen as only worthy of raping and were treated simply as sewers for the rapist's third body waste. Even in marriage, rape was acceptable and women were simply seen as vehicles for the bearing of male heirs.[7]

Muhammad had been orphaned at a young age, so to protect the children (as stated in Quran 4:3), he stipulated men may marry two to four mothers to ensure the protection of their children from this abuse. Unless the additional wives had orphans, i.e. fatherless children, men had to be content with one wife to avoid financial hardship.

Enemy tribal men had no intention of adopting monogamy and other men's children. To this day, 'hadith Islam' promotes that men can legally have up to four wives. There is no stipulation that they must only be women who have children and no means of support, as clearly stated in the Quran. These lust-driven men seek out virgins.

Burqas are a symptom of corrupt hadith rule, unrelated to faith. They are the most blatant proof of submission to tribal tradition and of women's fear of the controlling, tribal men that had subjugated them prior to 610 A.D., before Prophet Muhammad's conversion to the Abrahamic faith, and after his death in 632 A.D. These all-encompassing robes were not mentioned in the Quran, they were part of the thousands of fabrications added to the faith against the wishes of the prophet, Muhammad.[8-10] Male-dominated Sharia law is built on these fallacious hadiths and, consequently, the killing and vicious treatment of women who do not wear them, still occurs.

The burqa, masking the smile, makes a dangerous statement to the Western world: 'I am not your friend, infidel.' The burqa is the most concealing of all Islamic veils. It covers the face and body, leaving just a mesh screen to see through.[11] In Western cultures, covering the face and smile and having no eye contact when conversing with people is considered insulting. Many women continue wearing them because of fear of brutal repercussion from psychopathic men enslaved to the 'hadith Islam' cult offshoot.[12] Why should the world support this form of male control? Feminists should hang their heads in shame that they are supporting this form of dress, which has nothing to do with Muhammad's faith. It is supporting males who control women and generally lack sexual control. Followers of faith should read Quran 29:68, 'Who doeth greater wrong than he who inventeth a lie concerning Allah, or denieth the truth when it cometh unto him? Is not there a home in hell for disbelievers?'

My first experience of future foreboding was in 1974. I was travelling through France, by train, with a couple of other backpackers. We were heading down to the Costa del Sol and Monaco. There was a three-hour stopover in Paris, so I spent time soaking up the beauty and atmosphere of the city. I was waiting on a footpath, near the station, for my friends. It was late afternoon and the street was deserted. I was gazing up the street when an attractive, slim young French woman, with a laughing, small boy, caught my attention.

They stopped to look into the bay window of a patisserie. The little boy was smiling, pointing at the array of delicious cakes and pastries. He turned back to his mother, but his glance went beyond her, to further up the street. He cried out and hid his head in her skirt. My glance followed his up the street and I saw five faceless black shapes crossing the street to our side. At that time, Australia had never been exposed to this terrifying form of dress, the burqa, where the head and entire body are completely covered. They looked likes ghouls in a scene from some horror movie.

As kids, we would scare each other by throwing sheets over our heads and making ghostly sounds, but even in my late twenties, I shivered at the sight of those all-black menacing apparitions wafting towards us. As they were forms without faces, they looked so very tall. The mother knelt to console her little boy and shield him from the threatening and unfriendly forms. That moment, when innocent joy turned to such terror in the child, remains frozen in my mind, just like the tragedy of John Kennedy's assassination, or Princess Diana's death stays frozen in time. The burqa is not worn for religious belief: it is merely to promote male dominance in the world. It is the ethos of a cult intent on spreading terror to young and old. France subsequently banned the full-face covering, as the entire world should. It is an instance of tyrannical hadith rule, not the rule of God.

The practice of covering women from head to toe in sheets originated in Mesopotamia and is pre-Islam.[12] Mesopotamia has been identified as having 'inspired some of the most important developments in human history'. They developed a cursive script and a postal system using envelopes of clay; they developed a library system and constructed the masonry dam. Mathematically astute, they established that a circle could be divided into 360 units and used longitude and latitude. Babylonian astronomers discovered an 18.6-year cycle in the rising and setting of the moon: from this they created the first almanacs.[13] However, even as early as circa 3000 BC, the difference between the neighbouring sister-states of ancient Mesopotamia, Assyria and Babylonia revealed the difference between cultures ruled by more autocratic dictators (Assyria), and the state where the priesthood was the highest authority (Babylonia). Assyrians formed one of the most vicious and barbaric military dynasties, whereas Babylonians became merchants, doctors, scientists and agriculturalists, who planted the first cereal crops and used ploughs to harvest them.[14]

In Assyria, the status of women was deplorable. Assyrian men were harsh, violent, and cruel people, to enemies and their women.[15] With the conquests of the neighbouring lands, Assyria was flooded with an enormous number of slaves. The males were used for slave labour, while the females were used as concubines and domestic slaves. To be able to distinguish the free women from the slaves or concubines, laws were issued that forced them to wear a veil, while those who were considered unrespectable were forced to go with their heads uncovered.[16]

The veil became an exclusive symbol of respect, a privilege that slaves and women forced into prostitution were denied. If these women tried to hide their status by wearing a cloak, the clothing of a non-slave, to prevent street attacks and rape from the horrifically cruel men of that culture who lacked sexual control, they would be severely punished—in some cases sentenced to death.[17] These were cruel, bestial men who saw women as little better than animals. These men enforced veiling, and it is continued to this day, on the pretence that it is safer, by men following in the footsteps of the barbaric Assyrians. It is not safer: women encased in sheets do not cure men lacking in emotional development (EQ) and sexual control—rape has actually increased.[18&19]

Muslims worldwide are forced to believe corrupt clerics when they say that women are ordered to cover their face and hair. Yet, this command is not in the Quran. The verses that 'hadith Islamists' use to force women to cover themselves are hadith fabrications that overrule the Quran. These rules were made by the early deceptive 'jinn devils' that created the books of Sunnah. People of this culture, such as Ibn Warraq, who wrote *Why I Am Not a Muslim*, are, fortunately, beginning to recognise the corruption of the faith and removing themselves from the Sunni cult offshoot.[20] However, as protestants removed themselves from the corrupt rules introduced by the Catholic branch to start Protestant branches of faith, to ensure the monotheist Christian faith survived, so should these people commence 'protestant' branches of Islam, to ensure the original values Muhammad introduced, are restored.

Veiling is only the beginning of the process of abuse towards women in the Muslim world. Beating a wife is encouraged by illegal hadith fabrications, where it states that it is forbidden to interfere with a husband beating his wife—even if he beats her to death.[21] The full-body covering of the burqa has been proven to increase bad behaviour by psychopathic males, who are perpetually in denial and refuse to be accountable.[22] The men need to be assessed and treated for this serious mental disorder and forced to take responsibility for their cowardness.

Sunni 'hadith Islam' has allowed men to revert to the barbarianism of the early bestial Assyrians. Psychopaths within the Egyptian Muslim Brotherhood gave men permission to rape unveiled women.[23] The books by Cheri Berens, *An American woman living in Egypt: Life during an Islamic takeover*, and Ibn Warraq, *Why I Am Not a Muslim*, are very informative, revealing the downward spiral resulting from dictatorial Sunni control. While both are courageous books, in the foreword of Warraq's book, R. Joseph Hoffmann, wrote, 'Few books about religion deserve the attribution "courageous". This book, I am pleased to report, does. It is courageous because it is (as the term originally denoted) full of heart *(*coeur*)* and courageous because it is an act of intellectual honesty and bravery, an act of faith rather than of faithlessness.'

Veiling seems to have worked in reverse, as these monsters found veiling made females more tempting. Now women have to be constantly chaperoned for protection against these horrific predators. The male insistence on these all-encompassing robes in modern times broadcasts to the world that these men have not moved on from the uncivilised and brutish behaviour of times prior to the teachings of the prophet, Muhammad.

In March 2002, in the Muslim holy city of Mecca, fifteen teenage girls perished in a fire at their school when the Saudi religious police, the *mutaween*, would not let them out of the building. In the female-only school environment, the girls had removed the all-concealing burqas that Saudi women must wear. They had not put these robes back on before trying to flee from the fire. The godless *mutaween* preferred that they die rather than transgress their politically corrupt, man-made 'hadith Islamic' laws. These brainwashed men even fought against brave police and firemen who were trying to open the school doors to save the girls.[24] Because of such religious corruption across the Muslim world, women endure restrictions on their movements, their marital options, their professional opportunities and much more.

The burqa is the visual proof of the 'hadith Islam' contempt for all that Muhammad attempted to change. Arab conquerors, invading those countries where rape was common, were forced to adopt this dress code for their wives, for safety as well as status. It had nothing to do with religion: it is more of a reflection of devolution than evolution. Instead of moving on and teaching men, from childhood, to respect women and treat them as equals, we now see some corrupt, despotic religious leaders guaranteeing purgatory for their black souls by encouraging men to rape women for not wearing the burqa. Reverting to this barbarism, practised prior to the birth of the last great prophet, is almost beyond human comprehension.

Khadija, the wife of Muhammad, did not wear a burqa or mask: after all, the only rule in the Quran is to dress modestly. It was never suggested that women should be completely covered from head to toe, effectively shutting them off from society. This obsessive behaviour can be traits of the psychopathic or the sociopathic persona, as these individuals need complete control. A sad fact, which has been revealed from women's shelters across the world, is that far too often this offensive clothing masks the domestic violence inflicted by men on their wives.[25-26] Bruised and battered bodies can be hidden behind those dreadful burqas, effectively masking men's inhumanity towards women.

Sunni 'hadith Islam' and Sharia law allows this treatment, hence, vicious Muslim men with psychopathic tendencies can punch female faces and blacken the eyes with complete freedom, as these women are totally masked in public by the burqa.

Insidious hadith rules made by earthborn men have isolated Islamic women. Even in modern times sociopathic and psychopathic men, and occasionally women, will isolate their partners by separating them from family and shutting out their friends, making them more vulnerable and dependent on their partner.[27-29] This narcissistic need for sole and undivided attention often leads to domestic violence and can result in psychopathic personas inflicting psychological as well as physical harm on their partners.[30]

God expects more of women than to be simply vehicles for breeding, which male-dominated religions demand, to build their power and control. He expects bravery. Men and women should stand united, as Khadija did with her partner, and break away from 'hadith Islam' fabrications introduced by egocentric caliphates. This narrow-minded view of women is an insult to true Islam, the third Abrahamic faith, and shows complete contempt for both the rules of Allah and the third prophet.

The *True Islam* site confirms the contempt shown for the words of the Quran by dictatorial tribal men who have created the sacrilegious religious offshoot, 'hadith Islam', based on thousands of fake hadiths.[31-33] The *History of Hadith* article gives examples of the corruption of those early fabrications.[34] There are no words in the Quran which command women to cover their entire bodies—that is a man-made rule made by autocrats supporting female subjugation. In spurious books of Sunnah, 'hadith Islam' clerics have twisted the words in the Quran 24:31 and 33:59 to justify this falsehood.

The face and the smile are parts of the body that are necessary to reveal, as the smile separates friend from foe. Quran 24:31 says women should 'guard their private parts' and 'cover their cleavage', it does not mention covering their heads. Although the Quran 33:59 states believers should lower their garments, precise details were not given. The exact amount of lowering was for the women themselves to decide, as long as righteousness was maintained—to have hems dragging in the dust below their feet was a male decision, not God's:

> Quran 33:59, 'O you prophet, tell your wives and your daughters and the women of the believers to lower their garments. This is better so that they will be recognised and not harmed. God is Forgiver, Merciful.' [35&36]

Women who continue to follow false hadiths are not only in contempt of the third prophet, they are behaving in exactly the same manner as Eve in that symbolic *Garden of Eden* parable, told by the first prophet, Moses. They have listened and trusted, as Eve did, to the deceptive serpents, men who have twisted God's word to gain control of this small Eden we call Earth. However, those deceptive serpents have been warned of their final destiny: they will be 'cursed above all cattle, and above all wild animals', and 'upon their bellies' they will go, and 'dust' they shall eat for eternity (Genesis 3:14).[37]

All three Abrahamic religions (Judaism, Christianity and Islam) support that both men and women dress modestly. The symbolic parable in the first book of the Bible described how the occupants, Adam and Eve, decided to cover themselves when the evil creature that mingled with them (the serpent), was exposed. Quran 7:26 aligns with the biblical *Garden of Eden* parable, where humans were warned of the need to wear modest clothing, as there will always be evil snakes who will take advantage of the vulnerable and then blame them for their pathetic weakness:

> Quran7:26, 'O children of Adam, we have provided you with garments to cover your bodies, as well as for luxury. But the best garment is the garment of righteousness. These are some of GOD's signs, that they may take heed.'[38]

In all faiths, God's laws expect men and women to be moral and modest. While Islamic headscarves can be very beautiful, only emotionally bankrupt men would order women to cover their entire head and body with sheets. This has never been for religious reasons. The contempt for the value of women has moulded men who have an extreme lack of sexual control. Sharia law still blames women when rape occurs: raped women are whipped and jailed in some Muslim 'hadith Islam' countries. The perpetrators are not men of God, they have been moulded into a bestial psychopathic sub-set of humanity.

The misogynist male-dominated Sharia law blames women for rape, simply for being women and thus the cause of this temptation. It appears weakness, at being unable to control the urge to rape the female gender if they catch even a glimpse of their face, hair or body, has allowed Muslim cultures to force women to wear all-encompassing burqas. This is not a rule of Allah or the Quran; it is a rule instituted by seriously mentally skewed men. Men who can twist the blame of their own lack of sexual control onto women are virtually admitting they are little better than animals 'in heat'—and that is the world of the less evolved human subset of psychopathy.

Innocent women should not be imprisoned in this unsociable garb—it is the bestial men, no better than rutting animals, that should be in prison, or castrated, so they cannot continue to harm women.[39-41] Why do governments allow a culture that practises blatant female oppression and shocking gender-apartheid to continue these practises when they move to democratic countries? This behaviour is in contempt of the teachings of Muhammad. Muhammad, with his much-loved wife Khadija, who was a very successful career woman, tried to protect women and improve conditions for orphaned female children who were abysmally treated by many tribal men of that era.[42&43] Disregard for females has retarded evolution and intellectual advancement in all cultures where patriarchy is practised.

Where are the brave women of our past, who were prepared to go to prison to get equality? Presumably, feminists still prefer to cower behind that impenetrable wall of 'political correctness'. Phyllis Chesler, a Professor of psychology and women's studies and an American once married to a Muslim, is a strong advocate for the plight of women in the Middle East. Her book, *The death of feminism*,[44] is a brilliant critique of the feminist left's shameful neglect of the problems of 'sisters' outside of their personal world. As I was a supporter of Women's

Liberation in about the same era as her activist journey, I was surprised that she supported feminism. Of all three major female activist groups (Suffragettes, Women's Liberation and Feminists), it was feminism that seemed to be most self-serving. Feminism focused on the teacup world of domesticity and self, they seemed the least courageous—cowering behind the impenetrable wall of political correctness.

The feminist movement, originally created by married women with children, restricted their concerns to the more traditional roles of marital life and protection for their children. Women driven by their ovaries, needing children to make their lives complete, had divorced themselves from the brave Suffragettes and Women's Liberation movement. The latter, my preferred group, were possibly considered less feminine as we pursued careers, rather than marriage and dependence on men. The successful Women's Liberation group were women who fought for change in world attitudes, wanting equality and freedom from the societal and church indoctrination of male dependence and the life-sentence of parenting.

Unmarried 'liberationists' frequently gained greater work equality, it was only half a century later, in 2019, when feminists had to start the 'Me Too' movement to gain ground. This far less courageous and confrontational group was still struggling to reach that status. Even the hash-tag has rather a herd-following-the-leader ring to it, a term more demeaning than demanding. 'I am here—hear me roar' was the more aggressive mantra of earlier freedom fighters.

As a single career woman who really enjoyed working with my amusing male colleagues, I found the world of feminism—where many women seemed to genuinely dislike men—rather offensive. The appallingly sexist title alienates the male gender, something which also made me feel very uncomfortable. I much preferred to be a 'liberationist', representing a wider interest in world events than being linked with some gender-specific group. Chesler's book is an incredibly powerful book and should be a must-read for brave young women of the future. However, authoritative women of the future, and males that support them, should find a better, non-sexist title. Currently, men who support this cause have to use the emasculating term of feminist. This does suggest misandry, which is as bad as misogyny.

Chesler's book adds to the list of horrific crimes against women by psychopathic male Muslims to which some feminists turn a blind eye. In Tehran, in 2002, a father cut off his seven-year-old daughter's head after suspecting an uncle had raped her. How could siblings and others accept that the father's motive was to defend his honour, dignity, and name? That particular sub-human, totally devoid of conscience and empathy (C&E), had no honour, dignity, or honourable name to preserve: it was totally blackened by the paedophile uncle and his own behaviour. He was the 'spawn of Satan'—spitting in the face of Allah.

Debasing women, encouraging rape, and discouraging respect for the female gender by treating them as second-class citizens are powerful key elements for developing psychopathic personas. Males that have been raised in a world that shows contempt for women cannot fail to tick most, if not all, of the boxes of psychopathy.[45] Even banning women from praying with men as equals in the houses of God reveals horrendous male hubris and self-importance. This was not the behaviour of Muhammad and his wife Khadija, and was certainly not God's rule as defined in the Quran. It is the rule of men who have placed tribal tradition above, or equal to, Scripture; the sin of *Shirk*.[46]

Through apathy in the Muslim culture and the world, we now have the 'psychopaths running the asylum'. The good and honest members of the Islamic faith, particularly females, should stand against the 'infidels' within their midst and reclaim true Islam. Religions, not God, are suppressing the female gender. Promoting and preaching inequality in any form, continued gender bias, and supporting financial disparity have historically been the gangrenous rot of civilisation.

Tragically, when you subjugate women, men with a depraved sense of superiority are formed and brainwashed to believe that all females are just slabs of meat, commodities to be used and abused for personal pleasure. There are no bounds to the depravity of these rapists and murderers, whose corrupted religion has allowed them to treat women as second-class citizens.

India is rapidly transforming from a Hindu country to an Islamic country. In October 2015, a mother wrote about the rapes of two young girls in Delhi.[47] One was a five-year-old, the other barely two and a half years old—still too small to even be in a room alone. The man that assaulted them were either a 'Bhaiya' (brother) or an uncle. The week before, there had been yet another rape of a minor, a four-year-old. The esteemed religious leaders could not use the excuse that these females were roaming around at night after curfew, or that they were provocatively dressed, they were far too young.

In 2017, five years after Jyoti Singh died after being gang raped, nothing had changed,[48] as a 7-year-old girl, and two days later an eighteen-month-old girl, was gang-raped in the same city. Both girls needed surgery as a result of the attacks. In January 2018, an eight-month-old baby girl was raped, allegedly by her cousin, also in the Indian capital.[49] The Delhi Commission for Women, led by Chief Swati Maliwal, who visited the baby girl, described her injuries as 'horrific'. The baby underwent a three-hour operation and her cries could be heard throughout the hospital. A year earlier an eleven-month-old baby was raped for two hours by a 36-year-old construction worker in the locality of Vikaspuri in west Delhi. The baby was later found in an unconscious state bleeding profusely.[50] According to the latest National Crime Records Bureau data, 2016 saw 19,765 cases of child rape being registered in India – a rise of 82 per cent from 2015 when 10,854 cases were recorded. At least three cases of rape took place every day in the national capital.[51&52] When women are devalued, rape reaches horrific levels.[53&54]

Full castration for serial paedophiles (which actually improves long-term health and longevity), should be performed on these offenders to ensure their toxic genes do not spread to future generations. Male serial offenders have lost the right to be part of the male gender and should complete their lives as eunuchs—a constant reminder of their failure to behave as responsible humans.

The term 'honour killing' is a grotesque oxymoron. This godless form of killing was started by barbaric and cruel men who treated women as worse than animals. There is a strong chance MRI scans of these offenders would pick up a complete lack of activity in the area of the brain where emotions should be registering: scans would show a colourless void, where there should be vibrant colour.

A 'religion of peace'? Why Christianity is and Islam isn't, by Robert

Spencer[55] and *The violent oppression of women in Islam,* by Spencer and Phyllis Chesler[56] are must-read articles that reveal the insanity and grotesque brutality moulded by male-dominated religious corruption and cultural inbreeding. In this section I have used numerous quotes from Spencer and Chesler's report for readers who may not have internet access, however, it is an excellent report and should be read in full. It should be noted that in 2003 even the parliament of relatively moderate Jordan voted down a provision designed to stiffen penalties for honour killings. According to *Al-Jazeera,* Islamists and conservatives said false hadith laws violated religious traditions and would destroy families and values. There are no family values in 'hadith Islam', because there is no equality. It is a blatant transgression of Muhammad's 'religion of peace' as described in his famous last sermon and as written in the Quran (6: 111–113), he banned all false hadiths (laws) added by tribal leaders. Muhammad worked to change female subjugation and give women equality, as his wife Khadija had enjoyed—barbarous tribal leaders were never going to accept such a loss of control.

Sharia law reintroduced many barbaric tribal traditions. Many of the laws violate, in the most sacrilegious manner, the values of faith introduced by the three major messengers. If Allah never forgave the deceptive serpent in the Garden of Eden parable, then the bestial subset of humanity that commit or support honour killings will be the rotting souls that pave the path to hell.

As reported in the *Chicago Tribune,* on 31 May 1994, 16-year-old, Kifaya Husayn, a Jordanian girl, was lashed to a chair by her 32-year-old brother. He gave her a drink of water and told her to recite an Islamic prayer. Then he slashed her throat. Immediately afterward, he ran out into the street, waving the bloody knife and crying, 'I have killed my sister to cleanse my honour.'[57]

You may ask what Kifaya's crime was; she was raped by another brother, a twenty-one-year-old. Her judge and jury were her own uncles, mentally skewed old men who convinced her eldest brother that Kifaya was too much of a disgrace to the family honour to be allowed to live. The court that prosecuted Kifaya's brother showed how little they valued her life—he was given fifteen years in prison, which was later reduced to seven. This male should have been castrated, so he could not breed upon his release and continue to pass on the potential psychopathic genome; males like this are no longer worthy to call themselves men.

These psychopaths are an offence to civilisation, and they have been created by corrupt religious beliefs.[58] Such corruption of faith, as Muhammad warned, has destroyed the integrity of Islam. Their support of rape makes it appear they put the worship of sex well above the support of Allah. The existence of such objectionable males confirm there is a satanic force every bit as bad as all the dire warnings in the Holy Scriptures and the Quran.

In September 2003, *Time* magazine reported that in Iraq, 17-year-old Ali Jasib Mushiji shot his mother and half-brother because he suspected them of having an affair, and killed his four-year-old sister because he thought she was their child.[61] Sitting in a jail cell in a Baghdad slum, he said he wiped out his family 'to cleanse its shame.' These cultures must start directing their children towards studies in the field of neuroscience and build psychopathic clinics for research and analysis of these mentally skewed individuals.[59]

The same report also recounted that Qadisiyah Misad, sixteen, ran away from her family's home on the outskirts of Baghdad. Within days, one of her brothers and a cousin tracked her down on a city street and hauled her back home. According to Essam Wafik al-Jadr, the judge who prosecuted the case, one of Misad's brothers cornered his teenage sister in the living room, drew a pistol and shot several bullets into her. 'The parents requested that the brothers kill her,' says al-Jadr, who learned of the killing when Misad's body turned up in Baghdad's city morgue. He decided to prosecute the brother for an honour killing. The punishment hardly fitted the crime; Misad's brother received a year in jail, and (when interviewed for the article less than a year after the event) al-Jadr was not even certain he was still incarcerated, since he was eligible for parole within a few months of his conviction.

The report also told of a Baghdad coroner who reported the death of Mouna Adnan Habib, thirty-two, a mother of two who had been delivered to the city morgue with five bullets in her chest. Habib's left hand had been cut off—a practice common in family honour murders, in which men amputate the woman's left hand or index finger to display as proof to tribal leaders and relatives that the deed has been done. In Habib's case, relatives suspected her of having an affair. 'They saw her talking to a man a few times,' said al-Jadr, whose staff investigated the case. Local police told al-Jadr that they believe Mouna Habib was killed by her nephew, rather than her husband, but that the nephew had disappeared.

What part of the body do adulterous males have amputated? It should be the penis, if they truly lived by the literal, rather than the symbolic, meaning of an 'eye for an eye'. Family men, who through cancer have lost testicles, have commented on the close relationship of love and affection that continues with their partners—when their brain is no longer ruled by this organ.

In 2005, in Gaza, five masked members of Hamas shot Yusra Azzumi, a 20-year-old Palestinian woman to death, brutalised her corpse, and savagely beat both her brother, Rami, and her fiancé, Ziad Zaranda, whom she was to marry within days. This self-appointed Morality Squad wrongly suspected Yusra (herself a Hamas member) of immoral behaviour. A Palestinian Arab girl, Rofayda Qaoud, became pregnant in 2003 after her brothers raped her. Her mother then demanded she kill herself. Tragically, this evil woman killed her daughter when the innocent, assaulted girl refused. According to a news report, armed with a plastic bag, razor and wooden stick, this odious woman entered her sleeping daughter's room. 'Tonight, you die, Rofayda,' she told the girl, before wrapping the bag tightly around her head. Next, Qaoud sliced Rofayda's wrists, ignoring her muffled pleas of 'No, mother, no!' After her daughter went limp, Qaoud struck her in the head with the stick. Killing her sixth-born child took twenty minutes, Qaoud told a visitor through a stream of crocodile tears and cigarettes that she smoked in rapid succession. 'She killed me before I killed her,' said the 43-year-old mother of nine. 'I had to protect my children. This is the only way I could protect my family's honour.' This woman was seriously mentally damaged by inhumane cultural brainwashing.

Along with other violent and oppressive practices directed at

Muslim women, honour killings have migrated to the West. On 8 January 1999 in Cleveland, Ohio, a Palestinian woman, Methel Dayem, was murdered by two male cousins in what prosecutors termed an honour killing. Her crime? She had refused to marry a first cousin, insisted on attending college, drove her own car, and was deemed 'too independent'. The fact that the prosecution used the term honour killing led the Muslim community to attack the prosecution as 'inflammatory', 'anti-Arab' and 'anti-Islamic'—which in turn led to a bench trial, not a trial by jury. Despite enormous circumstantial evidence, the judge did not find that the prosecution proved its case beyond a reasonable doubt.

The anti-social males (i.e. sociopaths and psychopaths) corrupting faith with these actions have no morals—they are extremely adulterous (polygamous, taking numerous virgin wives), yet any independent action taken by an Arab or Muslim girl or woman is perceived as intrinsically sexual, immoral and dishonourable. Hence, if she wants to attend college, refuses to marry a first cousin, chooses a love match, tries to elope, leave her religion or convert to another religion, she runs the risk of being murdered in a most vicious way by woman-hating, male faux-religious psychopaths—males who obviously have seriously under-developed grey and/or white matter within the brain temporal zones.[63]

How can this community defend their dreadfully corrupted religion? What other culture would even consider this foul behaviour as honourable? It is unbelievably sexist, but as Muslim women are so oppressed, do they really fully comprehend the term 'sexism'? If they really want to prove to the world that this godless, inhumane treatment is not part of their lifestyle, they must make radical change—or live with the contempt they will receive from the Western world for allowing such barbarism. Do these religious clerics really think we are like their enslaved followers: deaf, dumb and blind to female abuse?

In September 2006, in Ottawa, a young woman, Khatera Sadiqi, was shot dead at a shopping mall. Her fiancé, Feroz Mangal, was shot by the same gun and was in a coma. Police announced that her brother, Hasibullah Sadiqi, was their prime suspect. Mangal's father explained that he wasn't happy because they were engaged. In March 2006 in

Birmingham, England, two young men set fire to a house. They did so because the sister of one of them, a 15-year-old girl named Meherun Khanum, was dating a young man named Abdul Hamid, and her brother did not approve. Those who were in the house got out through windows, except for Abdul Hamid's six-year-old sister, Alisha, who was severely burned and died shortly after. The young Muslim men who were involved in the attack fled to Bangladesh, where they would not be held accountable.

On 7 February 2005, Hatin Surucu made her way to a bus stop in the main Oberlandgarten Strasse in Berlin. Minutes later, a volley of pistol shots hit her. She died choking on her blood. A bus driver discovered the body and called the police. Hatin's three brothers, aged eighteen to twenty-five, were arrested and formally charged with the murder. They pleaded not guilty. At the time of the report, they were still awaiting trial. However, it is important to note that in a Berlin high school class discussion about her murder, teenage Turkish male students said that Hatin 'had only herself to blame' and that she 'deserved what she got—the whore lived like a German.'

These males are some of the most godless, immoral and disgraceful 'whores', rutting with anything and everything, raping without guilt or concern. Yet innocent women are frequently killed, because of the vile actions and lies, told by these godless men. A petition signed by two million people worldwide stopped the flogging of a 15-year-old rape victim in the Maldives. She was repeatedly raped by her own stepfather and had been sentenced to 100 lashes for 'fornication'. The authorities claimed she was being punished accordingly for having consensual pre-marital sex with a man, a punishable offense under the Islamic Sharia laws practiced in the country. The obscene injustice was that the man she supposedly had sexual relations with, was not identified or charged by the authorities. In fact, in 90 per cent of those flogged for fornication in Maldives are women and underage girls who have been potentially abused or raped, while men enjoy a culture of impunity. Fortunately, her sentence was quashed![60]

In March 2007, a 19-year-old Saudi woman received a sentence of ninety lashes. Her crime was that a man threatened to tell her father that they were having an affair unless she met him alone. When she did, she was kidnapped and repeatedly raped, after which her brother beat her because the rapes brought shame to the family. Rather than giving her justice, a Saudi court sentenced her to be lashed ninety times more because she had met a man alone who was not related to her.

This was far from an isolated case. In 2004, a 16-year-old girl, Atefeh Rajabi, was hanged in a public square in Iran.[61] Rajabi was charged with adultery, which generally means she was raped. Her rapist was not executed. Atefeh told the mullah-judge, Haji Rezaii, that he ought to punish men who rape, not their victims. The judge both sentenced and personally hanged Atefeh because, in addition to her crime, he said that she had a 'sharp tongue'. This is the human excrement that often fills the judiciary systems of these cultures, enslaved to autocratic 'hadith Islam' rule and dominated by Sharia law. The judge should have been stripped of his position and placed in a psychiatric clinic until his brain development was reactivated and once again aligned with that of mentally healthy men and women.

Time magazine reported in 2004 that in Iraq, a 16-year-old girl named Rana was raped by her neighbour in the city of Nasiriyah, and when her family discovered that she was no longer a virgin, her brother decided to kill her. A cousin who was aware of the plan took Rana to a nearby Italian military base; she was later moved to Baghdad and finally to a secret location farther north. Having fled her family, she is unlikely ever to return home.

Several recent high-profile cases in Nigeria have also revolved around rape accusations being transformed by Islamic authorities into charges of fornication. A 17-year-old Nigerian girl named Bariya Ibrahim Magazu was sentenced to 100 lashes for fornication after she was discovered to be pregnant. She accused one of the several men who had gang-raped her as possibly being the father; when they all denied having had relations with her, she received an additional eighty lashes for bearing false witness.

Corrupt Sharia law restricts the validity of a woman's testimony, particularly in cases involving sexual immorality. Islamic legal theorists have limited it even farther, in the words of one Muslim legal manual, to 'cases involving property, or transactions dealing with property, such as sales.' In other religion-driven judicial areas, only men can testify; they do not have the secular laws of the Western world, which are separated from corrupted religious ideology. It is virtually impossible, therefore, to prove rape in cultures that follow Sharia law. If the required male witnesses cannot be found to exonerate her (i.e. four men who testify to seeing the actual crime), the victim's charge of rape can become an admission of adultery. That accounts for the grim fact that as many as 75 per cent of the women in prison in Pakistan are, in fact, behind bars for the crime of having been raped.[62]

How can these men have the audacity to compare themselves as equals in a world that has moved far beyond the backward and misogynist lifestyle of tribal, emotionally stunted barbarians? Until they can wipe out this shocking behaviour, governments of the world should separate followers of 'hadith Islam' and Sharia law from Muslim dissidents, men and women who do have C&E (conscience and empathy) and who try to follow the original Quran Islam faith. 'Hadith Islam' is the tyrannical law of dictators, not faith in Allah. It is a complete violation of almost everything that was true Islamic faith, which followed the path of the two earlier Abrahamic faiths, Judaism and Christianity.

The contempt in which corrupt men hold Muhammad and his original Quranic faith is so shocking it is almost unfathomable. Female genital mutilation, daughter and wife-beating, child and arranged marriage, polygamy, *purdah* (female seclusion and segregation), easy divorce for men, female sexual and domestic slavery, veiling, routine rape, gang rape and honour killing have absolutely no connection to true Islam, or to the world. They are entirely the construct of misogynist men with the psychopathic genome that should have been bred out of the culture centuries ago by true faith and by making first-cousin marriages illegal, rather than preferable.

The article by Spencer and Chesler, *The violent oppression of women in Islam*, tells of an obviously mentally skewed 'hadith Islam' scholar, al-Rafihi, who was quoted as saying, 'If I came across a rape crime—kidnap and violation of honour—I would discipline the man and order that the woman be arrested and jailed for life.' This man (an Australian 'hadith

Islam' mufti), said women were 'weapons' used by 'Satan' to control men. He said adultery is the fault of women 90 per cent of the time. Why? This unevolved, sexist man's reply was, 'Because she possesses the weapon of enticement (*igraa*)'. This statement is further proof that 'hadith Islam' moulds psychopathic personas. Of course, he re-worded it for the media the following day, but this is the language of clerics of the 'hadith Islam' cult offshoot when they are in segregated rooms in the mosques, speaking to men only.

Fortunately, unlike 'hadith Islam', men of other religions are not so weak and can generally control their sexual urges. They also have criminal law that is separate from bogus religious laws: secular law, which protects women from such mentally skewed men. After such a comment, Hilali should have been arrested and placed in jail for a term for excusing this bestial behaviour towards women. Men who think like this should not be walking amongst us, after release from prison they should be assessed and put under treatment in clinics specialising in psychopathic research. He should have been tested for psychopathy, and if the test proved a lack of C&E, then transferred to a psychiatric clinic because, to date, psychopathy is incurable.[63] Psychopathy has a genetic link and to date DNA, in an individual after birth, cannot be altered.[64] Good Muslims must show more bravery because it is men like this that have brutalised them and caused them to flee from their homes to distant places.

The three major prophets risked their lives trying to spread moral integrity, but the subjugation of men and women, with cultural or gender apartheid, indicates evil still exists amongst us. If men and women do not fight for equality, it allows evil to prevail. The Catholic religion and 'hadith Islam' are both guilty of applying rules of compulsion, seen as a sin in the holy books of the three Abrahamic faiths. It is predominately from these religions that horrific crimes have flourished.

The current form of Islam, 'hadith Islam', is a corruption of faith. Dictators have moulded Muhammad's faith to suit their own preferences. Unfortunately, dictators rule by fear, and if followers dare to break away and restore the original Islamic faith, death or imprisonment follow. When Muslims come to free countries, they should have the courage to abandon such corruption and allow equality between men and women. Governments should not allow inequality to continue in places of worship and in their personal lives. If Muslims are not prepared to follow our secular law, they are free to return to cultures where this enslavement continues.

Good men and women of the world should unite and demand something similar to the Nuremberg trials, which were held to prosecute prominent Nazi criminals, monstrous psychopathic killers and torturers of Jewish people. The cruel and murderous followers of 'hadith Islam' and members of the Sharia legal system who support honour killings and the oppression of the female gender, have committed (and continue to commit daily) the same crimes against women and humanity. Treating women as second-class citizens, often with barbarous brutality, is as heinous as the Nazi holocaust. These men must be held accountable by the world and incarcerated in appropriate psychiatric institutions so they can never again target the female gender, the elderly, children and innocent animals.

Cultures that persist in male domination and the repression of the female gender will continue to mould monsters. Deceptive religious clerics that support this autocratic tyranny have shown the world how the corruption of religion can degrade civilisation and invite apocalyptic disaster to society. Men and women of the world, governments and Muslim immigrants that escape this oppression, must fight against this degradation of the original Islamic faith. Gender apartheid must not be allowed in the free world.

Feminists bow your heads in shame when we have young people like Ayla Ozturk who started this petition for the US and Turkish Governments, 'Turkish women are being killed every single day. In Turkey it's a full on femicide. In America, Turkish women are being abused, killed, and sexualized. I am a 14-year-old Turkish woman and I am scared for my life. Sign if you have a heart. We need this to stop. We need to put laws in place. If you supported Black Lives Matter, you should support this. If you don't, then you can't call yourself a good person.'

~ 9 ~

Should faith and science be adversaries: Where do we go from here?

'Isn't it time we asked ourselves, are we willing to accept any behaviour codified within religious or cultural practice? If honour killings are okay, then why not virgin sacrifices, or cannibalism, or sex with children outside the church? We have perversely taken our notion of tolerance to such extremes that we've become tolerant of intolerance.'
— **Bill Maher**

Sunni 'hadith Islam' mocks faith in Allah by breaking the basic Holy Commandments. Terrorists, and the corrupt clerics that mould them, are proving they are oblivious of the fact that religion was introduced to make humans more civilised. Individuals raised in harsh, unloving early environments are robbed of the full development of grey and white brain matter, which stunts the emotional development of C&E, the two traits that divide non-psychopaths from psychopathic personas.[1&2]

If people of faith believe this earth has a spiritual Creator, the Creator's greatest enemies are the foot soldiers of sin, evil men that support destruction of God's greatest gift to humanity—this Garden of Eden we call Earth. The 'scorched earth' policy of 'hadith Islam' terrorists is spitting in the face of Allah. The smashing and burning of all they conquer is creating environmental and health havoc in Mosul and other cities and countries these godless psychopaths invade. Environmental pollution has added 'complexity and danger' to the humanitarian crisis sparked by the military offensive in Mosul, fumes from burning stockpiles of sulphur dioxide and oil wells that had been set ablaze, led to further physical illness and suffering for civilians.[3]

Terrorists that destroy God's gifts are seriously mentally skewed if they think they will ever reach a place of eternal rest for showing such treachery. Humans have been given the responsibility to care for this planet to earn that place of golden light and timeless rest. Where in the Quran does it promise that trashing God's Eden, and killing and raping other humans, God's children, will bring rewards?

The prophet Jesus (described as an apostle in the Bible, Hebrews 3:1) and his twelve loyal disciples were the foundation of the Christian faith. Apostolic succession was in relation to these chosen loyal disciples who continued to spread the word of God. However, apostolic succession did not automatically follow down from the messengers and the disciples. It did not apply specifically to Catholic priests: forgiving sins and keeping them secret was not part of religious education, hence, 'confessionals' became an illegal ritual created by this branch of Christianity and it has caused immense damage in the civilised world.

Apostolic succession was also not passed down to Muslim tribal leaders who were promoted as successors of Muhammad after his death. On the presumption it did, dictatorial tribal leaders rewrote the Quranic religious laws, in books of Sunnah, which bore little relevance to Muhammad's original Quran. The dictatorial brain registers only anaemic levels of C&E, Dr Hare's research has revealed narcissism, manipulation and control, the primary traits of dictators, are all characteristics of the psychopathic persona.

Muhammad bravely followed in the footsteps of the two prophets before him. However, with the introduction of the apostasy rule, bestial tribal men protected themselves by murderous brute force from the same fatal outcomes that the brave earlier disciples of faith suffered. The men of God preached peace and love, not the hatred and slaughter now fuelled by ruthless 'hadith Islam' clerics and tribal leaders. This is more related to behaviour of men of the antichrist.

Faith, with its simple role of introducing a moral compass to a more barbarous world of tribal domination, has been almost submerged in the religious world created by men. So many cults and religions have strayed so far from the simple Abrahamic faith, they are virtually back in the early eras of male tribal control, which had stimulated three brave men to make change in this world. These cults have become massive money-making industries, exploiting the tax-exempt loophole, which has made their leaders millionaires and has placed the book value for their faux-faith institutions in the billionaire status. Government, by placing religions completely above the law, has made organised religion extremely attractive to sinister conmen: white-collar psychopaths, who flourish in this vulnerable world of trust. They have slithered into the upper echelons and moulded their cult offshoots around their personal choices, creating farce not faith.

For centuries, competitive, egocentric males have corrupted monotheist faith and its simple commandments. The enigmatic spiritual force we accept as God has no religion. Religion was entirely the creation of males after the deaths of the prophets. Many were well intentioned, but others sought personal adulation—these were the serpents in religious robes. They are far removed from the original simple values of GOD (Goodness, Order and Decency). Showing respect for a spiritual presence, obeying a few simple commandments and teaching goodness and emotional development (EQ) were the duties of religious clerics. That should have been the basic agenda of all religions. However, it is an insult to align many of the current cult offshoots, generally male-driven, with faith.

The Catholic Church failed its followers immensely by allowing psychopathic paedophiles to merge invisibly into their celibate male numbers, virtually unnoticed. Islam, in the same manner, has allowed extremist clerics to slither into positions of power and to mould men into monsters. Yet the world ignores a religion that has allowed egocentric tribal leaders to add thousands of irreverent and barbarous tribal traditions to that faith—rules that now permit rape within marriage, paedophilia, religious enslavement and the subjugation of women.

The world cannot start healing until this corrupted form of the Islamic religion, 'hadith Islam', is returned to the original intent of 'submission' (Islam) to God's word, away from 'submission' to false witness—i.e. enslavement to false hadiths and books of Sunnah. There must be change away from dictatorial segregation and gender apartheid, back to equality and true community.

Brave people dared to break away from the corruption forming in the Christian Catholic Church by celibate men who were becoming manipulative and powerful clerics by controlling rather than counselling.[4] Many religious protestors were persecuted and died, but Protestant churches reclaimed their faith in God and stopped being servile to dominating priests—and the world benefitted.

The current form of Islam, under the control of dictators, still punishes individuals if they consider breaking away from the corrupted form of Islam, fear is the control used by dictators. The United Nations should stand against this disgraceful gender apartheid and nations should not trade with countries that exploit women to this appalling degree. If Muslim clerics come to free countries and continue to practice gender segregation and do not accept gender equality, which their own prophet practised, they should be seen as law breakers and returned to cultures where this enslavement continues.

The world has had the last major Abrahamic prophet, now we need brave Muslims to rise like phoenixes from the ashes of their destroyed 'religion of peace' and return to the faith that Muhammad introduced. Females should fight for and be accepted as Islamic religious clerics in the Western world. We need people of monotheist faith to join as one, men and women, to walk together into the houses of God, be they churches, chapels, temples, mosques, or just open spaces of worship. We need Catholics to invite Muslim friends to their Church, Muslims to invite Christians to their services, Jews to invite both—and women must walk beside men and their partners, linking hands as equals and break down the barriers of godless male segregation.

Egocentric, autocratic men, acting as God rather than servants of an ethereal, spiritual Creator, have brought disgrace to religious learning institutions. Unfortunately, psychopathic personas are always attracted to positions of power and control, so these religious institutions became a magnet for deceptive and manipulative serpents. These subtle snakes, the white-collar psychopaths, have slithered into religious teaching institutions, as well as other management positions in business.

It appears psychopaths will continue to remain our most frightening predator, the necessary evil in the 'master plan' of life: the prime predator of the apex predator.[5-7] Perhaps our planet may need these mentally skewed people to start the occasional world war, if we cannot control population numbers, or protect the earth's environment and all creatures within it.

It appears humans were a huge evolutionary glitch—the most intelligent species, yet destined to become the most environmentally destructive. Now, with no existing predator, they are becoming the very worst plague species of all living creatures. Due to relentless over-breeding, encouraged by welfare governments and male-dominated religions, with the massive demand and waste of the environmental nuclear bomb, plastic, people's daily needs drive every environmentally damaging industry.

The human species has more than quadrupled the speed of the greatest threat to this planet: global warming. By covering fields of grass with inappropriate crops and tearing out millions of trees, humans have ruthlessly destroyed the Earth's cooling system, then covered that bare earth with bitumen, metal, bricks and mortar, which radiates blazing furnace heat into the atmosphere. Yet, it is irresponsible overpopulation that is the elephant in the room no one dares to mention.

With every environmentally destructive industry driven by increased human need, having a child has become the blackest environmental footprint. Men and women refusing to control the numbers of children they produce, in times of peace, create the most imminent danger for this planet of finite resources. People breeding over ZPG (Zero Population Growth: having over two children) should be shamed, not celebrated. Large families, possibly addicted to oxytocin, or enslaved to corrupt religious rules, are our worst environmental vandals. Large families creating overcrowded situations have resulted in the faster spread of illnesses and disease.

It has been shown that the millions of citizens that emigrate or flee from the Middle East reproduce at a much faster rate because Islam, like the Catholic faith, discourages birth control. This man-made rule introduced to increase religious numbers and power is an immoral and barbaric practice, but it is encouraged by governments that pay high levels of subsidies for every child born. Countries should adopt the system Singapore adopted because of their limited living space: full benefits for the first child, half for the next and a quarter for the third, leaving any further children as entirely the responsibility of the parents. This meant the larger families were those families with successful life skills and a good work ethic, who could afford to send their children to better schools and provide more stable family environments.

This form of population control improves the social skills and average intelligence of the overall population. Welfare-driven countries, like the UK and Australia, have the least competent individuals breeding the most children, which is tripling the crime rate and dumbing down second and third generations.[8-11] Excessive numbers beyond ZPG, or adults having further children with other partners after divorce or separation, should be taxed. Men and women must start being more accountable and stop having children they cannot afford to raise. This over-breeding forces taxpayers, who do show more responsibility in family numbers, to pay high taxes to meet the welfare costs created by these overlarge families. Countries should adopt the system Singapore adopted; DNA testing for parentage would stop men from having children in excess of ZPG.

Thuggish gangs of men have often come from overly large families, reduced to poverty because of excessive numbers. Forcing millions to survive in dreadful poverty is a root cause of vicious, ruthless, gang behaviour. These gangs include the Mafia, Cosa Nostra, the drug cartels of South America and the Philippines, and the Irish IRA. The 'hadith Islam' branch of true Islam has moulded some of the worst psychopaths, the four deadliest being Islamic State terrorists (ISIL), the Taliban, Al-Shabaab and Boko Haram.[12]

We are now in an age of atheist indifference and degraded levels of parenting, which means more children are being raised without EQ. In addition, the Middle Eastern practice of first-cousin marriages continues to increase the chances of genetic faults being passed to children. This may potentially increase the numbers being influenced by violent psychopathic terrorists. Governments need to make SEL (Social and Emotional Learning) classes compulsory, in all educational institutions.[13]

The first messenger gave warning of the psychopathic persona, circa 1400 BC, using a serpent as a metaphor for these predatory humans that prey on the vulnerable. Ruled by self-interest and greed, they are a subset of humanity and the most dangerous of all animal species that inhabit this earth. With brains that are virtually alien to C&E they are the reason humans, unlike other animal species, had to develop a moral compass, as those qualities when not instinctive and had to be learned. We were warned these evil people had the potential to destroy this planet.

Humans who are incapable of registering conscience and empathy (C&E) are the most dangerous of all living creatures. The thing of most concern is the fact they look exactly like us. They do not have razor-sharp teeth or claws, like animal predators, they mingle invisibly amongst us. White-collar psychopaths, in the corporate world, generally do not murder, however, heinous psychopaths—the serial killers and rapists—frequently do. Placing them in permanent confinement in psychiatric clinics (for research) until their brains can eventually be reactivated, should become a part of law across the world.

Moral integrity must be learned as the qualities are not innate, if they are not ingrained by mid-teens, we have a subset of society. School bullying is the apprenticeship for sociopathy or psychopathy—which includes the future conmen and occasionally women who put self before society, through to the anti-social creatures recognised as psychopaths, whose brains do not conceptualise normal emotional reactions. Sociopaths are the result of inappropriate or single parenting where children lack a positive male role model, whereas psychopaths have a genetic component but are still negatively impacted if they are not raised in a stable and happy early environment. Boys have the greater need for a two-parent team that sets firm routines and boundaries, while providing unconditional love. Psychopaths cope well in prison because they do not register anxiety, often misread by Parole Boards as good behaviour.

After they serve their prison time, these individuals should never be released back into society, any more than one would release a tiger or a crocodile from a zoo or reserve, onto the streets. If they cannot be maintained in permanent security, full castration should become the law. As psychopathy is a disorder of choice, knowing these were the two forms of sentencing outcomes would certainly have greater psychological impact on their decisions to start or repeat their crime than the pathetic electronic ankle bracelets currently in use.

Psychopaths are a much greater risk to humanity than other forms of mental disorder. If it is a genetic fault it should be reduced or erased from society with the same drive we have for trying to cure cancer. We have made gigantic strides in treating all areas of the body below the neck, now technology allows us to scan the brain it is time to focus on the most important organ in the entire body. We should be aware of the lack of 'grey' or 'white brain matter' development in psychopaths, years before the addiction to wrongdoing becomes ingrained for life, in mid-teens.[14-16] A cancer-damaged body kills the individual, the skewed thinking of the psychopathic brain can kill or financially destroy thousands.

This world will only survive if following generations recognise what is one of the greatest errors of judgement this world has ever made: ignoring the psychopathic persona, particularly in gender-apartheid religions. Numbers of psychopaths are increasing and they have become even more subtle, hiding under the pretence of religious observance. Men who are driven by self-interest, intent on personal power, should never be accepted in any institutions of faith—they are the face of evil that all three major prophets fought against.

Communism and backward tribal groups, like those of many Middle Eastern countries, are often ruled by men who lack MERC, and the quality of life for many, particularly women and children, varies from poor to appalling. As yet, there are still many unanswered questions as to the 'how and why' of this behaviour. Neuroscience is beginning to unravel this mystery, as advances in technology (MRI scanning) and DNA research are now revealing dramatic variations in the psychopathic brain. The evidence that psychopathy appears to have a genetic link, combined with the custom of first-cousin marriages in the Muslim world—which dramatically increases the risk of genetic disorders—may explain the spiralling numbers of heinous terrorists in the Muslim cultures. [17-19]

Young people should re-analyse those early words of wisdom from the three Holy Books. Scriptures should be used for textbook references in areas of modern philosophy. Why is there a problem in allowing people, with more advanced scientific and intellectual acumen, to interpret symbolism and meaning, rather than accepting inept and outdated literal translations? It has been observed that Christianity would have collapsed if Martin Luther had not allowed wider access to the Bible by having it translated from Latin into the language of the people.[20] People needed to be aware of how the powerful Catholic Church was in corrupting the original written word, with their own rules of compulsion, a transgression against faith. Compulsion was a sin in the eyes of all three messengers.

At least early Judeo-Christians did not replace the Old and New Testament with their own books of rules, as 'hadith Islam' has done, with the five books of Sunnah now more dominant in 'hadith Islam' than the original Quran. Books of Sunnah are substitute books of faith, consisting of thousands of false hadiths, condemned by Muhammad.[21] They were purportedly records of the sayings of Muhammad, although nearly all have been proven false. Hadith fabrications were banned in the Quran and by the prophet in his last famous sermon.[22]

Perhaps our jaded souls need to be revived and the values of GOD, which basically defines a moral compass, brought back into our children's lives. Is it time for a new reformation of faith, where people of all three Abrahamic faiths speak in the same voice, as did the three early prophets around which the three major Abrahamic religions were formed? Early Christians took great risks and many were killed, but faith gives great courage. There are equally wicked cults masquerading under Christianity, but Protestant faiths overall improved society in those early days, prior to atheism and the downward slide of moral and social integrity. Martin Luther, by setting the seeds of the Protestant Reformation, had a huge influence on the development of western society.[23] Unless there is similar substantial reform in Islam, away from political and male dominance, there will be ever-increasing bloodshed and loss of life. Like early

Catholic clerics, Islamic religious clerics who support the Sunni 'hadith Islam' offshoot are driven more by personal interests and control.

European women have suffered similar episodes of Muslim gang raping, but reporting on it is shut down by political correctness. Society, unaware of the religious corruption by the 'hadith Islam' cult, is deliberately turning a blind eye, now allowing tribal gender-apartheid and the exceptionally sexist Sharia law, simply because it masquerades as true Quranic Islam. By allowing tribal men to pull civilisation back into the 'dark ages' of dominant males, the Western world is spitting in the faces of brave women, Suffragettes and Women's Liberation, who fought long and hard for equality.

This behaviour is the inevitable result of years of male dominance and female oppression. Women across the world must continue to stand against males who support male domination and refuse to allow gender equality. Until religions are prepared to accept women as equals, especially in places of worship, these men should be barred from access to democratic countries. Unless brave Muslim men are prepared to walk into their mosques and sit, or kneel, with their wives and children and freely pray to God, there will be no safety on this earth from 'hadith Islam' terrorists. Female subjugation must cease.

'Hadith Islam' males, in total denial of their lack of personal control, blame the female victims of rape, because psychopathic personas are incapable of recognising they have a serious mental problem.[24] As stated by Dr Hare, a patient must recognise that there is a problem to seek help from a therapist, however, the crux of the issue is that, 'Psychopaths don't feel they have psychological or emotional problems, and they see no reason to change their behaviour to conform to societal standards with which they do not agree.'

Psychopaths have little aptitude for experiencing the emotional responses of fear and anxiety that are the mainsprings of conscience, hence, terrorist gangs brutally rape and kill, without remorse, and are the worst of all animal species that inhabit this earth. Driven by unrestrained sexual hunger, they are consistently seeking prey. Rape destroys a victim's entire life and worth, in these backward tribal communities that insist on virginity for the female. It is a culture of incredible male bigotry and misogyny, where the males celebrate immorality and adultery but brutalise or kill women if they commit the same crime. Under Sharia law, it is usually the woman that is jailed for rape. Rape for a woman is a life-destroying act, hence, the offender should suffer a similar life-changing outcome. Full castration should be the penalty.

As long as gender-apartheid remains, we will struggle to find equality and a better quality of life worldwide. By ignoring psychopathic behaviour, we deserve the threat of war, or whatever natural disasters our apathy towards societal and environmental damage may cause.

The bravery of women in the past has enforced equality in the Western world, creating a more civilised world for men, women and children. Concerned men and women of the world now have the biggest challenge: to empower Muslim women. We should bring democracy and peace back into the world and make corrupted religions accountable under secular law. The United Nations must force equality and rights for women in all countries and stop the 'hadith Islamic' war against women—stop their killing, stop their torture and stop their subjugation by emotionally retarded, godless males who demand control and dominance.

Other cultures cannot break through the cultural and personality barriers of 'hadith Islam'; only Muslims faithful to the Quran can convert their people who follow hadith fabrications introduced in books of Sunnah, words of earthborn men not Muhammad. They must follow the example of their prophet by reining in barbaric misogyny, financial disparity and male chauvinism. They must look seriously at the problem of the inherited psychopathic lack of emotional development (EQ) and, most importantly, be faithful to their prophet's plea to destroy all hadiths additional to the Quran. Governments must support brave Islamic dissidents who try to make change back to the true Islamic faith.

The world has allowed the serpent of pure evil to once again unfurl. Neuroscience has proved the accuracy of the Bible's first prophetic parable. We have the capacity to destroy this Garden of Eden by listening to the whisperings of the snakes we call psychopaths, who are now some of our most powerful and wealthy individuals.

The atheist contempt for social and emotional learning (SEL) once provided by religious institutions is creating increasing numbers of white-collar psychopaths (WCPs). Psychopaths choose the path of evil. When parental apathy ignores the early signs of this disorder in children, behaviour like persistent animal cruelty, deception and school bullying, it encourages this eventual path of evil and thus emboldens these snakes in suits.

As a pantheist believer in a spiritual divinity, I have always thought Nature was our hardest taskmaster. As we continue to abuse Earth's surface, it appears to lash back with terrifying and deadly catastrophic events to protect itself. Even if planet Earth ends up as bare and barren as Mars, it will still be spinning in its orbit, while we will have wiped ourselves into extinction because of our greed and out-of-control consumerism.

Verses of the Quran and the Bible can be twisted and misconstrued, translated with good or bad intent. How they are interpreted defines the man or woman. Sadly, skewed brains that believe we can show our gratitude for life on this incredible planet by turning it into 'killing fields' are proof that this world needed those three good men to show the vast chasm between good and evil, godly and godless. The Quran, dictated by a man who was influenced by the Judeo-Christian faiths before him, has many verses that concentrate on the same virtues as the Judeo-Christian faiths. In True Islam, The Holy Quran, translated by Dr. Rashad Khalifa, shows a vast majority of the Quran deals with morality.[25] Numerous examples are also listed on the Islamic Virtues and 'Islam on demand' sites.[26&27]

While I believe in a Spiritual Presence, as a pantheist–monotheist I also believe that final access to that place of 'golden light' will be given to all faiths with good moral codes, such as Buddhists and Hindus. If there is purpose to this life that leads us to a place of eternal rest, that drive would be met by good souls, not by those that have lived lives of greed, deception and brutality. That divine presence, which most faiths believe in, does not have a preferred religion. An honourable man, or woman, who genuinely lived a good and caring life, who did not kill any of God's creatures because their faith forbade it, has more chance of reaching that place of eternal rest than a mean hypocrite with regular attendance at a powerful male-dominated house of worship.

I believe we are all judged by our actions on this earth, not by the church we attend or how faithfully we follow man-made religious rules. Individuals whose daily lives instinctively followed those basic *Ten Commandments* are the people the messengers (Moses, Jesus and Muhammad) were trying to empower and give hope. The messengers did not die to save us—they introduced the values of faith to save us. If we live godforsaken lives, trashing those values, then we will be forsaken by that source of spiritual strength in which people of faith believe. Living up to the values they spread is the only chance of eternal rest, in a golden afterlife.

Scientists tell us this planet and all life was formed from the dust of a Big Bang—the *Theory of Evolution*. What if the *Theory of Intelligent Design*, based on the three prophets' message of eternal rest versus the blackness of hellish unrest(the foundation of religious instruction), also has accuracy? It is a gamble atheists and non-believing communist and fascist regimes are prepared to take, but not one I am prepared to risk. This world is filled with incredible things—can science really guarantee that our souls (the goodness neuroscience has only partly explained) will just turn to compost, or ashes, along with the physical body after death?

This world should not accept the continued bloodshed of terrorist behaviour. Let Muslims, faithful only to the Quran who want real change, be the nemesis of 'hadith Islam'. I finish with a quote from Christian Scriptures—the Old Testament, which was the first of the three Holy Scriptures. While the whole of Amos, Chapter 5 is worth reading, Amos 5: 24 is the verse I have chosen.[28]

'Let justice roll down like waters
and righteousness like an
ever-flowingstream.'

>>><<<

~ References~

Preface

1. Cleland DA (2018), *Why the White Horse of Revelation 6 CANNOT be the Antichrist!*
    <https://revelation6.com/white-horse-revelation-6-really-antichrist/>
2. Bolinger, H (2019), *Why the White Horse of Revelation 6 CANNOT be the Antichrist!* Crosswalk.com Editor, Christianity.com.
    <https://www.christianity.com/wiki/end-times/who-are-the-four-horsemen-in-revelation-their-meaning-and-significance.html>
3. The Editors of Encyclopaedia Britannica (2021), *Four horsemen of the apocalypse: Christianity.*
    <https://www.britannica.com/topic/four-horsemen-of-the-Apocalypse>
4. Holy Bible Revised Standard Version (1971), Collins Publishers, New York and Cleveland.
5. Ibid
6. Cleland DA (2018), *Why the Black Horse of Revelation CANNOT be the Horse of Famine!*
    <https://revelation6.com/why-the-black-horse-of-revelation-cannot-be-the-horse-of-famine/>
7. BibleRef (2021), *What does Revelation chapter 6 mean?*
    <https://www.bibleref.com/Revelation/6/Revelation-chapter-6.html>
8. Major Religions of the World Ranked by Number of Adherents (2009).
    <http://chartsbin.com/view/3nr>
9. Wikipedia (2020). *List of religious populations.*
    <https://en.wikipedia.org/wiki/List_of_religious_populations>

10. Itani T (2015), *Quran: English Translation. Clear, Easy to Read, Modern English, Pure.*
    <https://www.amazon.com.au/Quran-English-Translation-Clear-Modern/dp/0986136808>

11. Zielinski S (2015), *Modern Humans Have Become Superpredators*, Smithsonian.com.
    <https://www.smithsonianmag.com/science-nature/modern-humans-have-become-superpredators-180956348/>

12. Kingsford R, Maron M, Wintle B (2016), *Australia's land clearing rate is once again among the highest in the world*, UNSW Newsroom, Sydney.
    <https://newsroom.unsw.edu.au/news/science-tech/australia per centE2 per cent80 per cent99s-land-clearing-rate-once-again-among-highest-world>

13. Morton A and Davies A (2019), *Australia spends billions planting trees – then wipes out carbon gains by bulldozing them*, The Guardian, Australia.
    <https://www.theguardian.com/environment/2019/oct/17/australia-spends-billions-planting-trees-then-wipes-out-carbon-gains-by-bulldozing-them>

14. Wikipedia (2020), *Big Pharma conspiracy theory.*
    <https://en.wikipedia.org/wiki/Big_Pharma_conspiracy_theory>

15. SBS Movies (2019), *The Crown Prince of Saudi Arabia.*
    <https://www.sbs.com.au/movies/movie/crown-prince-saudi-arabia-0>

16. Wikipedia (2017), *Intra-species recognition.*
    <https://en.wikipedia.org/wiki/Intra-species_recognition>

17. Borg MJ (2001), *Reading the Bible again for the first time: taking the Bible seriously but not literally*, HarperCollins, New York.

18. Balk AP (2012), *Balderdash: a treatise on ethics*, Thelema Publication LLC, London.

19. Babiak P and Hare RD (2007), *Snakes in Suits*, HarperCollins Publishers, New York.

20. Hare RD (1993), *Without Conscience.*

21. Goleman D (2006), *Emotional intelligence: why it can matter more than IQ*, 10th anniversary ed., Bantam Books, New York.

22. Moir A and Jessel D (1989), *Brainsex: the real difference between men and women*, Mandarin Paperbacks, London.

23. Mindframe (2020), *For Suicide Prevention and Mental Health Sector.*
<https://mindframe.org.au/industry-hubs/for-suicide-prevention-and-mental-health-sector>

24. Coulter A (2009), *Guilty*, Three Rivers Press, New York.

25. Howes R (2012), *A Client's Guide to Transference*, Psychology Today.
<https://www.psychologytoday.com/au/blog/in-therapy/201206/clients-guide-transference>

26. Fruno A (2016), *Who's the animal? Stop domestic violence by punishing animal abusers*, The Daily Telegraph, NSW, Australia.
<https://www.dailytelegraph.com.au/rendezview/whos-the-animal-stop-domestic-violence-by-punishing-animal-abusers/news-story/1355da29c8b77fa9087b4d075363aae3>

27. Martin J (2018), *What Do ALL the Mass Shooters Have in Common? No Father in the Home*, TBE, USA.
<http://thebullelephant.com/what-do-all-the-mass-shooters-have-in-common-no-father-in-the-home/>

28. Zimmermann A (2018), *An inconvenient truth about child abuse*, Spectator Australia.
<https://www.spectator.co.uk/2018/07/an-inconvenient-truth-about-child-abuse/>

29. Hasson P (2015), *Guess which mass murderers came from a fatherless home*, The Federalist, USA.
<https://thefederalist.com/2015/07/14/guess-which-mass-murderers-came-from-a-fatherless-home/>

30. Early Childhood Learning & Knowledge Centre (2020), *Appreciating How Fathers Give Children a Head Start*, U.S. Department of Health & Human Services.
<https://eclkc.ohs.acf.hhs.gov/family-engagement/article/appreciating-how-fathers-give-children-head-start>

31. Howell N (2015), *A Link Between Single Parent Families and Crime*, Olivet Nazarene University, USA.
<https://digitalcommons.olivet.edu/cgi/viewcontent.cgi?article=1078&context=edd_diss>

32. Blackwood N, et al. (2012), *Psychopathy linked to brain abnormalities,* King's College, London.
    <https://www.kcl.ac.uk/archive/news/ioppn/records/2012/may/the-antisocial-brain>
33. Bakermans-Kranenburg MJ, van IJzendoorn MH, Riem MME, et al. (2012), *Oxytocin decreases handgrip force in reaction to infant crying in females without harsh parenting experiences,* Social Cognitive and Affective Neuroscience 7(8): 951–957.
    <https://www.ncbi.nlm.nih.gov/pmc/articles/PMC3501699/>
34. Dewar G (2019), *Oxytocin affects social bonds and our responses to toxic stress. Can we influence oxytocin in children?* Parenting Science.
    <https://www.parentingscience.com/oxytocin-in-children-and-parents.html>

Essay 1: The enigma of golden light

1. Babiak P, Hare RD (2007), *Snakes in Suits,* HarperCollins Publishers, New York.
2. Wikipedia (2020), *Port Arthur massacre (Australia).*
   <https://en.wikipedia.org/wiki/Port_Arthur_massacre_(Australia)>
3. Wikipedia (2020), *Christchurch mosque shootings.*
   <https://en.wikipedia.org/wiki/Christchurch_mosque_shootings>
4. Wikipedia (2020), *List of mass shootings in the United States in 2019.*
   <https://en.wikipedia.org/wiki/List_of_mass_shootings_in_the_United_States_in_2019>
5. Wikipedia (2020), *List of mass shootings in the United States in 2018.*
   <https://en.wikipedia.org/wiki/List_of_mass_shootings_in_the_United_States_in_2018>
6. Wikipedia (2020), *List of school shootings in the United States.*
   <https://en.wikipedia.org/wiki/List_of_school_shootings_in_the_United_States>

7. Carrega C (2019), *School shootings are more common than you may think: A look at the incidents that went under the radar in 2019*, ABC News. <https://abcnews.go.com/US/schools-shootings-common-incidents-radar-2019/story?id=67040402>

8. Epstein Z (2016), *These aren't Steve Jobs's last words, but they still managed to inspire a billionaire.* <https://bgr.com/2016/04/29/steve-jobs-last-words-branson/>

9. Wikipedia (2019), *Steve Jobs.* <https://en.wikipedia.org/wiki/Steve_Jobs#Biological_and_adoptive_family>

10. Neal MC (2011), *To Heaven and back*, WaterBrook & Multnomah, Division of Random House Inc., New York.

11. Alexander E (2012), *Proof of Heaven: A Neurosurgeon's Journey into the Afterlife*, Simon & Schuster Paperbacks, New York.

12. Alimurung G (2014), *Dr. Rajiv Parti's Hellish Out-of-Body Experience Changed His Life.* <http://www.laweekly.com/arts/dr-rajiv-partis-hellish-out-of-body-experience-changed-his-life-4448860>

13. Wikipedia (2020), *I Am (2010 American documentary film).* <https://en.wikipedia.org/wiki/I_Am_(2010_American_documentary_film)>

Essay 2. Three courageous men of faith changed the world

1. Goleman D (2006), *Emotional intelligence: why it can matter more than IQ*, 10th anniversary edn, Bantam Books, New York.

2. Hare RD (1993), *Without Conscience*, The Guilford Press, New York

3. Kiehl KA and Hoffman MB (2011), *The criminal psychopath: history, neuroscience, treatment, and economics*, Jurimetrics: 355-397. <https://www.ncbi.nlm.nih.gov/pmc/articles/PMC4059069/>

4. Biography Newsletter (2014), *Pontius Pilate Biography.* <https://www.biography.com/religious-figure/pontius-pilate>

5. Hare RD (1993), *Without Conscience:* p195.

6. Wikipedia (2020), Category: Four Horsemen of the Apocalypse. <https://en.wikipedia.org/wiki/Four_Horsemen_of_the_Apocalypse>

7. Turchin P (2013), *Return of the Oppressed,* Aeon Media Group Ltd. <https://aeon.co/essays/history-tells-us-where-the-wealth-gap-leads>

8. Mason M (2019), *Revealed: How much tax Netflix pays*, Financial Review, Australia. <https://www.afr.com/companies/media-and-marketing/revealed-how-much-tax-netflix-pays-20191025-p534aa>

9. Holy Bible Revised Standard Version (1971), Collins Publishers, New York and Cleveland.

10. Keyser JD (2012), *The Ancient Beginnings of the Virgin Birth Myth*, Hope of Israel Ministries, Azusa, USA. <http://www.hope-of-israel.org/originsVBmyth.html>

11. Vanderbilt University (2016), *Neanderthal DNA has subtle but significant impact on human traits*, American Association for the Advancement of Science, US. <https://phys.org/news/2016-02-neanderthal-dna-subtle-significant-impact.html>

12. Beyond Today (2011), *The Surprising Origins of the Trinity Doctrine*, Posted by United Church of God. <https://www.ucg.org/bible-study-tools/booklets/is-god-a-trinity/the-surprising-origins-of-the-trinity-doctrine>

13. Rath J (1997), *Historical Background of the Trinity*, Christadelphia World Wide. <http://www.christadelphia.org/trinityhistory.php>

14. Islamic Research (2014), *Examples of Hadith that Insult Prophet Muhammad.* <https://yaqeeninstitute.org/mohammad-elshinawy/how-the-prophet-muhammad-rose-above-enmity-and-insult>

15. Submission.org (2013), *Hadith and the Corruption of the great religion of Islam.* <http://submission.org/Corruption_of_Religion.html>

16. True Islam (2020), *The history of hadith, Prophet Muhammad forbids the writing of his hadith*, Part 1 (7).
    <http://www.quran-islam.org/articles/part_1/history_hadith_1_(P1148).html>

17. ING (2020), *Apostasy in Islam*, Islamic Networks Group (ING), San Jose, CA.
    <https://ing.org/apostasy-in-islam/>

18. Brown J (2017), *The issue of apostasy in Islam,* Yaqeen Institute for Islamic Research, Irving, TX.
    <https://yaqeeninstitute.org/jonathan-brown/the-issue-of-apostasy-in-islam/>

19. Wikipedia (2020), *Apostasy.*
    <https://en.wikipedia.org/wiki/Apostasy>

20. Wikipedia (2020), *Shirk (Islam)*.
    <https://en.wikipedia.org/wiki/Shirk_(Islam)>

21. Wikiversity (2020), *Council of Nicaea (325 A.D.)*, The First Ecumenical Council at Nicaea: The Arian Controversy.
    <https://en.m.wikiversity.org/wiki/Council_of_Nicea_(325_A.D.)>

22. Shelley BL (1990), *The First Council Of Nicaea, Christian History*, CT (Christianity Today).
    <https://www.christianitytoday.com/history/issues/issue-28/325-first-council-of-nicea.html>

23. Hare RD, *Without Conscience.*

24. Zielinski S (2015), *Modern Humans Have Become Superpredators*, Smithsonian.com.
    <https://www.smithsonianmag.com/science-nature/modern-humans-have-become-superpredators-180956348/>

25. Word Press (2016), *Intraspecies Predators.*
    <https://kiasherosjourney.wordpress.com/2016/02/27/interspecies-predators/>

26. Elkins K (2018), *How much money you need to be part of the 1 percent worldwide*, NBC Universal.
    <https://www.cnbc.com/2018/11/01/how-much-money-you-need-to-be-part-of-the-1-percent-worldwide.html>

27. Goodreads, Inc. (2020), *Albert Einstein Quotes* , <https://www.goodreads.com/quotes/33738-all-religions-arts-and-sciences-are-branches-of-the-same>

28. Goalcast (2017), *Top 30 most inspiring Albert Einstein quotes.* <https://www.goalcast.com/2017/03/29/top-30-most-inspiring-albert-einstein-quotes/>

29. Minford E (2000), *'Science without religion is lame, religion without science is blind.'* UniMed Publishing. <https://www.universalmedicine.com.au/blog/science-without-religion-lame-religion-without-science-blind>
    Wikipedia (2020), *Religious and philosophical views of Albert Einstein.* <https://en.wikipedia.org/wiki/Religious_and_philosophical_views_of_Albert_Einstein>

Essay 3. Psychopathy – genetic and inappropriate early nurture

1. Encyclopaedia of Mental Disorders (2019), *Hare Psychopathy Checklist,* Advameg Inc, Illinois, US. <http://www.minddisorders.com/Flu-Inv/HarePsychopathy-Checklist.html>

2. Balm J (2014), *The subway of the brain – Why white matter matters,* Springer Nature, BioMed Central Ltd (BMC), London. <http://blogs.biomedcentral.com/on-biology/2014/03/14/the-subway-of-the-brain-why-white-matter-matters/>

3. Hare RD (2010), *Intraspecies Predator: How a psychopath sees the world,* Sott video (www.sott.net). <https://www.sott.net/article/218599-Intraspecies-Predator-How-A-Psychopath-Sees-The-World>

4. Diamond J (1992), *The third chimpanzee: the evolution and future of the human animal,* HarperCollins Publishers, New York.

5. Hare RD (1993), *Without Conscience,* The Guilford Press, New York.

6. Ponerology News (2013), *Neuroscientist James Fallon's Work & Life Shed Light on How Psychopathic Killers are Made… and Perhaps Prevented.*

<https://www.ponerologynews.com/neuroscientist-james-fallon-how-psychopathic-killers-made-prevented/

7. Swenson RS (2006), *Limbic System,* Review of Clinical and Functional Neuroscience, Dartmouth Medical School, UK. <https://www.dartmouth.edu/~rswenson/NeuroSci/chapter_9.html>

8. Howell BR, et al. (2013), *Brain white matter microstructure alterations in adolescent rhesus monkeys exposed to early life stress: associations with high cortisol during infancy.* <https://biolmoodanxietydisord.biomedcentral.com/articles/10.1186/2045-5380-3-21>

9. Delobel-Ayoub M, et al. (2015), *Socioeconomic Disparities and Prevalence of Autism Spectrum Disorders and Intellectual Disability.* <https://www.ncbi.nlm.nih.gov/pmc/articles/PMC4635003/>

10. Stein J (2017), *Humour Is Serious Business,* Stanford Graduate School of Business. <https://www.gsb.stanford.edu/insights/humor-serious-business>

11. Bakermans-Kranenburg MJ, et al. (2012), *Oxytocin decreases handgrip force in reaction to infant crying in females without harsh parenting experiences.* <https://www.ncbi.nlm.nih.gov/pmc/articles/PMC3501699/>

12. Dewar G (2019), *Oxytocin affects social bonds and our responses to toxic stress. Can we influence oxytocin in children?* Parenting Science. <https://www.parentingscience.com/oxytocin-in-children-and-parents.html>

13. Mann D (2008), *C-Section Affects Moms' Response to Baby,* WebMD. <https://www.webmd.com/baby/news/20080904/c-section-affects-moms-response-to-baby#1>

14. Khamsi R (2006), *Maternal hormone protects baby's brain during birth,* New Scientist. <https://www.newscientist.com/article/dn10805-maternal-hormone-protects-babys-brain-during-birth/>

15. Meyer JH, et al. (2006), *Elevated Monoamine Oxidase A Levels in the Brain: of major depression an explanation for the Monoamine Imbalance.* <http://jamanetwork.com/journals/jamapsychiatry/fullarticle/668227>

16. Emery LR (2009), *11 Terrifying Serial Killers with Extremely High IQs,* Ranker.com.
    <https://www.ranker.com/list/smart-serial-killers/lea-rose-emery>

17. Oleson JC (2016), *Criminal Genius: A Portrait of High-IQ Offenders,* University of California Press, Oakland, US.

18. Witt K (2012), *Males Inherit More Intelligence from their Mothers*, Cultural Commentary, Neurobiology.
    <https://drkeithwitt.com/males-inherit-more-intelligence-from-mothers-63/>

19. Badcock C (2011), *The incredible expanding adventures of the X-chromosome,* Psychology Today, Sussex publishers.
    <https://www.psychologytoday.com/au/articles/201109/the-incredible-expanding-adventures-the-x-chromosome>

20. Silman A (2019), *What Ever Happened to the Mysterious Nobel Prize Sperm Bank?* The Cut, Vox Media Network.
    <https://www.thecut.com/2019/08/what-ever-happened-to-the-mysterious-nobel-prize-sperm-bank.html>

21. Australian Association for Infant Mental Health (2013), *Child Care.*
    <https://www.aaimhi.org/key-issues/position-statements-and-guidelines/AAIMHI-paper-Background-to-child-care.pdf>

22. Adams, KM (2011), *Silently seduced: when parents make their children partners,* HCI Books, Florida.

23. Adams KM, Morgan AP (2007), *When he's married to mom,* Simon & Schuster, New York.

24. Biddulph S (1998), *Raising boys,* Celestial Arts, Berkeley, California.

25. Blankenhorn D (1996), *Fatherless America,* HarperCollins Publishers, New York.

26. Brown NW (2001)), *Children of the self-Absorbed*, New Harbinger Publications, Oakland, CA.

27. Buckingham J (2000), *Boy troubles: understanding rising suicide, rising crime and education failure,* The Centre of Independent Studies, St Leonards, NSW, Australia.

28. Corneau G (1991), *Absent fathers, lost sons,* Shambhala Publications, Boston, Massachusetts.

29. Forward S, Buck C (1989), *Toxic parents: overcoming their hurtful legacy and reclaiming your life*, Bantam Books, New York.
30. Garbarino J (1999)), *Raising children in a socially toxic environment*, Jossey-Bass Publishers, San Francisco.
31. Garbarino J (2000), *Lost boys: why our sons turn violent and how we can save them*, Anchor Books, Random House Inc, New York.
32. Miller D (2010), *Father fiction: chapters for a fatherless generation*, Hodder & Stoughton, London.
33. Garcia-Arocena D (2015), *The genetics of violent behaviour*, The Jackson Laboratory, USA.
    <https://www.jax.org/news-and-insights/jax-blog/2015/december/the-genetics-of-violent-behavior>
34. Wikipedia (2020), *Y chromosome*.
    <https://en.wikipedia.org/wiki/Y_chromosome>
35. NIH (2020), *X Chromosome*, National Human Genome Research Institute, USA.
    <https://www.genome.gov/genetics-glossary/X-Chromosome>
36. Wikipedia (2020), *X chromosome*.
    <https://en.wikipedia.org/wiki/X_chromosome>
37. Sohrabi S (2015), *The criminal gene: the link between MAOA and aggression (Review)*, BMC Proceedings.
    <https://www.ncbi.nlm.nih.gov/pmc/articles/PMC4306065/>
38. Bonn SA (2014), *How to tell a sociopath from a psychopath*, Psychology Today.
    <https://www.psychologytoday.com/blog/wicked-deeds/201401/how-tell-sociopath-psychopath>
39. Blackwood N, et al. (2012), *Psychopathy linked to brain abnormalities*, King's College, London.
    <https://www.kcl.ac.uk/archive/news/ioppn/records/2012/may/the-antisocial-brain>
40. Hare RD (1993), *Without Conscience*: p.200.
41. Wikipedia (2017), *Intra-species recognition*.
    <https://en.wikipedia.org/wiki/Intra-species_recognition>
42. Hare RD, *Intraspecies Predator: How a psychopath sees the world*.

43. S.P.E.C.T. Study (2007), *Psychopath MRI- general psychology.*
<https://www.youtube.com/watch?v=oaTfdKYbudk&amp=&feature=player_embedded>

44. Hare RD (1998), *Psychopathy, Affect, and Behavior,* in Psychopathy: Theory, Research, and Implications for Society, eds. Cooke, DJ Forth, AE & Hare RD, Dordrecht, The Netherlands: Kluwer: p.105-137.
<https://link.springer.com/chapter/10.1007/978-94-011-3965-6_6>

45. Ponerology News (2013), *Neuroscientist James Fallon's Work & Life Shed Light on How Psychopathic Killers are made…and Perhaps Prevented.*
<https://www.ponerologynews.com/neuroscientist-james-fallon-how-psychopathic-killers-made-prevented/>

46. Kim-Cohen J, Caspi A, Taylor A, et al. (2006), *MAOA, maltreatment, and gene-environment interaction predicting children's mental health: new evidence and a meta-analysis,* Mol. Psychiatry; 11(10): p.903-13.

47. Prescott JW (2002), *Touch the Future*: How Culture Shapes the Developing Brain & the Future of Humanity.
<www.violence.de/prescott/ttf/cultbrain.pdf>

48. Magid K (1989), *High Risk: children without conscience,* Bantam Books, New York

49. Wójciak PI, Remlinger-Molenda A, Rybakowski J (2012), *The role of oxytocin and vasopressin in central nervous system activity and mental disorder,* National Centre for Biotechnology Information (NCBI).
<https://www.ncbi.nlm.nih.gov/pubmed/23479945>

50. Mitchell H, Aamodt MG (2005), *The Incidence of Child Abuse in Serial Killers,* Radford University, in Journal of Police and Criminal Psychology, 2005, Volume 20, No1.
<https://link.springer.com/article/10.1007/BF02806705>

51. Blackwood N, et al., *Psychopathy linked to brain abnormalities.*

52. Tiede R (2014), *Trauma in the Child Welfare and Public Health Systems,* USA.
<http://alfredadler.edu/sites/default/files/Tiede   per cent20Presentation per cent20201df4.p>

53. Juvenile Crime, Juvenile Justice (2001), *The Development of delinquency,* National Academies Press, National Academy of Sciences, Washington.
<https://www.nap.edu/read/9747/chapter/5>

54. Hare RD (1993), *Without Conscience.*

55. Goleman D (2006), Emotional intelligence: why it can matter more than IQ, Bantam Books, New York.

56. Kiehl KA (2015), *The Psychopath Whisperer: The Science of Those Without Conscience,* Penguin Random House, New York.

57. Hare RD (1993), *Without Conscience.*

58. Bonn SA (2014), *Psychopathic Criminals Cannot Be Cured.*
<https://www.psychologytoday.com/au/blog/wicked-deeds/201408/cure-psychopathic-criminals?amp=>

59. Hare RD (1993), *Without Conscience.*

60. Wikipedia (2020, *Religious views on female genital mutilation.*
<https://en.wikipedia.org/wiki/Religious_views_on_female_genital_mutilation>

61. Miltimore J (2017), *Muslim inbreeding is a huge problem--and people don't want to talk about it,* Charlemagne Institute, Bloomington, MN.
<https://www.intellectualtakeout.org/article/muslim-inbreeding-huge-problem-and-people-dont-want-talk-about-it/>

62. *Arnold* N (2017), *People should know the risks of marrying their cousin,* BBC
<https://www.bbc.co.uk/bbcthree/article/6af25e7b-0545-42ba-a6fa- 82ac1023b4ed>

63. Fallon J (2014), *How I discovered I have the brain of a psychopath.*
<https://www.theguardian.com/commentisfree/2014/jun/03/how-i-discovered-i-have-the-brain-of-a-psychopath>

64. McLeod S (2017), *Bowlby's Attachment Theory,* Simply Psychology.
<https://www.simplypsychology.org/bowlby.html>

65. McLeod S (2008), *Privation - Failure to Form an Attachment,* Simply Psychology.
<https://www.simplypsychology.org/privation.html>

66. Chesler P (1996), *What is justice for a rape victim?*
<https://www.ontheissuesmagazine.com/1996winter/w95chesler.php>.

67. Bennoune K (2015), *Acting TOGETHER to Stop Those Who Are Killing Us*, International Law and the Civil Society Struggle against Jihadist Terrorism. *Proceedings of the Annual Meeting (American Society of International Law): 109*, 143-152. <https://www.jstor.org/stable/10.5305/procannmeetasil.109.2015.0143?seq=1>

68. Hanson JL, et al. (2013), *Early neglect is associated with alterations in white matter integrity and cognitive functioning.* <https://www.ncbi.nlm.nih.gov/pmc/articles/PMC3690164/>

69. Chow TW, (2000), *Personality in Frontal Lobe Disorders.* <https://www.ncbi.nlm.nih.gov/pmc/articles/PMC5786154/>

70. Babao-Guballa C (2013), *The link between animal cruelty and antisocial personality disorders,* Philippine Daily Inquirer. <https://lifestyle.inquirer.net/129343/the-link-between-animal-cruelty-and-antisocial-personality-disorders/>

71. Griffiths M (2016), *The psychology of animal torture*, Psychology Today. <https://www.psychologytoday.com/au/blog/in-excess/201611/the-psychology-animal-torture>

72. Worthylake M (2014), *Family Pets Teach Children Empathy*, Butte Humane Society, California. <https://buttehumane.org/family-pets-teach-children-empathy/>

Essay 4. Sociopaths and psychopaths are not interchangeable titles

1. Babiak P, et al. (2012), *Psychopathy - An Important Forensic Concept for the 21st Century,* FBI law Enforcement Bulletin, United States Department of Justice. <https://leb.fbi.gov/2012/july/psychopathy-an-important-forensic-concept-for-the-21st-century>

2. Hare RD and Logan MH (2008), *Criminal Psychopathy: An Introduction for Police*, The Psychology of Criminal Investigations: The Search for the Truth, eds. St-Yves M, Tanguay M (Cowansville, QC: Editions Yvon Blais, 2009).

<https://www.yumpu.com/en/document/read/6607147/criminal-psychopathy-an-introduction-for-police-dr-matt-logan->

3. Hare RD (1993), *Without Conscience*, The Guilford Press, New York: p.113

4. IDS 302 Project (2010), *The Fatherless Generation*, USA. <https://thefatherlessgeneration.wordpress.com/statistics/>

5. Sabrina (2017), *The Fatherless Generation: My story*. <https://thefatherlessgeneration.wordpress.com/my-story/>

6. Sabrina (2017), *My Analysis-Hope for the Fatherless*. <https://thefatherlessgeneration.wordpress.com/my-analysis-hope-for-the-fatherless/>

7. Frick PJ and Marsee MA (2018), *Psychopathy and Developmental Pathways to Antisocial Behaviour in Youth*, in Handbook of Psychopathy, ed. Christopher J. Patrick (New York, NY: Guilford Press, (2006): p.353-374. <https://psycnet.apa.org/record/2018-14405-019>

8. Lynam DR (1996), *Early Identification of Chronic Offenders: Who is the Fledgling Psychopath?*, Psychological Bulletin 120, no. 2: 209-234.

9. Kolla NJ, Malcolm CP, Attard S, et al. (2013), *Childhood Maltreatment and Aggressive Behaviour in Violent Offenders with Psychopathy*. <https://www.ncbi.nlm.nih.gov/pubmed/23972111>

10. Cornell DG, Warren J, Hawk G, et al. (1996), *Psychopathy in Instrumental and Reactive Violent Offenders*, Journal of Consulting and Clinical Psychology 64, no. 4 (p. 783-790). <https://www.ncbi.nlm.nih.gov/pubmed/8803369>

11. Woodworth M, Porter S (2002), *In Cold Blood: Characteristics of Criminal Homicides as a Function of Psychopathy*, Journal of Abnormal Psychology 111, no. 3: 436-445.

12. Storey JE, Hart SD, Meloy JR, et al. (2009), *Psychopathy and Stalking*. Law and Human Behavior 33: 237–246. <https://doi.org/10.1007/s10979-008-9149-5>

13. Hare RD, *Without Conscience*: p.2.

14. Fallon J (2014), *The Psychopath Inside: A Neuroscientist's Personal Journey into the Dark Side of the Brain*, Penguin Putnam Inc., New York, USA.

15. Fallon J (2014), *How I discovered I have the brain of a psychopath.* <https://www.theguardian.com/commentisfree/2014/jun/03/how-i-discovered-i-have-the-brain-of-a-psychopath>

16. Hagerty BB (2010), *Neuroscientist Uncovers A Dark Secret,* NPR Morning Edition. <https://www.npr.org/templates/story/story.php?storyId=127888976>

17. Wójciak PI, Remlinger-Molenda A, Rybakowski J (2012), *The role of oxytocin and vasopressin in central nervous system activity and mental disorder,* National Center for Biotechnology Information(NCBI). <https://www.ncbi.nlm.nih.gov/pubmed/23479945>

18. Mount H (2013), *Scientist who found he'd the brain of a psychopath... and what it taught him about human nature,* Daily Mail, UK. <http://www.dailymail.co.uk/news/article-2514670/Scientist-James-Fallon-hes-brain-psychopath-related-Lizzie-Borden.html>

19. ABC All in the Mind (2014), *The psychopath within.* <https://www.abc.net.au/radionational/programs/allinthemind/the-psychopath-within/5415302#transcript>

20. Oleson JC (2016), *Criminal Genius: A Portrait of High-IQ Offenders,* University of California Press, Oakland, California.

21. Emery LR (2019), *Terrifying Serial Killers with Extremely High IQs,* Ranker. <https://www.ranker.com/list/smart-serial-killers/lea-rose-emery>

22. Bonn SA (2019), *Wicked Deeds: Understanding What Drives Serial Killers.* <https://www.psychologytoday.com/blog/wicked-deeds>

23. Wikipedia (2020), *Edmund Kemper.* <https://en.wikipedia.org/wiki/Edmund_Kemper>

24. Goleman D (2006), *Emotional intelligence: why it can matter more than IQ,* Bantam Books, New York.

25. Ponerology News (2013), *Neuroscientist James Fallon's Work & Life Shed Light on How Psychopathic Killers are Made…and Perhaps Prevented.* <https://www.ponerologynews.com/neuroscientist-james-fallon-how-psychopathic-killers-made-prevented/>

26. Hercz R (2001), *Psychopaths among us.*
    <http://www.Hare.org/links/saturday.html>
27. Hare RD, *Without Conscience*: p.198.
28. Fruno A (2016), *Who's the animal? Stop domestic violence by punishing animal abusers*, The Daily Telegraph.
    <https://www.dailytelegraph.com.au/rendezview/whos-the-animal-stop-domestic-violence-by-punishing-animal-abusers/news-story/>
29. Hare RD (2003), *Hare Psychopathy Checklist-Revised*, 2nd ed. Toronto, ON: Multi-Health Systems.
    <https://sk.sagepub.com/reference/psychologylaw/n138.xml>
30. Bright Side (2020), *7 Signs That a Child Will Be a Psychopath in the Future.*
    <https://brightside.me/inspiration-family-and-kids/7-signs-that-a-child-will-be-a-psychopath-in-the-future-444660/>
31. Menon MK & Sharland A (2010), *Narcissism, Exploitative Attitudes, and Academic Dishonesty: An Exploratory Investigation of Reality Versus Myth*, Journal of Education for Business: Pages 50-55.
    <https://www.tandfonline.com/doi/abs/10.1080/08832321003774772>
32. Dingfelder S F (2011), *Reflecting on narcissism*, American Psychological Association.
    <https://www.apa.org/monitor/2011/02/narcissism>
33. Daily Mail Reporter (2013), *How college students think they are more special than EVER: Study reveals rocketing sense of entitlement on U.S. campuses*, Mail Online.
    <https://www.dailymail.co.uk/news/article-2257715/Study-shows-college-students-think-theyre-special--read-write-barely-study.html>
34. Hotchkiss S (2003), *Why is it always about you? The seven deadly sins of narcissism*, Free Press, New York.
35. Manne A (2014), *The life of I: the new culture of narcissism*, Melbourne University Press, Carlton, Victoria, Australia.
36. Twenge JM, Campbell WK (2009), *The narcissism epidemic: living in the age of entitlement*, Free Press, Simon & Schuster Inc, New York.

37. Brown NW (2001)), *Children of the self-Absorbed*, New Harbinger Publications, Oakland, CA.

38. Forward S, Buck C (1989), *Toxic parents: overcoming their hurtful legacy and reclaiming your life,* Bantam Books, New York.

39. Garbarino J (1999), *Raising children in a socially toxic environment,* Jossey-Bass Publishers, San Francisco.

40. Golomb E (1992), *Trapped in the mirror: adult children of narcissists in their struggle for self,* Harper, New York.

41. Martinez-Lewi L (2008), *Freeing yourself from the narcissist in your life,* Tarcher, Penguin Books, New York.

42. Miller A (1990), *For your own good: hidden cruelty in child-rearing and the roots of violence,* 3rd edn, The Noonday Press, New York.

43. Frias S (2017), *15 Reasons autism begins in pregnancy,* BabyGaga, Valnet Property, Quebec.
    <http://www.babygaga.com/15-reasons-autism-begins-in-pregnancy/>

44. El-Guebaly N (2005), *Don't drink and drive: the successful message of Mothers Against Drunk Driving (MADD),* World Psychiatry: 4(1): 35–36.
    <https://www.ncbi.nlm.nih.gov/pmc/articles/PMC1414720/>

45. Fell JC & Voas R (2006), *Mothers Against Drunk Driving (MADD): the first 25 years,* ResearchGate.
    <https://www.researchgate.net/publication/6804716_Mothers_Against_Drunk_Driving_MADD_the_first_25_years>

46. Editorial Staff (2020), *Effectiveness of Mothers Against Drunk Driving,* American Addiction Centers.
    <https://www.alcohol.org/teens/mothers-against-drunk-driving/>

47. MADD (2020), *Saving lives, serving people,* Irving, Texas, US.
    <https://www.madd.org/history/>

48. MADD (2020), *Statistics: Fight back against misinformation. Get the facts.* Irving, Texas, US.
    <https://www.madd.org/statistics/>

49. Goleman D (2006), *Emotional intelligence.*

50. ABC News (2015), *Rising compensation claims for teachers under stress.* <https://www.abc.net.au/news/2015-09-01/rising-compensation-claims-for-teachers-under-stress/6739248>

51. Stroud G (2017), *Why do teachers leave?* ABC News. <https://www.abc.net.au/news/2017-02-04/why-do-teachers-leave/8234054>

52. The Guardian, Australian edition (2018), *Two-thirds of teachers think of quitting over bad behaviour, survey finds.* <https://www.theguardian.com/education/2018/dec/16/two-thirds-of-teachers-think-of-quitting-over-bad-behaviour-survey-finds>

53. Adams R (2019), *One in four teachers 'experience violence from pupils every week',* The Guardian, Belfast. <https://www.theguardian.com/education/2019/apr/20/one-in-four-teachers-experience-violence-from-pupils-every-week>

54. Tiede R (2014), *Trauma in the Child Welfare and Public Health Systems,* USA. <http://alfredadler.edu/sites/default/files/Tiede per cent20Presentation per cent20201df4.p>

55. McLanahan S (2001), *The Consequences of Single Motherhood,* The American Prospect, Inc. <https://prospect.org/health/consequences-single-motherhood/>

56. Goleman D (2006), *Emotional intelligence.*

57. Cohen P (2012), *Single moms can't be scapegoated for the murder rate anymore* <https://www.theatlantic.com/sexes/archive/2012/11/single-moms-cant-be-scapegoated-for-the-murder-rate-anymore/265576/>

58. Dalrymple T (2001)), *Life at the bottom,* Ivan R Dee, Publisher, Chicago.

59. Biddulph, S (2006), *Raising babies: Should under 3s go to nursery?* Harper Thorsons, United Kingdom.

60. The Urban Child Institute (2010), *Baby's brain begins now: Conception to age 3,* Tennessee, US. <http://www.urbanchildinstitute.org/why-0-3/baby-and-brain>

61. Narvaez DF (2017), *Be worried about boys, especially baby boys,* Psychology Today.
<https://www.psychologytoday.com/au/blog/moral-landscapes/201701/be-worried-about-boys-especially-baby-boys>

62. Winston R, Chicot R (2016), *The importance of early bonding on the long-term mental health and resilience of children,* The London Journal of Primary Care; 8(1): 12–14.
<https://www.ncbi.nlm.nih.gov/pmc/articles/PMC5330336/>

63. Australian Association for Infant Mental Health (2013), *Child Care.*
<https://www.aaimhi.org/key-issues/position-statements-and-guidelines/AAIMHI-paper-Background-to-child-care.pdf>

64. Balm J (2014), *The subway of the brain – Why white matter matters,* Springer Nature, BioMed Central Ltd (BMC), London.
<http://blogs.biomedcentral.com/on-biology/2014/03/14/the-subway-of-the-brain-why-white-matter-matters/>

65. IDS 302 Project, *The Fatherless Generation.*

66. Magid K, McKelvey CA (1989), *High risk: children without conscience,* Bantam Books, New York.

67. Tiede R (2014), *Trauma in the Child Welfare and Public Health Systems.*

68. Juvenile Crime, Juvenile Justice (2001), *The Development of delinquency,* National Academies Press, National Academy of Sciences, Washington.
<https://www.nap.edu/read/9747/chapter/5>

69. Weebly Education (2000), *Statistics on fatherless homes,* San Francisco.
<http://endparentalalienation.weebly.com/uploads/1/1/2/2/11226479/statistics_on_fatherless_homes.pdf>

70. Sullivan L (2000), *Behavioural Poverty,* Policy Monograph 45, The Centre for Independent Studies Ltd., St Leonards, NSW.

71. Facts for Life, 4th edn (2010), *Facts for Life saves lives!* United Nations Children's Fund, New York.
<http://www.factsforlifeglobal.org/03/>

72. UNICEF (2014), *The First Seven Years Are Key to a Successful Life,* The World Bank.
<https://www.worldbank.org/en/news/press-release/2014/06/05/the-first-seven-years-are-key-to-a-successful-life>

73. Fraga J (2017), *Do the first 7 years of life really mean everything?* Healthline Media.
<https://www.healthline.com/health/parenting/first-seven-years-of-childhood#By-the-age-of-7,-kids-are-putting-the-pieces-together->

74. Goleman D, *Emotional intelligence.*

75. Halliday J (2019), *Teachers strike over pupils 'carrying knives and brawling,'* *The* Guardian, UK.
<https://www.theguardian.com/uk-news/2019/jun/27/teachers-strike-pupils-carrying-knives-brawling-starbank-birmingham>

76. Adams (2020, *Behaviour battleground: isolation booths divide opinion among teachers,* The Guardian, UK.
<https://www.theguardian.com/education/2020/jan/17/behaviour-battleground-isolation-booths-divide-opinion-among-teachers>

77. Coulter, *Guilty*: Ch 2.

78. Saunders P (2004), *Australia's welfare habit and how to kick it*, Duffy & Snellgrove, Sydney.

79. IDS 302 Project (2010), *The Fatherless Generation.*

80. Hare RD (1993), *Without Conscience.*

81. Goleman D (2006), *Emotional intelligence.*

82. Boba Ambassadors (2017), *The Importance of Dads: Expert findings about involved fathers,* US.
<https://boba.com/pages/the-importance-of-dads>

83. Garcia-Arocena D (2015), *The genetics of violent behaviour,* The Jackson Laboratory, US.
<https://www.jax.org/news-and-insights/jax-blog/2015/december/the-genetics-of-violent-behavior>

84. Sohrabi S (2015), *The criminal gene: the link between MAOA and aggression* (Review), BMC Proceedings.
<https://www.ncbi.nlm.nih.gov/pmc/articles/PMC4306065/>

85. Kiehl KA, Hoffman M (2011), *The criminal psychopath: history, neuroscience, treatment, and economics.*
<https://www.ncbi.nlm.nih.gov/pmc/articles/PMC4059069/>

86. Ponerology News (2013), *Neuroscientist James Fallon's Work & Life Shed Light on How Psychopathic Killers are Made…and Perhaps Prevented.* <https://www.ponerologynews.com/neuroscientist-james-fallon-how-psychopathic-killers-made-prevented/>
87. Blackwood N, et al. (2012), *Psychopathy linked to brain abnormalities,* King's College, London. <https://www.kcl.ac.uk/archive/news/ioppn/records/2012/may/the-antisocial-brain>
88. Garcia-Arocena D (2015), *The genetics of violent behavior,* The Jackson Laboratory. <https://www.jax.org/news-and-insights/jax-blog/2015/december/the-genetics-of-violent-behavior>
89. Narvaez DF (2017), *Be worried about boys, especially baby boys,* Psychology Today. <https://www.psychologytoday.com/au/blog/moral-landscapes/201701/be-worried-about-boys-especially-baby-boys>
90. Schore AN (2017), *All our sons: the developmental neurobiology and neuroendocrinology of boys at risk.* <https://pubmed.ncbi.nlm.gov/29842663/>
91. Sohrabi S (2015), *The criminal gene: the link between MAOA and aggression.*
92. Bussing K (2018), *13 signs you're dealing with a psychopath, according to experts,* Readers Digest. <https://www.businessinsider.com/13-signs-youre-dealing-with-a-psychopath-according-to-experts-2018-2/?r=AU&IR=T>
93. Hudson RA (1999), *The sociology and psychology of terrorism: Who becomes a terrorist and why?* Federal Research Division, Library of Congress, Washington DC. <https://fas.org/irp/threat/frd.html>
94. Balm J (2014), *The subway of the brain – Why white matter matters,* Springer Nature, BioMed Central Ltd (BMC), London. <http://blogs.biomedcentral.com/on-biology/2014/03/14/the-subway-of-the-brain-why-white-matter-matters/>
95. Blackwood N, et al. (2012, *Psychopathy linked to brain abnormalities.*
96. Fact check (2016), *Does Australia have one of the 'highest loss of species anywhere in the world'?*

<http://www.abc.net.au/news/2015-08-19/fact-check-does-australia-have-one-of-the-highest-extinction/6691026>

97. The World Bank, *Arable land (per cent of land area) - Arable land (hectares per person)*.
    <https://data.worldbank.org/indicator/AG.LND.ARBL.ZS>

98. Global Footprint Network (2019), *Advancing the science of sustainability*, Oakland, USA.
    <https://www.footprintnetwork.org/resources/glossary/>

99. Wikipedia (2020), *List of countries and dependencies by population density*.
    <https://en.wikipedia.org/wiki/List_of_countries_and_dependencies_by_population_density>

100. Wikipedia (2020), *Global catastrophic risk*.
    <https://en.wikipedia.org/wiki/Global_catastrophic_risk#Global_warming>

101. Balm J, *The subway of the brain – Why white matter matters*.

102. IDS 302 Project, *The Fatherless Generation*.

103. Moir A & Jessel D, *Brainsex: the real difference between men and women*.

104. Hare RD (1993), *Without Conscience*.

105. Islam Question and Answer (2003), *Singing and dancing at celebrations*.
    <https://islamqa.info/en/answers/9290/singing-and-dancing-at-celebrations>

106. Islam Question and Answer (2000), *Ruling on music, singing and dancing*
    <https://islamqa.info/en/answers/5000/ruling-on-music-singing-and-dancing>

107. Webb S (2016), *Executed for 'refusing a dance'*, The Sun, UK.
    <https://www.thesun.co.uk/news/2330904/shocking-moment-pregnant-woman-is-shot-dead-at-wedding-after-she-refused-to-dance-with-a-drunk-stranger/>

108. Pleasance C (2020), *Dancer is shot in the face at a wedding in India after she stopped for a break between songs*, Mail Online, Daily Mail, UK.
    <https://www.dailymail.co.uk/news/article-7764271/Dancer-shot-face-wedding-India-stopped-break.html>

109. Berens C (2017), *Veiling and the Rise in Rapes*.
    <http://www.cheriberens.net/veiling-and-the-rise-in-rapes.html>

110. MacDorman M (1987), *Contemporary marriage practices in North India: evidence from three Uttar Pradesh villages.*
<https://openresearch-repository.anu.edu.au/handle/1885/123772>
111. Chesler P (2006), *The death of feminism*, Palgrave Macmillan, New York.
112. Ponerology News, *Neuroscientist James Fallon's Work & Life Shed Light on How Psychopathic Killers are Made.*
113. Blackwood N, et al., *Psychopathy linked to brain abnormalities.*
114. Hanson JL, et al. (2013), *Early neglect is associated with alterations in white matter integrity and cognitive functioning.*
<https://www.ncbi.nlm.nih.gov/pmc/articles/PMC3690164/>

Essay 5. Religion above the law has allowed gender apartheid

1. Buhler R & Staff (2017), *Donald Trump: Being an Atheist Gives Me a Business Edge-Fiction!* What's True Incorporated.
<https://www.truthorfiction.com/donald-trump-atheist-business-edge/>
2. Grigg R (1997), *Who wrote the first book of the Bible—Genesis?* Creation Ex Nihilo Dec 93 - Feb 1994, Vol. 16 No. 1, p38-41, Christian Answers Network, Marysville, USA.
<http://christiananswers.net/q-aig/aig-c021.html>
3. Hare RD (1993), *Without Conscience*, The Guilford Press, New York.
4. Marks G (2016), *21 percent of CEOs are psychopaths. Only 21 percent?* Washington Post.
<https://www.washingtonpost.com/news/on-small-business/wp/2016/09/16/gene-marks-21-percent-of-ceos-are-psychopaths-only-21-percent/>
5. Wikipedia (2020), *Psychopathy in the workplace.*
<https://en.wikipedia.org/wiki/Psychopathy_in_the_workplace>
6. Brogaard B (2019), *Are Psychopaths Mad or Bad?* Psychology Today
<https://www.psychologytoday.com/au/blog/the-superhuman-mind/201909/are-psychopaths-mad-or-bad>

7. Moir A & Jessel D (1989), *Brainsex: the real difference between men and women*, Mandarin Paperbacks, London.
8. Knoblauch JA (2009), *Some Food Additives Mimic Human Hormones*, Scientific American.
   <https://www.scientificamerican.com/article/food-additives-mimic-hormones/>
9. BBC News (2019), *Catholic Church child sexual abuse scandal*,
   <https://www.bbc.com/news/world-44209971>
10. Wright KS (2017), *The principles of Catholic social teaching: A guide for decision making from daily clinical encounters to national policy-making*, The Linacre Quarterly, US.
    <https://www.ncbi.nlm.nih.gov/pmc/articles/PMC5375653/>
11. Holy Bible Revised Standard Version (1971), Collins Publishers, New York & Cleveland.
12. Williams J (2017), *The principles of Catholic social teaching: A guide for decision making from daily clinical encounters to national policy-making*, The New York Times.
    <https://www.nytimes.com/2017/12/14/world/australia/australia-sexual-abuse-children.html>
13. Moir A & Jessel D, *Brainsex*: Ch 2.
14. Schmalz M (2019), *Why ending the secrecy of 'confession' is so controversial for the Catholic Church*, Dateline, NSW.
    <https://www.sbs.com.au/news/dateline/why-ending-the-secrecy-of-confession-is-so-controversial-for-the-catholic-church>
15. Pettinger T (2014), *Biography of Martin Luther*, Oxford, UK.
    <http://www.biographyonline.net/spiritual/martin-luther.html>
16. Rosenberg ML, Smith JC, Davidson LE & Conn JM (1987), *The emergence of youth suicide: An Epidemiologic Analysis and Public Health Perspective*, Annual Review Public Health, USA.
    <https://pubmed.ncbi.nlm.nih.gov/3580062/ >
17. Zubrick SR, Hafekost J, Johnson SE, et al. (2016), *Suicidal Behaviours: Prevalence estimates from the second Australian Child and Adolescent Survey of Mental Health and Wellbeing*, Aust N Z J Psychiatry: p.899-910.
    <https://www.ncbi.nlm.nih.gov/pubmed/26764371>

18. The Urban Child Institute (2020), *Baby's Brain Begins Now: Conception to Age 3.*
    <http://www.urbanchildinstitute.org/why-0-3/baby-and-brain>
19. Word Press (2016), *Intraspecies Predators.*
    <https://kiasherosjourney.wordpress.com/2016/02/27/interspecies-predators/>
20. Simon G (2013), *Predators Among Us: The Psychopaths.*
    <https://www.drgeorgesimon.com/predators-among-us-the-psychopaths/>
21. Zielinski S (2015), *Modern Humans Have Become Superpredators,* Smithsonian.com.
    <https://www.smithsonianmag.com/science-nature/modern-humans-have-become-superpredators-180956348/>
22. Wani MS (2020), *7 of the Richest Dictators In History,* Investopedia, New York.
    <https://www.investopedia.com/financial-edge/0912/8-of-the-richest-dictators-in-history.aspx>
23. Encyclopaedia Britannica (2020), *Dictatorship.*
    <https://www.britannica.com/topic/dictatorship>
24. Wikipedia (2020), *State of atheism.*
    <https://en.wikipedia.org/wiki/State_atheism>
25. Niiler E (2011), *How dictators keep control,* NBC News.
    <http://www.nbcnews.com/id/45751914/ns/technology_and_science-science/t/how-dictators-keep-control/>
26. Cline A (2019), *Hitler, Nationalism, and Positive Christianity,* Learn Religions, Dotdash publishing, New York.
    <https://www.learnreligions.com/adolf-hitler-and-christian-nationalism-248189>
27. Cline A (2019), *Was Hitler an Atheist?* Learn Religions, Dotdash publishing, New York.
    <https://www.learnreligions.com/hitler-was-an-atheist-250215>
28. Holocaust Encyclopaedia, *The German Churches and the Nazi State,* United States Holocaust Memorial Museum, Washington, DC.
    <https://encyclopedia.ushmm.org/content/en/article/the-german-churches-and-the-nazi-state>

29. Wilson, William D, (2016), *The Orthodox Betrayal: How German Christians Embraced and Taught Nazism and Sparked a Christian Battle*, University Honors Program Theses. 160.
<https://digitalcommons.georgiasouthern.edu/honors-theses/160>

30. Four Corners (2017), *Syria's Disappeared*, ABC.
<https://www.abc.net.au/4corners/syrias-disappeared-social/8468570>

31. Hare RD, *Without Conscience*: Preface (p.xii).

32. Babiak P, Hare RD (2007), *Snakes in Suits*, HarperCollins Publishers, New York.

33. Holy Bible Revised Standard Version (1971), Collins Publishers, New York & Cleveland.

34. Wikipedia (2020), *Usury*.
<https://en.wikipedia.org/wiki/Usury>

35. Ackerman JM (1981), *The History of Usury*, Interest Rates and the Law, Arizona, US.
<https://americansforfairnessinlending.wordpress.com/the-history-of-usury/>

36. Mayyasi A (2017), *Of Money and Morals*, Aeon Media Group Ltd.
<https://aeon.co/essays/how-did-usury-stop-being-a-sin-and-become-respectable-finance>

37. Rowlingson K (2011), *Does income inequality cause health and social problems?* Joseph Rowntree Foundation, York.
<https://www.drugsandalcohol.ie/15970/>

38. Keeley B (2015), *How does income inequality affect our lives?* Income Inequality: The Gap between Rich and Poor, OECD Publishing, Paris.
<https://doi.org/10.1787/9789264246010-6-en>

39. Holmes A (2013), *Some economic effects of inequality*, The Parliamentary Library, Department of Parliamentary Services, Australia.
<https://www.aph.gov.au/About_Parliament/Parliamentary_Departments/Parliamentary_Library/pubs/BriefingBook44p/EconEffects>

40. Neate R (2017), *Richest 1 per cent own half the world's wealth, study finds,* Guardian Australia, New South Wales.
    <https://www.theguardian.com/inequality/2017/nov/14/worlds-richest-wealth-credit-suisse>

41. Elliott L (2019), *World's 26 richest people own as much as poorest 50 per cent, says Oxfam,* Guardian Australia, NSW, Australia.
    <https://www.theguardian.com/business/2019/jan/21/world-26-richest-people-own-as-much-as-poorest-50-per-cent-oxfam-report>

42. Staton T (2014), *The top 20 highest-paid biopharma CEOs,* FiercePharma, USA.
    <https://www.fiercepharma.com/special-report/top-20-highest-paid-biopharma-ceos>

43. Sullivan L (2000), *Behavioural Poverty,* Policy Monograph 45, The Centre for Independent Studies Ltd., St Leonards, NSW, Australia.

44. Hill SS and Mead FS (1994), *Handbook of Denominations in the United States,* Abingdon, US.
    <http://www.mesacc.edu/~thoqh49081/handouts/denominations.html>

45. Goleman D (2006), *Emotional intelligence: why it can matter more than IQ,* Bantam Books, New York.

46. David Barrett's statistics Part II (2019), *The Facts and Stats on '33,000 Denominations'.*
    <http://www.philvaz.com/apologetics/a106.htm>

47. Matthews C (2015), *How much does Scientology pocket from its tax exempt status?* Fortune, New York.
    <http://fortune.com/2015/04/08/scientology-tax-exempt/>

48. Tarico V (2013), *10 ways religious groups steal public money,* Salon Media Group, US.
    <http://www.salon.com/2013/09/19/10_ways_religious_groups_take_public_money_partner/>

49. Celebrity Net Worth (2020), *Creflo Dollar Net Worth: $27 Million.*
    <https://www.celebritynetworth.com/richest-celebrities/creflo-dollar-net-worth/>

50. Crane E (2019), *'It's an offense to the Lord': Televangelist Benny Hinn*, Daily Mail, UK.
    <https://www.dailymail.co.uk/news/article-7432887/Christian-televangelist-Benny-Hinn-rejects-prosperity-gospel.html#comments>

51. Tuttle B (2018), *Billy Graham Was One of America's Richest Pastors*, Money.com, Guaynabo, PR.
    <https://money.com/billy-graham-net-worth-quotes-money-greed/>

52. Celebrity Net Worth (2020), *Bishop Eddie Long Net Worth: $5 Million*.
    <https://www.celebritynetworth.com/richest-celebrities/bishop-eddie-long-net-worth/>

53. Goleman D, *Emotional intelligence: why it can matter more than IQ*.

54. Hare RD, *Without Conscience*.

55. Black A (2010), *Legal recognition of Sharia law: Is this the right direction for Australian family matters?* Family Matters No. 84, Australian Institute of Family Studies, Australian Government.
    <https://aifs.gov.au/publications/family-matters/issue-84/legal-recognition-sharia-law>

Essay 6. Religious rules of compulsion have sabotaged faith

1. Hare RD (1993), *Without Conscience*, Guilford Press, New York.

2. Hercz R (2001), *Psychopaths among us*.
   <http://www.Hare.org/links/saturday.html>

3. Hunter P (2010), *The psycho gene*, EMBO reports, U.S. National Library of Medicine, Bethesda MD, USA.
   <https://www.ncbi.nlm.nih.gov/pmc/articles/PMC2933872/#b3>

4. Hare RD (1993), *Without Conscience*, p.98.

5. Hare RD (1993), *Without Conscience*, p.160

6. Hare RD (1993), *Without Conscience*, p.198

7. Harris GT, Rice ME & Cormier C (1991), *Psychopathy and violent recidivism*, Law and human behaviour 15: 625-37

8. Neumann CS, Hare RD and Newman JP (2011), *The super-ordinate nature of the psychopathy checklist-revised,* Journal of Personality Disorders. USA: NCBI, 2007; 21(2).
<https://www.ncbi.nlm.nih.gov/pmc/articles/PMC3136810/>

9. Blackwood N, et al. (2012), *Psychopathy linked to brain abnormalities,* King's College, London.
<https://www.kcl.ac.uk/archive/news/ioppn/records/2012/may/the-antisocial-brain>

10. Wikipedia (2020), *Broadmoor Hospital.*
<https://en.wikipedia.org/wiki/Broadmoor_Hospital>

11. Hercz R, *Psychopaths among us.*

12. Australian Public Service Commission (2020), *APS Agencies – size and function.*
<https://www.apsc.gov.au/aps-agencies-size-and-function>

13. IDS 302 Project (2010), *The Fatherless Generation,* USA.
<https://thefatherlessgeneration.wordpress.com/statistics/>

14. Australian Institute of Health and Welfare (2012), *Child protection Australia 2010–11.*
<https://www.aihw.gov.au/reports/child-protection/child-protection-australia-2010-11/contents/summary>

15. Thomas JR and Högnäs RS (2015), *The Effect of Parental Divorce on the Health of Adult Children.*
<https://www.ncbi.nlm.nih.gov/pmc/articles/PMC4651447/>

16. Balm J (2014), *The subway of the brain – Why white matter matters,* Springer Nature, BioMed Central Ltd (BMC), London.
<http://blogs.biomedcentral.com/on-biology/2014/03/14/the-subway-of-the-brain-why-white-matter-matters/>

17. Hare RD (1998), *Psychopaths and Their Nature: Implications for the Mental Health and Criminal Justice Systems*, in Psychopathy: Antisocial, Criminal, and Violent Behaviour, (p.188–212), ed. Millon T, Simonsen E, Birket-Smith M & Davis RD, The Guilford Press, New York

18. Babiak P, et al. (2012), *Psychopathy - An Important Forensic Concept for the 21st Century,* FBI law Enforcement Bulletin, United States Department of Justice.

<https://leb.fbi.gov/2012/july/psychopathy-an-important-forensic-concept-for-the-21st-century>
19. Hare RD (2003), *Hare Psychopathy Checklist-Revised*, 2nd ed. Toronto, ON: Multi-Health Systems.
<https://sk.sagepub.com/reference/psychologylaw/n138.xml>
20. Häkkänen-Nyholm H, Hare RD (2009), *Psychopathy, Homicide, and the Courts: Working the System*, in *Criminal Justice and Behavior* 36, no. 8 (2009): 761-777.
<https://journals.sagepub.com/doi/10.1177/0093854809336946>
21. Porter S, Brinke L, Wilson K (2009), *Crime Profiles and Conditional Release Performance of Psychopathic and Nonpsychopathic Sexual Offenders*, Legal and Criminological Psychology 14, no. 1 (February 2009): 109-118.
<https://onlinelibrary.wiley.com/doi/abs/10.1348/135532508X284310>
22. Meloy JR (1988), *The Psychopathic Mind: Origins, Dynamics, and Treatment*, Jason Aronson Inc., USA
23. Harris GT, Rice ME & Cormier C (1991), *Psychopathy and violent recidivism*, Law and human behaviour 15: 625-37.
<https://psycnet.apa.org/record/1992-13227-001>
24. Wikipedia (2020), *Emotional detachment*.
<https://en.wikipedia.org/wiki/Emotional_detachment>
25. Babiak P, et al., *Psychopathy - An Important Forensic Concept for the 21st Century*.
26. Babiak P and Hare RD (2007), *Snakes in Suits*, HarperCollins Publishers, New York.
27. Neumann CS, Hare RD, and Newman JP (2015), *The super-ordinate nature of the psychopathy checklist-revised*, (last para. 'Discussion') NCBI, US.
<https://www.ncbi.nlm.nih.gov/pmc/articles/PMC3136810/>
28. Hare RD, *Without Conscience*: p.198-200.
29. Hare RD (2010), *Intraspecies Predator: How a psychopath sees the world*, Sott video (www.sott.net).
<https://www.sott.net/article/218599-Intraspecies-Predator-How-A-Psychopath-Sees-The-World>

30. Kiehl KA (2015), *The Psychopath Whisperer: The Science of Those Without Conscience*, Penguin Random House, New York.

31. Parry W (2011), *How to Spot Psychopaths: Speech Patterns Give Them Away.*
<https://www.livescience.com/16585-psychopaths-speech-language.html>

32. Inspector of Custodial Services (2018), *The management of radicalised inmates in NSW*, Sydney, Australia.
<www.custodialinspector.justice.nsw.gov.au › Documents PDF>

33. Graham-Harrison E (2009), *China's last eunuch spills sex secrets.*
<https://www.reuters.com/article/us-china-eunuch-idUSTRE52E06H20090316>

34. Wikipedia (2020), *Eunuch.*
<https://en.wikipedia.org/wiki/Eunuch>

35. Wong J & ABC News Medical Unit (2012), *Eunuchs May Hold Key to Longevity.*
<http://abcnews.go.com/Health/castration-men-live-longer-eunuchs-studied-korean-records/story?id=17310420>

36. Sifferlin A (2012), *Do eunuchs really live longer?*
<https://edition.cnn.com/2012/09/25/health/eunuchs-lifespan/index.html>

37. Gallagher J (2012), *Eunuchs reveal clues to why women live longer than men.*
<https://www.bbc.com/news/health-19699266>

38. Norman-Eady S (2006), *Castration of sex offenders*, OLR Research Report, Connecticut, USA.
<https://www.cga.ct.gov/2006/rpt/2006-R-0183.htm>

39. Weinberger LE, Sreenivasan S, Garrick T, Osran H (2005), *The Impact of Surgical Castration on Sexual Recidivism Risk Among Sexually Violent Predatory Offenders*, Journal of the American Academy of Psychiatry and the Law, Vol. 33 (1) 16-36.
<http://jaapl.org/content/33/1/16>

40. Hare RD, *Without Conscience.*

41. Pollock A (2016), *Why I Don't Use the Word 'Forgiveness' in Trauma Therapy*, GoodTherapy.

<http://www.goodtherapy.org/blog/why-i-dont-use-the-word-forgiveness-in-trauma-therapy-0120164>

42. Forward S, Buck, C (1989), *Toxic parents: overcoming their hurtful legacy and reclaiming your life*, Bantam Books, New York.

43. Forward S & Frazier D (1997), *Emotional Blackmail: When the people in your life use fear, obligation and guilt to manipulate you*, Thorsons Audio, HarperCollins Publishers, Glasgow.

44. Catholic Answers (2004), *The Forgiveness of Sins*.
    <https://www.catholic.com/tract/the-forgiveness-of-sins>

45. Intelligent Design, *What is Intelligent Design*, Discovery Institute.
    <https://intelligentdesign.org/whatisid/>

46. Black, A (2010), *Legal recognition of Sharia law: Is this the right direction for Australian family matters?* Family Matters, 84, 64-67, Australian Institute of Family Studies, Australian Government.
    <https://aifs.gov.au/publications/family-matters/issue-84/legal-recognition-sharia-law>

47. Goleman D (2006), *Emotional intelligence: why it can matter more than IQ*, Bantam Books, New York.

48. BBC News (2019), *Catholic Church child sexual abuse scandal*.
    <https://www.bbc.com/news/world-44209971>

49. Perkins, M (2019), *'I cannot comprehend': Sex abuse royal commissioner slams Catholic leaders*, The Sydney Morning Herald.
    <https://www.smh.com.au/national/i-cannot-comprehend-sex-abuse-royal-commissioner-slams-catholic-leaders-20191210-p53inr.html>

50. Millar GH (2002), *Inquiry into children in institutional care*, Senate Community Affairs References Committee, Canberra, ACT.
    <www.aph.gov.au › inst_care › submissions › sub135_doc>

51. Hare RD, *Without conscience:* p.33.

52. Sennels N (2013), *Reports on Muslim immigration, first cousin inbreeding and high numbers of birth defects, lack of integration*, Norway and Sweden.

53. Coulter, A (2009), *Guilty (Ch2)*, Three Rivers Press, New York.

54. Bodissey B (2011), *Why Multiculture Will Always Fail*.
    <http://gatesofvienna.blogspot.com/2011/03/why-multiculture-will-always-fail.html>

55. Sennels N (2010), *The Connection Between Muslim Inbreeding and Terrorism.*
    <http://gatesofvienna.blogspot.com.au/2010/12/connection-between-muslim-inbreeding.html>

56. Sennels N (2018), *Holy Wrath: Among criminal Muslims,* Logik Förlag, Sweden.

57. Schmidlin W (2016), *The Muslim dilemma and their conflict with Western Culture.*
    <http://www.wernercairns.com/2016/04/the-muslim-dilemma-and-their-conflict.html>

58. Dymphna (2010), *Islam Means Never Having to Say You're Sorry.*
    <http://gatesofvienna.blogspot.com/2010/05/islam-means-never-having-to-say-youre.html>

59. Whitton E (2013), *The Parliament of Australia (n lawyers).*
    <https://independentaustralia.net/politics/politics-display/the-parliament-of-australian-lawyers,5652>

60. Drutman L (2016), *There are too many lawyers in politics. Here's what to do about it,* Vox Media.
    <https://www.vox.com/polyarchy/2016/6/30/12068490/too-many-lawyers-politics>

61. Watts A (2017), *Legal challenge: Knowing the law inside out is not always the best preparation* for government, The Spectator, London, UK.
    <https://www.spectator.co.uk/article/legal-challenge>

62. Ambrosius T (2009), *Youths, Crime, and Islam.*
    <http://gatesofvienna.blogspot.com/2009/02/youths-crime-and-islam.html>

63. The Local (2017), *So... are they no-go zones? What you need to know about Sweden's vulnerable areas.*
    <https://www.thelocal.se/20170621/no-go-zones-what-you-need-to-know-about-swedens-vulnerable-areas>

64. Streuning F (2010*), Family Security Matters.*
    <https://2010-14.newenglishreview.org/blog_direct_link.cfm?blog_id=26947&Danish per cent2DPsychologist>

65. McIntyre A (2014), *In Denmark, a Bruising Multiculturalism.*
    <https://quadrant.org.au/opinion/qed/2014/08/denmark-bruising-multiculturalism/>

66. Spencer R (2016), *Sweden: Memorial for murdered social worker banned to avoid upsetting Muslim migrants.*
    <http://www.jihadwatch.org/2016/02/sweden-memorial-for-murdered-social-worker-banned-to-avoid-upsetting-muslim-migrants>

67. Prison Planet (2017), *Sweden: Muslim migrants throw firecracker at baby.*
    <https://www.prisonplanet.com/sweden-muslim-migrants-throw-firecracker-at-baby.html>

68. The Mirror (2016), *Jyoti Singh, Delhi rape victim*, UK.
    <http://www.mirror.co.uk/all-about/jyoti-singh>

69. Wikipedia (2020), *2012 Delhi gang rape.*
    <https://en.wikipedia.org/wiki/2012_Delhi_gang_rape>

70. Independent News, (2015), *Delhi bus rapist blames dead victim for attack because 'girls are responsible for rape'*, UK.
    <http://www.independent.co.uk/news/world/asia/delhi-bus-rapist-blames-dead-victim-for-attack-because-girls-are-responsible-for-rape-10079894.html>

71. India Today (2013), *Delhi gang rape victim's friend relives the horrifying 84 minutes of December 16 night.*
    <http://indiatoday.intoday.in/story/delhi-gangrape-victims-friend-relives-the-horrifying-84-minutes-of-december-16-night/1/309573.html>

72. The Australian (2013), *Father names rape victim as Jyoti Singh Pandey to hearten others.*
    <https://www.theaustralian.com.au/news/world/father-names-rape-victim-as-jyoti-singh-pandey-to-hearten-others/news-story/>

73. Chamberlain G and Bhabani S (2017), *Five years after the gang-rape and murder of Jyoti Singh, what has changed for women in India?* The Guardian, India.
    <https://www.theguardian.com/society/2017/dec/03/five-years-after-gang-murder-jyoti-singh-how-has-delhi-changed>

74. Norman-Eady, *Castration of sex offenders.*

75. Hare RD, *Without conscience.*

76. Wikipedia (2020), *Bilal Skaf: Australian serial gang rapist.*
    <https://en.wikipedia.org/wiki/Bilal_Skaf>

77. Wikipedia (2020), *Sydney gang rapes.*
    <https://en.wikipedia.org/wiki/Sydney_gang_rapes>
78. Alchetron.com (2018), Bilal Skaf.
    <https://alchetron.com/Bilal-Skaf>
79. Hare RD, *Without conscience:* p.195.
80. Hare RD, *Without conscience:* p.198.
81. Norman-Eady S (2006), *Castration of sex offenders,* OLR Research Report, USA.
    <https://www.cga.ct.gov/2006/rpt/2006-R-0183.htm>
82. Weinberger LE, Sreenivasan S, Garrick T and Osran H (2005), *The Impact of Surgical Castration on Sexual Recidivism Risk Among Sexually Violent Predatory Offenders,* Journal of the American Academy of Psychiatry and the Law Online: March 2005, 33 (1) 16-36.
    <http://jaapl.org/content/33/1/16>
83. Wong J & ABC News Medical Unit, *Eunuchs May Hold Key to Longevity.*
84. Sennels, *The Connection Between Muslim Inbreeding and Terrorism.*

Essay 7. Male domination in religion has moulded monsters

1. Human Rights Watch (2017), *Russia: Bill to Decriminalize Domestic Violence Parliament Should Reject Measure That Harms Families*, New York.
   <https://www.hrw.org/news/2017/01/23/russia-bill-decriminalize-domestic-violence>
2. Beccaria F and White HR (2012), *Underage Drinking in Europe and North America,* OpenEdition Books, Chapter 1: p. 21-78.
   <https://books.openedition.org/pucl/3274?lang=en>
3. Gilligan C, Kuntsche E, Gmel G (2012), *Adolescent Drinking Patterns Across Countries: Associations with Alcohol Policies,* Alcohol and Alcoholism, Volume 47, Issue 6: Pages 732–737. <https://academic.oup.com/alcalc/article/47/6/732/204327>
4. Rosen S (2018), *These 10 Countries Drink the Most per Capita,* The Points Guy.

<https://thepointsguy.com/news/these-10-countries-drink-the-most-per-capita/>

5. Weatherall TJ, Conigrave KM, Conigrave JH, et al. (2020), *What is the prevalence of current alcohol dependence and how is it measured for Indigenous people in Australia, New Zealand, Canada and the United States of America?* <https://pubmed.ncbi.nlm.nih.gov/32943111/>

6. True Islam (2020), *The history of hadith, Prophet Muhammad forbids the writing of his hadith*, Part 1 (7). <http://www.quran-islam.org/articles/part_1/history_hadith_1_(P1148).html>

7. Wikipedia (2020), *Apostasy*. <https://en.wikipedia.org/wiki/Apostasy>

8. Wikipedia (2020), *Ashtiname of Muhammad*. <https://en.wikipedia.org/wiki/Ashtiname_of_Muhammad>

9. Wikipedia (2020), *Shirk (Islam)*. <https://en.wikipedia.org/wiki/Shirk_(Islam)>

10. Wikipedia (2020), *God in Islam*. <https://en.wikipedia.org/wiki/God_in_Islam>

11. Görke A, Pink J (2015), *Tafsir and Islamic Intellectual History: Exploring the Boundaries of a Genre*, Oxford University Press (OUP): p.478. <https://www.iis.ac.uk/publication/tafsir-and-islamic-intellectual-history-exploring-boundaries-genre>

12. Holy Bible Revised Standard Version (1971), Collins Publishers, New York & Cleveland.

13. Wikipedia, *Ashtiname of Muhammad*.

14. True Islam (2020), *The history of hadith: Prophet Muhammad forbids the writing of his hadith*, Part 1 (7). <http://www.quran-islam.org/articles/part_1/history_hadith_1_(P1148).html>

15. Wikipedia), *Shirk (Islam)*.

16. Submission.org (2013), *Hadith and the Corruption of the great religion of Islam*. <http://submission.org/Corruption_of_Religion.html>

17. Singh M (2014), *Some Early Childhood Experiences Shape Adult Life, But Which Ones?* NPR.org.
    <https://www.npr.org/sections/health-shots/2014/12/19/371679655/some-early-childhood-experiences-shape-adult-life-but-which>
18. Fuller K (2020), *5 Ways Childhood Trauma Affects Adulthood.*
    <https://www.akuamindbody.com/mental-health/5-ways-childhood-trauma-affects-adulthood/>
19. Hare RD (1993), *Without Conscience*, Guilford Press, New York.
20. Pettinger T (2014), *Biography of Martin Luther*, Oxford, UK.
    <http://www.biographyonline.net/spiritual/martin-luther.html>
21. Wikipedia (2020), *Stockholm syndrome.*
    <https://en.wikipedia.org/wiki/stockholm_syndrome>
22. Momynkulov Z (2017), *Why Muslim world lagged behind in science*, Egemen Qazaqstan.
    <https://en.egemen.kz/article/188580-why-muslim-world-lagged-behind-in-science>
23. Bardsley D (2017), *How did the Muslim world fall behind on science - and how can it thrive again?* The National.
    <https://www.thenational.ae/uae/how-did-the-muslim-world-fall-behind-on-science-and-how-can-it-thrive-again-1.680685>
24. Wikipedia (2020), *Islamic attitudes towards science.*
    <https://en.wikipedia.org/wiki/Islamic_attitudes_towards_science>
25. Giambrone A (2015*), Coping after captivity: The mental-health effects of being held hostage.*
    <https://www.theatlantic.com/health/archive/2015/01/coping-after-captivity/384577/>
26. ABC Science (2009), *Understanding psychopaths.*
    <https://www.abc.net.au/science/articles/2009/10/01/2701728.htm>
27. Kadivar, M (2014), *An Introduction to Apostasy, Blasphemy, & Religious Freedom in Islam.*
    <http://en.kadivar.com/2014/07/23/an-introduction-to-apostasy-blasphemy-religious-freedom-in-islam/>

28. Wikipedia (2020), *Apostasy.*
    <https://en.wikipedia.org/wiki/Apostasy>

29. Wikipedia (2020), *Ridda wars.*
    <https://en.wikipedia.org/wiki/Ridda_wars>

30. Library of Congress (2020), *Laws Criminalizing Apostasy*, Washington, DC
    <https://www.loc.gov/law/help/apostasy/index.php>

31. True Islam (2020), *The history of hadith: Prophet Muhammad forbids the writing of his hadith,* Part 1 (7).
    <http://www.quran-islam.org/articles/part_1/history_hadith_1_(P1148).html>

32. True Islam (2020), *The history of hadith: Why and when it was written,* (Part 2).
    <http://www.quran-Islam.org/articles/part_1/history_hadith_2_(P1308).htm/>

33. The Prophet of Mercy Website (2006), *Did Prophet Muhammad spread Islam by the sword and force people to accept his religion?*
    <http://mercyprophet.org/mul/node/3331>

34. Wikipedia (2020), *Forced conversion.*
    <https://en.wikipedia.org/wiki/Forced_conversion>

35. Wikipedia (2020), *Muhammad Quraish Shihab.*
    <https://en.m.wikipedia.org/wiki/Muhammad_Quraish_Shihab>

36. The Islamic Information (2020), *When Muhammad was Depressed.*
    <https://theislamicinformation.com/muhammad-pbuh-depressed/>

37. Simon G (2013), *Predators among us: The psychopaths.*
    <https://www.drgeorgesimon.com/predators-among-us-the-psychopaths/>

38. Blackwood N, et al. (2012), *Psychopathy linked to brain abnormalities,* King's College, London.
    <https://www.kcl.ac.uk/archive/news/ioppn/records/2012/may/the-antisocial-brain>

39. Hare RD (1993), *Without Conscience.*

40. Pruitt S (2019), *Islam's Sunni-Shia Divide, Explained,* This day in history.

<https://www.history.com/news/sunni-shia-divide-islam-muslim>

41. True Islam (2020), *'Halal Meat' – The Quranic truth.*
<http://www.quran-Islam.org/articles/halal_meat_(P1156).html>

42. Hermann HR (2007), *Killing Humans,* Dominance and Aggression in Humans and Other Animals: The Great Game of Life, Ch 15: Pages 229-249.
<https://www.sciencedirect.com/topics/social-sciences/cruelty-to-animals>

43. Babao-Guballa C (2013), *The link between animal cruelty and antisocial personality disorders*
<https://lifestyle.inquirer.net/129343/the-link-between-animal-cruelty-and-antisocial-personality-disorders/>

44. Islamic Research (2014), *Examples of Hadith that Insult Prophet Muhammad.*
<https://yaqeeninstitute.org/mohammad-elshinawy/how-the-prophet-muhammad-rose-above-enmity-and-insult>

45. TheReligionofPeace.com (2020), *Deception, Lying and Taqiyya: Does Islam permit Muslims to lie?*
<https://www.thereligionofpeace.com/pages/quran/taqiyya.aspx>

46. True Islam (2021), English translation of the Quran.
<https://www.quran-islam.org/main_topics/quran_in_english_(P1223).html>

47. Hare RD, *Without Conscience:* p. 195-198.

48. Wikipedia, *Ashtiname of Muhammad.*

49. True Islam (2020), *Why* Prophet *Muhammad is innocent of the fabricated hadith that fills the hadith books.*
<http://www.quran-islam.org/.../hadith_not_from_prophet_(P1177).html>

50. The Religion of Peace (2020), *Is the Quran Hate Propaganda?* Developed by TROP (The Religion Of Peace).
<http://www.thereligionofpeace.com/pages/articles/quran-hate.aspx>

51. Wikipedia (2020), *Sawda bint Zamʿa.*

<https://en.wikipedia.org/wiki/Sawda_bint_Zam per centCA per centBFa>

52. Joukowsky Institute for ArchaeologyIslamic (2009), *Civilizations: Ridda wars,* Brown University, Providence, USA.
<https://www.brown.edu/Departments/Joukowsky_Institute/courses/islamiccivilizations/8026.html>

53. Wikipedia, *Ridda wars.*

54. Hurtado L (2009), *Why Was Jesus Crucified?* Slate, U.S. and Canada.
<http://www.slate.com/articles/life/faithbased/2009/04/why_was_jesus_crucified.html>

55. Biography.com Editors (2014), *Pontius Pilate Biography.*
<https://www.biography.com/religious-figure/pontius-pilate>

56. Wikipedia (2020), *Alois Hitler.*
<https://en.wikipedia.org/wiki/Alois_Hitler>

57. Wikipedia (2020), *List of Islamist terrorist attacks.*
<https://en.wikipedia.org/wiki/List_of_Islamist_terrorist_attacks>

58. Kiehl KA and Hoffman MB (2014), *The criminal psychopath: history, neuroscience, treatment, and economics.*
<https://www.ncbi.nlm.nih.gov/pmc/articles/PMC4059069/>

59. Ahlul Bayt Digital Islamic Library Project 1995-2017, *Arabia before Islam.*
<https://www.al-islam.org/restatement-history-islam-and-muslims-sayyid-ali-ashgar-razwy/arabia-islam#social-conditions>

60. Spencer, R & Chesler, P (2007), *The violent oppression of women in Islam,* David Horowitz Freedom Center, Los Angeles.
<https://jenseyatvajameh.files.wordpress.com/2008/07/the-violent-oppression-of-women-in-Islam.pdf>

61. Wikipedia (2020), *Dictators.*
<https://en.wikipedia.org/wiki/Dictator>

62. PBS (2002), *Muhammad: Legacy of a Prophet.*
<https://www.pbs.org/muhammad/ma_women.shtml>

63. Callimachi, R (2015), *ISIS enshrines a theology of rape.*
<https://www.nytimes.com/2015/08/14/world/middleeast/isis-enshrines-a-theology-of-rape.html>

64. The New York Times (2016), *The Culture of Rape Within ISIS, and the Questions That Arise.*
<https://www.nytimes.com/2016/03/20/world/middleeast/the-culture-of-rape-within-isis-and-the-questions-that-arise.html>

65. Norman-Eady S (2006), *Castration of sex offenders*, OLR Research Report, Connecticut, USA.
<https://www.cga.ct.gov/2006/rpt/2006-R-0183.htm>

66. Weinberger LE, Sreenivasan S, Garrick T, Osran H (2005), *The Impact of Surgical Castration on Sexual Recidivism Risk Among Sexually Violent Predatory Offenders,* Journal of the American Academy of Psychiatry and the Law, Vol. 33 (1) 16-36.
<http://jaapl.org/content/33/1/16>

67. Wong J & ABC News Medical Unit (2012), *Eunuchs May Hold Key to Longevity.*
<http://abcnews.go.com/Health/castration-men-live-longer-eunuchs-studied-korean-records/story?id=17310420>

68. Burrows T (2015), *ISIS vow to eradicate 'disease' of Judaism from the world,* Daily Mail, UK.
<https://www.dailymail.co.uk/news/article-3286429/ISIS-vow-kill-eradicate-disease-Judaism-world-chilling-new-video-produced-Hebrew.html>

69. Submission.org, *Hadith and the Corruption of the great religion of Islam.*

70. Religious Forums (2017), *List of traditions (Hadiths) that contradict explicitly the holy Quran.*
<https://www.religiousforums.com/threads/list-of-traditions-hadiths-that-contradict-explicitly-the-holy-quran.194319/>

71. Semple K (2014), *Yazidi girls seized by ISIS speak out after escape.*
<http://www.nytimes.com/2014/11/15/world/middleeast/yazidi-girls-seized-by-isis-speak-out-after-escape.html?_r=0>

72. Wikipedia (2017), *Genocide of Yazidis by ISIL.*
<https://en.wikipedia.org/wiki/Persecution_of_Yazidis_by_ISIL#Abduction_of_women.3B_sexual_slavery>

73. Find a Grave (2012), *Stewart John "The Magician" Regan.*
<https://www.findagrave.com/memorial/89608108/stewart-john-regan>

74. Kiehl KA and Hoffman MB, *The criminal psychopath: history, neuroscience, treatment, and economics.*
75. Hare RD, *Without Conscience.*

Essay 8. Terrorists, murderers and rapists are soldiers of sin, not God

1. Wikipedia (2020), *Bigamy.*
   <https://en.wikipedia.org/wiki/Bigamy>
2. RANZCP (2020, *Borderline personality disorder,* Royal Australian & New Zealand College of Psychiatrists.
   <https://www.yourhealthinmind.org/mental-illnesses-disorders/bpd>
3. Holy Bible Revised Standard Version (1971), Collins Publishers, New York & Cleveland.
4. Wikipedia (2017), *Muhammad's wives.*
   <https://en.wikipedia.org/wiki/Muhammad per cent27s_wives>
5. Wikipedia (2020), *Stockholm syndrome.*
   <https://en.wikipedia.org/wiki/Stockholm_syndrome>
6. Wikipedia (2017), *Children of Muhammad.*
   <https://en.wikipedia.org/wiki/Children_of_Muhammad>
7. Spencer R & Chesler P (2007), *The violent oppression of women in Islam,* David Horowitz Freedom Center, Los Angeles.
   <https://jenseyatvajameh.files.wordpress.com/2008/07/the-violent-oppression-of-women-in-Islam.pdf>
8. Kinias A (2010), *History of the Veil: Part 3: Early days of Islam.*
   <https://alexandrakinias.wordpress.com/2010/07/11/history-of-the-veil-part-3-early-days-of-islam/>
9. Moore C (2020), *The Burqa – Islamic or Cultural?* True Islam (Pt 3).
   <http://www.quran-islam.org/articles/part_3/the_burqa_(P1357).html>
10. Jdemarai (2014), *Should Muslim women be forced to wear a veil in public?* World Religion News.
    <https://worldreligionnews.wordpress.com/2014/05/27/should-muslim-women-be-forced-to-wear-a-veil-in-public/>

11. BBC Newsround (2018), *What's the difference between a hijab, niqab and burka?*
    <https://www.bbc.co.uk/newsround/24118241>
12. Berens C (2017), *Veiling and the Rise in Rapes.*
    <http://www.cheriberens.net/veiling-and-the-rise-in-rapes.html>
13. Facts and Details (2019), *Babylonian and Mesopotamian mathematics.*
    <http://factsanddetails.com/world/cat56/sub402/entry-6083.htm >
14. Facts and Details (2019), *Agriculture, crops, irrigation and livestock in Mesopotamia.*
    <http://factsanddetails.com/world/cat56/sub363/item1513.html>
15. Kivumbi (2011), 'Difference between Assyrian and Babylonian', DB DifferenceBetween.net.
    <http://www.differencebetween.net/miscellaneous/difference-between-assyrian-and-babylonian/>
16. Kinias A (2010), *History of the Veil. Part 2: Veil in pre-Islamic Arabia.*
    <https://alexandrakinias.wordpress.com/2010/06/29/history-of-veil-part-2-veil-in-pre-islamic-arabia/>
17. Kinias A (2010), *History of the Veil. Part One: Veil in the Ancient World.*
    <https://alexandrakinias.wordpress.com/2010/06/27/history-of-the-veil-part-one-veil-in-the-ancient-world/>
18. Berens C (2017), *Women's March towards Islam?*
    <http://www.cheriberens.net/womenrsquos-march-towards-islam.html>
19. Wikipedia (2020), *Muslim Brotherhood in Egypt.*
    <https://en.wikipedia.org/wiki/Muslim_Brotherhood_in_Egypt>
20. Warraq I (2003), *Why I Am Not a Muslim*, Prometheus Books, New York.
21. Spencer R & Chesler P, *The violent oppression of women in Islam.*
22. Berens, *Women's March towards Islam?*
23. Berens C (2019), *An American woman living in Egypt: Life during an Islamic takeover*, MASR Academic Press.
24. BBC News (2002), *Saudi police 'stopped' fire rescue.*
    <http://news.bbc.co.uk/2/hi/middle_east/1874471.stm>

25. NZ Herald (2013), *Burqa hid injuries of teen repeatedly bashed.* <http://www.nzherald.co.nz/nz/news/article.cfm?c_id=1&objectid=11173066>

26. Simon, G (2008), *Understanding the Predatory Aggressive Personality,* Psychology, Philosophy and Real Life. <https://counsellingresource.com/features/2008/11/24/predatory-aggressive-personality/>

27. Pozueco-Romero JM, Manso JMM, Alonso MB, et al. (2013), *Socialized/subclinical psychopaths in intimate partner relationships: profile, psychological abuse and risk factors.* <https://www.researchgate.net/publication/267208193_>

28. Decision Making Confidence (2019), *It's not always easy to detect a sociopath, unless you know what you are looking for...* <https://www.decision-making-confidence.com/detect-a-sociopath.html>

29. Eddy B (2018), *Are You the Target of a Sociopath? Part I of 2,* Psychology Today. <https://www.psychologytoday.com/au/blog/5-types-people-who-can-ruin-your-life/201803/are-you-the-target-sociopath-part-i-2>

30. Psychopaths in Life (2020), *How & Why Psychopaths Isolate Their Victims.*

31. True Islam (2020), *The history of hadith, Prophet Muhammad forbids the writing of his hadith,* Part 1 (7). <http://www.quran-Islam.org/articles/part_1/history_hadith_1_(P1148).html>

32. True Islam (2020), *False Accusations against the Quran.* <http://www.quran-islam.org/main_topics/false_accusations_(P1215).html>

33. True Islam (2020), *The misinterpretation and manipulation of Quranic verses.* <http://www.quran-islam.org/main_topics/misinterpreted_verses_(P1224).html>

34. True Islam (2020), *The History of Hadith (Why and when it was written),* Part 2.

<http://www.quran-Islam.org/articles/part_1/history_hadith_2_
(P1308).html>

35. True Islam (2020), *The Dress Code in the Quran for Women*.
<http://www.quran-Islam.org/articles/women_dress_code_
(P1150).html>

36. True Islam (2020), *English Translation of the Quran, Sura 31-37 (33:59)*.
<http://www.quran-islam.org/main_topics/quran_in_english_
(P1223).html>

37. Holy Bible Revised Standard Version (1971), Collins Publishers,
New York and Cleveland.

38. True Islam (2020), *7- The Purgatory (Al-A'araf)*.
<http://www.quran-islam.org/main_topics/quran/quran_in_
english/sura_5_to_9_(P1323).html>

39. Norman-Eady S (2006), *Castration of sex offenders*, OLR Research
Report, Connecticut, USA.
<https://www.cga.ct.gov/2006/rpt/2006-R-0183.htm>

40. Weinberger LE, Sreenivasan S, Garrick T, Osran H (2005), *The
Impact of Surgical Castration on Sexual Recidivism Risk Among Sexually
Violent Predatory Offenders,* Journal of the American Academy of
Psychiatry and the Law, Vol. 33 (1) 16-36.
<http://jaapl.org/content/33/1/16>

41. Wong J & ABC News Medical Unit (2012), *Eunuchs May Hold Key to
Longevity*.
<http://abcnews.go.com/Health/castration-men-live-longer-
eunuchs-studied-korean-records/story?id=17310420>

42. Al-Jibouri YT (2017), '*Khadijah, Daughter of Khuwaylid, Wife of Prophet
Muhammad*', Ahlul Bayt Digital Islamic Library Project.
<https://www.al-islam.org/articles/khadijah-daughter-khuwaylid-
wife-prophet-muhammad-yasin-t-al-jibouri>

43. Wikipedia (2017), '*Khadija bint Khuwaylid*'.
<https://en.wikipedia.org/wiki/Khadija_bint_Khuwaylid>

44. Chesler P (2006), *The death of feminism*, Palgrave Macmillan, New
York.

45. Encyclopaedia of Mental Disorders (2019), *Hare Psychopathy Checklist*,
Advameg Inc, Illinois, US.

<http://www.minddisorders.com/Flu-Inv/Hare -Psychopathy-Checklist.html>

46. Wikipedia (2020), *Shirk (Islam)*.
    <https://en.wikipedia.org/wiki/Shirk_(Islam)>

47. Bhargava JM (2017), *A Parent Reacts to Rapes of Young Delhi Girls*, New Delhi Television (NDTV).
    <http://www.ndtv.com/blog/a-parent-reacts-to-rapes-of-young-delhi-girls-1233807>

48. Chamberlain G & Bhabani S (2017), *Five years after the gang-rape and murder of Jyoti Singh, what has changed for women in India?* The Guardian, Delhi, India.
    <https://www.theguardian.com/society/2017/dec/03/five-years-after-gang-murder-jyoti-singh-how-has-delhi-changed>

49. BBC News (2018), *India outcry after eight-month-old baby raped.*
    <https://www.bbc.com/news/world-asia-india-42869010>

50. Gella N (2017), *Daughters of Mother India... You're not safe here Unfortunately!!*
    <https://www.huffingtonpost.in/2016/09/03/11-months-old-baby-raped-for-two-hours-in-delhi_a_21465113/>

51. The Times of India (2016), *In Delhi, three kids face sex abuse daily: NCRB data.*
    <https://timesofindia.indiatimes.com/city/delhi/In-Delhi-three-kids-face-sex-abuse-daily-NCRB-data/articleshow/53998943.cms>

52. Hindustan Times (2016), *No let-up in number of rape cases against children in Delhi.*
    <https://www.hindustantimes.com/delhi/no-let-up-in-number-of-rape-cases-against-children-in-delhi/story-cCKMzaOoptKuq1Nz2OWctL.html>

53. BBC News (2016), *The Indian girls who survived being raped.*
    <https://www.bbc.com/news/world-asia-india-35379221>

54. Tavaana (2020), *Nirbhaya - fearless one: ending gender-based violence in India with institutional and cultural changes.*
    <https://tavaana.org/en/case-studies/Nirbhaya_Fearless_One_En>

55. Spencer R (2007), *A religion of peace? Why Christianity is and Islam isn't*, Regnery Publishing, Inc., Washington, DC.

56. Spencer R, Chesler P (2007), *The violent oppression of women in Islam*, David Horowitz Freedom Center, Los Angeles.
<https://jenseyatvajameh.files.wordpress.com/2008/07/the-violent-oppression-of-women-in-Islam.pdf>.

57. Choo K (1998), *Kifaya Hussein*, Chicago Tribune.
<http://www.chicagotribune.com/news/ct-xpm-1998-05-03-9805030063-story.html>

58. Croffie S (2020), *Duty or Faith?: The Evolution of Pakistani Rape Laws and Possibility for Non-Domestic Redress for Victims*, Emory Law, Atlanta, US.
<https://law.emory.edu/eilr/content/volume-30/issue-4/comments/duty-faith-pakistani-rape-non-domestic-redress.html>

59. Balm J (2014), *The subway of the brain – Why white matter matters*, Springer Nature, BioMed Central Ltd (BMC), London.
<http://blogs.biomedcentral.com/on-biology/2014/03/14/the-subway-of-the-brain-why-white-matter-matters/>

60. AVAAZ (2015), *Prevent the flogging of 15 year old rape victim in Maldives*.
<https://secure.avaaz.org/community_petitions/en/Prevent_a_rape_victim_from_being_punished/>

61. Wikipedia (2021), *Execution of a teenage girl – hanging* of *Atefeh Rajabi, 16-year-old-girl (2016)*, Discovery Channel, Cosmo Learning.
<https://cosmolearning.org/documentaries/execution-of-a-teenage-girl/>

62. McDougall D (2006), *Fareeda's fate: rape, prison and 25 lashes*, The Guardian, Western Pakistan.
<https://www.theguardian.com/world/2006/sep/17/pakistan.theobserver>

63. Hare RD (1993), *Without Conscience*, Guilford Press, New York.

64. Quora (2019), *Can DNA change after birth?*
<https://www.quora.com/Can-DNA-change-after-birth>

Essay 9. Should faith and science be adversaries: Where do we go from here?

1. Balm J (2014), *The subway of the brain – Why white matter matters*, Springer Nature, BioMed Central Ltd (BMC), London. <http://blogs.biomedcentral.com/on-biology/2014/03/14/the-subway-of-the-brain-why-white-matter-matters/>
2. Blackwood N, et al. (2012), *Psychopathy linked to brain abnormalities*, King's College, London. <https://www.kcl.ac.uk/archive/news/ioppn/records/2012/may/the-antisocial-brain>
3. UN News (2016), *ISIL's 'scorched earth policy' creating environmental and health havoc in Mosul, warns UN*. <https://news.un.org/en/story/2016/10/543902-isils-scorched-earth-policy-creating-environmental-and-health-havoc-mosul-warns>
4. Veith WJ (2009), *Paganism and Catholicism*, Amazing Discoveries Canada. <http://amazingdiscoveries.org/S-deception_end-time_paganism_Catholic_Mithraism>
5. Zielinski S (2015), *Modern Humans Have Become Superpredators*, Smithsonian Institution, US. <https://www.smithsonianmag.com/science-nature/modern-humans-have-become-superpredators-180956348/>
6. Simon G (2013), *Predators Among Us: The Psychopaths*. <https://www.drgeorgesimon.com/predators-among-us-the-psychopaths/>
7. Hare RD (2010), *Intraspecies Predator: How a psychopath sees the world*, Sott video (www.sott.net). <https://www.sott.net/article/218599-Intraspecies-Predator-How-A-Psychopath-Sees-The-World>
8. Payne R (1998), *A framework for understanding poverty*, RFT Publishing, Texas, USA.
9. Saunders P (2004), *Australia's welfare habit: and how to kick it*, Duffy & Snellgrove, Sydney.

10. Dalrymple, T (2001)), *Life at the bottom*, Ivan R Dee, Publisher, Chicago.

11. Sullivan L (2000), *Behavioural Poverty*, Policy Monograph 45, The Centre for Independent Studies Ltd., St Leonards, NSW.

12. Dudley D (2018), *The deadliest terrorist groups in the world today*, Forbes. <https://www.forbes.com/sites/dominicdudley/2018/12/05/deadliest-terrorist-groups-in-the-worlAd/#7ab316842b3e>

13. Goleman D (2006), *Emotional intelligence: why it can matter more than IQ*, Bantam Books, New York.

14. Meyer JH, et al. (2006), *Elevated Monoamine Oxidase A Levels in the Brain: of major depression an explanation for the Monoamine Imbalance.* <http://jamanetwork.com/journals/jamapsychiatry/fullarticle/668227>

15. Balm J (2014), *The subway of the brain – Why white matter matters*, Springer Nature, BioMed Central Ltd (BMC), London. <http://blogs.biomedcentral.com/on-biology/2014/03/14/the-subway-of-the-brain-why-white-matter-matters/>

16. Blackwood N, et al. (2012), *Psychopathy linked to brain abnormalities*, King's College, London. <https://www.kcl.ac.uk/archive/news/ioppn/records/2012/may/the-antisocial-brain>

17. Miltimore J (2017), *Muslim Inbreeding is a Huge Problem--And People Don't Want to Talk About It*, Intellectual Takeout, Charlemagne Institute, Bloomington, US. <https://www.intellectualtakeout.org/article/muslim-inbreeding-huge-problem-and-people-dont-want-talk-about-it/>

18. Edlund L (2018), *Cousin Marriage Is Not Choice: Muslim Marriage and Underdevelopment*, AEA Papers and Proceedings: 108:353-57. <https://www.researchgate.net/publication/325303709_Cousin_Marriage_Is_Not_Choice_Muslim_Marriage_and_Underdevelopment>

19. *Arnold N* (2017), *People should know the risks of marrying their cousin*, BBC, UK <https://www.bbc.co.uk/bbcthree/article/6af25e7b-0545-42ba-a6fa-82ac1023b4ed>

20. Pettinger T (2014), *Biography of Martin Luther*, Oxford, UK.
    <http://www.biographyonline.net/spiritual/martin-luther.html>
21. True Islam (2020), *The History of Hadith: True Islam is derived from the Quran and not from the traditions and cultures of Muslim people.*
    <http://www.quran-islam.org/articles/part_1/history_hadith_1_ (P1148).html>
22. True Islam (2020), *The history of hadith, Prophet Muhammad forbids the writing of his hadith*, Part 1 (7).
    <http://www.quran-islam.org/articles/part_1/history_hadith_1_ (P1148).html>
23. Pettinger T, *Biography of Martin Luther*.
24. Hare RD (1993), *Without Conscience*, Guilford Press, New York: p.195
25. True Islam (2020), *The Holy Quran,* translated by Dr. Rashad Khalifa.
    <http://www.quran-islam.org/main_topics/quran/quran_in_ english/sura_1_to_4_(P1322).html>
26. Zayn A (2016), *Islamic Virtues,* 30 Facts about Islam.
    <http://www.Islamondemand.com/Islamic_virtues.html>
27. Islam on Demand (2020), *Islamicity.*
    <https://www.islamicity.org/source/islam-on-demand>
28. Holy Bible Revised Standard Version (1971), Collins Publishers, New York & Cleveland.

~ Abbreviations and glossary ~

AD – Anno Domini (in the year of the Lord); used to number years in Gregorian and Julian calendars.

Ashtiname of Muhammad – The Covenant of the Prophet Muhammad made with the monks of Mt Sinai.

ASPD – Anti-social personality disorder: sociopathy.

ASPD+P – Anti-social personality disorder: psychopathy.

BBB – Blood-brain barrier.

BC – Before Christ.

Bhaiya– Hindi word, means 'big brother'.

BPD – Borderline personality disorder.

C&E –conscience and empathy.

CEO – Chief Executive Officer; the position with the highest numbers of WCPs (21 per cent).

CSC – Correctional Service of Canada.

DNA – Deoxyribonucleic acid.

EQ – emotional intelligence (quotient); includes morality, empathy, respect and conscience.

FGM – female genital mutilation.

GOD – used as an acronym for the values of faith—**G**oodness, **O**rder (including gender and cultural equality) and **D**ecency.

Hadiths – rules added to the Islamic faith after the death of the prophet; corrupt fabrications allegedly from conversations with Muhammad; also called 'Sunnah'.

HECS – Higher Education Contribution Scheme.

ISIL – Islamic State of Iraq and the Levant.

IQ – intelligence quotient.

Infidels – unbelievers or followers of religious 'fabrications' (e.g. hadiths and Sunnah, alternative books to the three books of Abrahamic faiths: Old and New Testaments and Quran).

'jinn devils'– enemies of the Prophets, term used by Muhammad to condemn creators of religious 'fabrications' (hadiths and Sunnah).

Kafir – Arabic term for 'unbeliever'.

MADD – Mothers against drunk driving.

MAOA – Monoamine oxidase A (the 'warrior gene'); low-activity MAOA relates to high levels of aggression.

MENSA – an international society whose only qualification for membership is a score in the top 2 per cent of the general population on a standardised intelligence test (132+ or 148+).

MERC – morality, empathy, respect and conscience.

Monotheist, monotheism – belief in the one God.

MRI – Magnetic Resonance Imaging.

Pantheist, pantheism – from the Ancient Greek expression 'all in God'. Religious belief that identifies God with the universe or regards the universe as a manifestation of God. It involves the denial of the humanisation of God and expresses a tendency to identify God with nature.

PCL-R – *Psychopathy Checklist*–Revised, the internationally recognised psychopathy testing process developed by Dr Robert Hare.

Psychopathic persona – a self-centred, callous, and remorseless person profoundly lacking in empathy and the ability to form warm and deep emotional relationships with others; a person who functions without the restraints of conscience. There appears to be a genetic link, with the outcome dependent on early parenting. To date, psychopathic personas are beyond rehabilitation after mid-teens, if early symptoms of bullying and cruelty to animals are ignored.

PTSD – Post-Traumatic Stress Disorder.

Purdah – meaning 'curtain', it is the godless and backward cultural practise of female seclusion and segregation.

SEL – Social and emotional learning classes, adopted in the US to help counter inadequate parenting.

Shirk – Arabic term for equating oneself with God, or substituting the words of the Holy Scriptures with the words of earthborn men.

Sociopaths – hotheads driven by rage; less organised than psychopaths. Not genetic, caused by dysfunctional early life. Some chance of rehabilitation unless combined with psychopathy genome.

Sunnah –'fabrications' added to Islamic faith to reintroduce harsh tribal traditions. Alternative term for false hadiths; strongly forbidden by Muhammad and the Quran.

WCP – White-collar psychopath: the charming and successful psychopaths attracted in greater numbers to CEO positions in finance (brokerage and banks), property development and positions where money can be easily drawn from ratepayers and clients. Also attracted to law, politics and religion, particularly male-dominated religions.

ZPG – Zero population growth

~ Attachment A: List of Islamic terror attacks since 1979 ~

Terrorist attacks by Islamic extremists to further a perceived Islamic religious or political cause have occurred globally. Faith, introduced by three incredibly enlightened Messengers, was to provide a moral compass to make humans more humane. As the most intelligent of all species, it was our responsibility to be 'shepherds' and care for this Garden of Eden, not become its most horrendous saboteurs.

Human slaughter is never the work of people of faith. Islamic terrorists have used such tactics as arson, vehicle rampage attacks, bombings and bomb threats, suicide attacks, spree shootings, stabbings, hijackings, kidnappings and beheadings. These godless acts are by men moulded by corruptions of the Islamic faith. Hadith fabrications, added under the guise of faith by men of the antichrist, enemies of God, Allah, have destroyed the 'religion of peace'. Dictatorial leaders, who wanted personal power and control, were the "jinn devils" of which the third messenger, Muhammad, warned (Quran 6:112-113).

For a full list of the hundreds of worldwide terror attacks made since 1979, visit Wikipedia's 'List of Islamic terrorist attacks'[11]. It shows the horror of men moulded by the corruption of the Islamic faith by early dictatorial tribalrulers.

---

1   https://en.wikipedia.org/w/index.php?title=Special:CiteThisPage&page=List_of_
Islamist_terrorist_attacks&id=935946402

~ Additional Reading ~

1. Adams KM (2011), *Silently seduced: when parents make their children partners*, HCI Books, Florida.
2. Adams KM & Morgan AP (2007), *When he's married to mom*, Simon & Schuster, New York.
3. Alexander E (2012), *Proof of Heaven: a neurosurgeon's journey into the afterlife*, Simon & Schuster Paperbacks, New York.
4. Babiak P,Hare RD (2007), *Snakes in Suits*, HarperCollins Publishers, New York.
5. Balk AP (2008), *Saints&sinners: an account of western civilization*, Thelema Publication LLC, London.
6. Balk AP (2012), *Balderdash: a treatise on ethics*, Thelema Publication LLC, London.
7. Beers W (1992)), *Women and sacrifice: male narcissism and the psychology of religion*, Wayne State University Press, Detroit.
8. Behe MJ (1996), *Darwin's black box*, Simon & Schuster, New York.
9. Biddulph S. (1998), *Raising boys*, Celestial Arts, Berkeley, California.
10. Biddulph S (2006), *Raising babies: should under 3s go to nursery?*, Harper Thorsons, United Kingdom.
11. Blair J, Mitchell D, Blair K (2005)), *The psychopath: emotion and the brain*, Blackwell Publishing, Malden, MA.
12. Blankenhorn D (1996), *Fatherless America*, HarperCollins Publishers, New York.
13. Borg MJ (2001), *Reading the Bible again for the first time: taking the Bible seriously but not literally*, HarperCollins, New York.
14. Borg MJ (2012), *Evolution of the word*, Harper Collins Publishers, the New York.
15. Borg MJ, (2004), *Jesus & Buddha: the parallel sayings*, Ulysses Press, USA.
16. Brown NW (2001), *Children of the self-absorbed*, New Harbinger Publications, Oakland, CA.

17. Brown SL (2005), *How to spot a dangerous man workbook: a survival guide for women*, Hunter House Publishers, Alameda, CA.

18. Buckingham J (2000), *Boy troubles: understanding rising suicide, rising crime and education failure*, The Centre of Independent Studies, St Leonards, NSW, Australia.

19. Chesler P (2006), *The death of feminism*, Palgrave Macmillan, New York.

20. Cleckley H (2015),*The mask of sanity*,(reprint of 1950 edn), Martino Fine Books, USA.

21. Cohen P (2018), *Enduring Bonds: Inequality, Marriage, Parenting, and Everything Else That Makes Families Great and Terrible*, University of California Press, California.

22. Corneau G (1991), *Absent fathers, lost sons*, Shambhala Publications, Boston, Massachusetts.

23. Coulter A (2009), *Guilty*, Three Rivers Press, New York.

24. Davies P (1992), *The Mind of God: science and the search for ultimate meaning*, Penguin Books, London.

25. Dawkins R (2006)), The God Delusion, Transworld Publishers, London.

26. Diamond J (1992), *The third chimpanzee: the evolution and future of the human animal,* HarperCollins Publishers, New York.

27. Douthat R (2018), *To change the church: Pope Francis and the future of Catholicism,* Simon & Schuster, New York.

28. Duffy B (2018), *The Perils of Perception,* Atlantic Books, London.

29. Dutton K (2012), *The wisdom of psychopaths: what saints, spies, and serial killers can teach us about success,* Scientific American / Farrar, Straus and Giroux, New York.

30. Esposito JL (2002), *What everyone needs to know about Islam*, Oxford University Press, Oxford.

31. Eide B, Eide F (2011), *The dyslexic advantage: unlocking the hidden potential of the dyslexic brain*, Hay House UK Ltd., London.

32. Fallon J (2014), *The Psychopath Inside : A Neuroscientist's Personal Journey into the Dark Side of the Brain*, Penguin Putnam Inc., New York, United States

33. Feldman D (2012), *Unorthodox: the scandalous rejection of my Hasidic roots*, Simon & Schuster, New York.

34. Fersch EL (2006), *Thinking about psychopaths and psychopathy*, iUniverse Inc., Lincoln, NE.

35. Forward S, Buck C (1989), *Toxic parents: overcoming their hurtful legacy and reclaiming your life*, Bantam Books, New York.

36. Forward S, Frazier D (1998), *Emotional blackmail: when the people in your life use fear and guilt to manipulate you*, Thorsons Audio, HarperCollins Publishers, Glasgow.

37. Frick PJ, Marsee MA (2006), *Psychopathy and Developmental Pathways to Antisocial Behaviour in Youth*, in Handbook of Psychopathy, ed. Christopher J. Patrick (New York, NY: Guilford Press, 2006): 353-374

38. Gaita R (2014), *A sense for humanity*, Monash University Publishing, Victoria, Australia.

39. Garbarino J (1999), *Raising children in a socially toxic environment*, Jossey-Bass Publishers, San Francisco.

40. Garbarino J (2000), *Lost boys: why our sons turn violent and how we can save them*, Anchor Books, Random House Inc, New York.

41. Goleman D (2006), *Emotional intelligence: why it can matter more than IQ*, 10th anniversary edn, Bantam Books, New York.

42. Golomb E (1992), *Trapped in the mirror: adult children of narcissists in their struggle for self*, Harper, New York.

43. Guggenbühl-Craig A (2008), *The emptied soul: on the nature of the psychopath*, Spring Publications Inc, Putnam, Conn.

44. HareRD (1993), *Without conscience*, The Guilford Press, New York.

45. Hare RD(2003), *Hare Psychopathy Checklist-Revised*, 2nd ed. Toronto, ON: Multi-Health Systems.

46. Hare RD, Logan MH (2008), *Criminal psychopathy: an introduction for police*, in The Psychology of Criminal Investigations: The Search for the Truth, eds. St-Yves M, Tanguay M (Cowansville, QC: Editions Yvon Blais, 2009).

47. Hett BC (2018), *The Death of Democracy*, Henry Holt & Co, New York.

48. Hotchkiss S (2003), *Why is it always about you? The seven deadly sins of narcissism*, Free Press, New York.

49. Keane B (2018), *The mess we're in: how our politics went to hell and dragged us with it*, Allen & Unwin, Australia.

50. Kiehl KA (1914), *The psychopath whisperer: the science of those without conscience*, Penguin Random House, New York.
51. Kobrin NH (2010), *The banality of suicide terrorism*, Potomac Books Inc, Washington, DC.
52. Kristof ND, WuDunn S (2010), *Half the sky: turning oppression into opportunity for women worldwide*, Vintage Books, Random House Inc, New York.
53. Kushner HS (1981, *When bad things happen to good people*, Pan Books Ltd, London.
54. Lane B, Gregg W (2011), *The encyclopaedia of mass murder*, Magpie Books, Constable & Robinson Ltd., London.
55. McCoy D (2006), *The manipulative man: identify his behaviour, counter the abuse, regain the control*, Adams Media, Avon, Massachusetts.
56. McCullough L (2014), *The religious philosophy of Simone Weil: an introduction*, I.B. Tauris & Co Ltd, London.
57. Mackie JL (1982), *The miracle of theism: arguments for and against the existence of God*, Clarendon Press, Oxford.
58. Magid K, McKelvey CA (1989), *High risk: children without conscience*, Bantam Books, New York
59. Manne A (2014), *The life of I: the new culture of narcissism*, Melbourne University Press, Carlton, Vic, Australia.
60. Martinez-Lewi L (2008), *Freeing yourself from the narcissist in your life*, Tarcher, Penguin Books, New York.
61. Miller A (1990), *For your own good: hidden cruelty in child-rearing and the roots of violence*, 3rd edn, The Noonday Press, New York.
62. Miller D (2010), *Father fiction: chapters for a fatherless generation*, Hodder & Stoughton, London.
63. Moir A, Jessel D (1989), *Brainsex: the real difference between men and women*, Mandarin Paperbacks, London.
64. Moubayed S (2015), *Under the black flag: at the frontier of the new Jihad*, I.B. Tauris & Co. Ltd, London.
65. Neal MC (2011), *To Heaven and back*, WaterBrook Multnomah, Division of Random House Inc., New York.
66. Oleson JC (2016), *Criminal genius: a portrait of high-IQ offenders*, University of California Press, Oakland, California.

67. MacKenzie J (2015), *Psychopath free: recovering from emotionally abusive relationships with narcissists, sociopaths and other toxic people*, Penguin Random House, New York.

68. Ronson J (2011), *The psychopath test: a journey through the madness industry*, Riverhead Books, Penguin Group (USA) Inc, New York.

69. Rogers CR (1989), *On becoming a person: a therapist's view of psychotherapy*, Mariner Books, Houghton Mifflin Co, New York

70. Salter AC (2003), *Predators: Paedophiles, Rapists, and Other Sex Offenders*, Basic Books, Hachette Book Group, New York.

71. Saunders P (2004), *Australia's welfare habit and how to kick it*, Duffy &Snellgrove, Sydney.

72. Schouten R, Silver J (2012), *Almost a psychopath: do I (or does someone I know) have a problem with manipulation and lack of empathy*, Hazelden, Center City, Minnesota.

73. Sheridan T (2011), *Puzzling people: the labyrinth of the psychopath*, Velluminous Press, UK.

74. Simon GK (2011), *Character disturbance: the phenomenon of our age*, Parkhurst Brothers Inc. Publishers, Little Rock, Arkansas.

75. Spencer R (2007), *A religion of peace? Why Christianity is and Islam isn't*, Regnery Publishing, Inc., Washington, DC.

76. Strudwick S (2010), *Dark soul: healing and recovering from toxic relationships*, SS Products, Kettering, UK.

77. Tibi B (2005), *Islam between Culture and Politics*, Palgrave Macmillan, New York.

78. TwengeJM, Campbell WK (2009), *The narcissism epidemic: living in the age of entitlement*, Free Press, Simon & Schuster Inc, New York.

79. Unwin SD (2003), *The probability of God*, Three Rivers Press, New York.

80. Wallace-Wells D (2019), *The uninhabitable earth: life after warming*, Tim Duggan Books, Penguin Random House, New York.

81. Warraq I (2003), *Why I Am Not a Muslim*, Prometheus Books, New York.

82. Webster R (1990), *A Brief History of Blasphemy*, The Orwell Press, Suffolk, UK

www.ingramcontent.com/pod-product-compliance
Lightning Source LLC
Chambersburg PA
CBHW031149270326
41931CB00006B/200